D0236660

THIS BOOK
BELONGS
· TO ·

....

....

....

The Ode Less Travelled

Unlocking the Poet Within

Stephen Fry

The Ode Less Travelled

Unlocking the Poet Within

HUTCHINSON
LONDON

Published by Hutchinson in 2005

10 9 8 7 6 5 4 3

Copyright © Stephen Fry 2005

First published in 2005 in the United Kingdom by Hutchinson

HUTCHINSON
The Random House Group Limited
20 Vauxhall Bridge Road, London SW1V 2SA

Random House Australia (Pty) Limited
20 Alfred Street, Milsons Point, Sydney
New South Wales 2061, Australia

Random House New Zealand Limited
18 Poland Road, Glenfield
Auckland 10, New Zealand

Random House South Africa (Pty) Limited
Isle of Houghton, Corner Boundary Road & Carse O'Gowrie,
Houghton, 2198, South Africa

The Random House Group Limited Reg. No. 954009

www.randomhouse.co.uk

A CIP catalogue record for this book is available
from the British Library

Papers used by Random House are natural, recyclable products made
from wood grown in sustainable forests. The manufacturing processes
conform to the environmental regulations of the country of origin

Designed and typeset in Bembo by Peter Ward
Printed and bound in Great Britain by
William Clowes Ltd, Beccles, Suffolk

ISBN 0 09 179661 X

The mediocre teacher tells. The good teacher explains.
The superior teacher demonstrates. The great teacher inspires.

For Rory Stuart, a good, superior and great teacher.

Table of Contents

2 Rhyme

3 Form

4 Diction and Poetics Today

Foreword

I HAVE A DARK AND DREADFUL SECRET. I write poetry.

This is an embarrassing confession for an adult to make. In their idle hours Winston Churchill and Noël Coward painted. For fun and relaxation Albert Einstein played the violin. Hemingway hunted, Agatha Christie gardened, James Joyce sang arias and Nabokov chased butterflies. But *poetry*?

I have a friend who drums in the attic, another who has been building a boat for years. An actor I know is prouder of the reproduction eighteenth-century duelling pistols he makes in a small workshop than he is of his knighthood. Britain is a nation of hobbyists – eccentric amateurs, talented part-timers, Pooterish potterers and dedicated autodidacts in every field of human endeavour. But *poetry*?

An adolescent girl may write poetry, so long as it is securely locked up in her pink leatherette five-year diary. Suburban professionals are permitted to enter jolly pastiche competitions in the *Spectator* and *New Statesman*. At a pinch, a young man may be allowed to write a verse or two of dirty doggerel and leave it on a post-it note stuck to the fridge when he has forgotten to buy a Valentine card. But that's *it*. Any more forays into the world of Poesy and you release the beast that lurks within every British breast – and the name of the beast is Embarrassment.

And yet . . .

I believe poetry is a primal impulse within us all. I believe we are all capable of it and furthermore that a small, often ignored corner of us positively yearns to try it. I believe our poetic impulse

xi

is blocked by the false belief that poetry might on the one hand be academic and technical and on the other formless and random. It seems to many that while there is a clear road to learning music, gardening or watercolours, poetry lies in inaccessible marshland: no pathways, no signposts, just the skeletons of long-dead poets poking through the bog and the unedifying sight of living ones floundering about in apparent confusion and mutual enmity. Behind it all, the dread memory of classrooms swollen into resentful silence while the English teacher invites us to 'respond' to a poem.

For me the private act of writing poetry is songwriting, confessional, diary-keeping, speculation, problem-solving, storytelling, therapy, anger management, craftsmanship, relaxation, concentration and spiritual adventure all in one inexpensive package.

Suppose I want to paint but seem to have no obvious talent. Never mind: there are artist supply shops selling paints, papers, pastels, charcoals and crayons. There are 'How To' books everywhere. Simple lessons in the rules of proportion and guides to composition and colourmixing can make up for my lack of natural ability and provide painless technical grounding. I am helped by grids and outlines, pantographs and tracing paper; precise instructions guide me in how to prepare a canvas, prime it with paint and wash it into an instant watercolour sky. There are instructional videos available; I can even find channels on cable and satellite television showing gentle hippies painting lakes, carving pine trees with palette knives and dotting them with impasto snow. Mahlsticks, sable, hogs-hair, turpentine and linseed. Viridian, umber, ochre and carmine. Perspective, chiaroscuro, *sfumato*, grisaille, tondo and *morbidezza*. Reserved modes and materials. The tools of the trade. A new jargon to learn. A whole initiation into technique, form and style.

Suppose I want to play music but seem to have no obvious talent. Never mind: there are music shops selling instruments, tuning forks, metronomes and 'How To' books by the score. And scores by the score. Instructional videos abound. I can buy digital keyboards linked to programmes that plug into my computer and guide me through the rudiments, monitoring my progress and accuracy. I start with scales and move on to chords and arpeggios. There are horsehair, rosin and catgut, reeds, plectrums and mouthpieces. There are diminished sevenths, augmented fifths, relative minors, trills and accidentals. There are riffs and figures, licks and vamps. Sonata, adagio, crescendo, scherzo and twelve-bar blues. Reserved modes and materials. The tools of the trade. A new jargon to learn. A whole initiation into technique, form and style.

To help us further there are evening classes, clubs and groups. Pack up your easel and palette and go into the countryside with a party of like-minded enthusiasts. Sit down with a friend and learn a new chord on the guitar. Join a band. Turn your watercolour view of Lake Windermere into a tablemat or T-shirt. Burn your version of 'Stairway to Heaven' onto a CD and alarm your friends.

None of these adventures into technique and proficiency will necessarily turn you into a genius or even a proficient craftsman. Your view of *Snow on York Minster*, whether languishing in the loft or forming the basis of this year's Christmas card doesn't make you Turner, Constable or Monet. Your version of 'Für Elise' on electric piano might not threaten Alfred Brendel, your trumpet blast of 'Basin Street Blues' could be so far from Satchmo that it hurts and your take on 'Lela' may well stand as an eternal reproach to all those with ears to hear. You may not sell a single picture, be invited even once to deputise for the church organist when she goes down with shingles or have any luck at all when you try out for the local Bay City Rollers tribute band. You are neither Great Artist, sessions professional, illustrator or admired amateur.

So what? You are someone who paints a bit, scratches around on the keyboard for fun, gets a kick out of learning a tune or discovering a new way of rendering the face of your beloved in charcoal. You have another life, you have family, work and friends but this is a hobby, a pastime, FUN. Do you give up the Sunday kick-around because you'll never be Thierry Henry? Of course not. That would be pathologically vain. We don't stop talking about how the world might be better just because we have no chance of making it to Prime Minister. We are all politicians. We are all artists. In an open society everything the mind and hands can achieve is our birthright. It is up to us to claim it.

And you know, you *might* be the real thing, or someone with the potential to give as much pleasure to others as you derive yourself. But how you will ever know if you don't try?

As the above is true of painting and music, so it is true of cookery and photography and gardening and interior decoration and chess and poker and skiing and sailing and carpentry and bridge and wine and knitting and brass-rubbing and line-dancing and the hundreds of other activities that enrich and enliven the daily toil of getting and spending, mortgages and shopping, school and office. There are rules, conventions, techniques, reserved objects, equipment and paraphernalia, time-honoured modes, forms, jargon and tradition. The average practitioner doesn't expect to win prizes, earn a fortune, become famous or acquire absolute mastery in their art, craft, sport – or as we would say now, their chosen leisure pursuit. *It really is enough to have fun.*

The point remains: it isn't a burden to learn the difference between acid and alkaline soil or understand how f-stops and exposure times affect your photograph. There's no drudgery or humiliation in discovering how to knit, purl and cast off, snowplough your skis, deglaze a pan, carve a dovetail or tot up your bridge hand according to Acol. Only an embarrassed adolescent or deranged coward thinks jargon and reserved languages are pretentious and that detail and structure are boring. Sensible people are above simpering at references to colour in music, structure in wine or rhythm in architecture. When you learn to sail you are literally shown the ropes and taught that they are called sheets or painters and that knots are hitches and forward is aft and right is starboard. That is not pseudery or exclusivity, it is precision, it is part of initiating the newcomer into the guild. Learning the lingo is the beginning of our rite of passage.

In music, tempo is not the same as rhythm, which is not the same as pulse. There are metronomic indications and time signatures. At some point along the road between picking out a tune with one finger and really playing *we need to know* these distinctions. For some it comes naturally and seems inborn, for most of us the music is buried deep inside but needs a little coaxing and tuition to be got out. So someone shows us, or we progress by video, evening class or book. *Talent is inborn but technique is learned.*

Talent without technique is like an engine without a steering wheel, gears or brakes. It doesn't matter how thoroughbred and powerful the V12 under the bonnet if it can't be steered and kept under control. Talented people who do nothing with their gifts often crash and burn. A great truth, so obvious that it is almost a secret, is that most people are embarrassed to the point of shame by their talents. Ashamed of their gifts but proud to bursting of their achievements. Do athletes boast of their hand-eye coordination, grace and natural sense of balance? No, they talk of how hard they trained, the sacrifices they made, the effort they put in.

> Ah, but a man's reach should exceed his grasp
> Or what's a heaven for?

Robert Browning's cry brings us back, at last, to poetry. While it is perfectly possible that you did not learn music at school, or drawing and painting, it is almost certain that you did learn poetry. Not how to do it, almost never how to write your own, but how, God help us, to *appreciate* it.

We have all of us, *all of us*, sat with brows furrowed feeling incredibly dense and dumb as the teacher asks us to respond to an image or line of verse.

> *What do you think Wordsworth was referring to here?*
> *What does Wilfred Owen achieve by choosing this metaphor?*

How does Keats respond to the nightingale?
Why do you think Shakespeare uses the word 'gentle' as a verb?
What is Larkin's attitude to the hotel room?

It brings it all back, doesn't it? All the red-faced, blood-pounding humiliation and embarrassment of being singled out for comment.

The way poetry was taught at school reminded W. H. Auden of a *Punch* cartoon composed, legend has it, by the poet A. E. Housman. Two English teachers are walking in the woods in springtime. The first, on hearing birdsong, is moved to quote William Wordsworth:

TEACHER 1: Oh cuckoo, shall I call thee bird
　　　　　　Or but a wandering voice?

TEACHER 2: State the alternative preferred
　　　　　　With reasons for your choice.

Even if some secret part of you might have been privately moved and engaged, you probably went through a stage of loathing those bores Shakespeare, Keats, Owen, Eliot, Larkin and all who came before and after them. You may love them now, you may still hate them or perhaps you feel entirely indifferent to the whole pack of them. But however well or badly we were taught English literature, how many of us have ever been shown how to write our own poems?

Don't worry, it doesn't have to rhyme. Don't bother
with metre and verses. Just express yourself. Pour out
your feelings.

Suppose you had never played the piano in your life.

Don't worry, just lift the lid and *express yourself*. Pour
out your feelings.

We have all heard children do just that and we have all wanted to treat them with great violence as a result. Yet this is the only instruction we are ever likely to get in the art of writing poetry:

Anything goes.

But that's how modern poetry *works*, isn't it? Free verse, don't they call it? *Vers libre?*

Ye-e-es . . . And in avant-garde music, John Cage famously wrote a piece of silence called '4 Minutes 33 Seconds' and created other works requiring ball-bearings and chains to be dropped on to prepared pianos. Do music teachers suggest that to children? Do we encourage them to ignore all harmony and rhythm and just make noise? It is important to realise that Cage's first pieces were written in the Western compositional tradition, in movements with conventional Italian names like lento, vivace and fugato. Picasso's early paintings are flawless models of figurative accuracy. Listening to music may inspire an extraordinary emotional response, but extraordinary emotions are not enough to make music.

Unlike musical notation, paint or clay, language is inside every one of us. For free. We are all proficient at it. We already have the palette, the paints and the instruments. We don't have to go and buy any reserved materials. Poetry is made of the same stuff you are reading now, the same stuff you use to order pizza over the phone, the same stuff you yell at your parents and children, whisper in your lover's ear and shove into an e-mail, text or birthday card. It is common to us all. Is that why we resent being told that there is a technique to its highest expression, poetry? I cannot ski, so I would like to be shown how to. I cannot paint, so I would value some lessons. But I can speak and write, so do not waste my time telling me that I need lessons in poetry, which is, after all, no more than emotional writing, with or without the odd rhyme. Isn't it?

Jan Schreiber in a review of Timothy Steele's *Missing Measures*, says this of modern verse:

> The writing of poetry has been made laughably easy. There
> are no technical constraints. Knowledge of the tradition is
> not necessary, nor is a desire to communicate, this having
> been supplanted in many practitioners by the more urgent

desire to express themselves. Even sophistication in the manipulation of syntax is not sought. Poetry, it seems, need no longer be at least as well written as prose.

Personally, I find writing without form, metre or rhyme not 'laughably easy' but fantastically difficult. If you can do it, good luck to you and farewell, this book is not for you: but a word of warning from W. H. Auden before you go.

> The poet who writes 'free' verse is like Robinson Crusoe on his desert island: he must do all his cooking, laundry and darning for himself. In a few exceptional cases, this manly independence produces something original and impressive, but more often the result is squalor – dirty sheets on the unmade bed and empty bottles on the unswept floor.

I cannot teach you how to be a great poet or even a good one. Dammit, I can't teach *myself* that. But I can show you how to have fun with the modes and forms of poetry as they have developed over the years. By the time you have read this book you will be able to write a Petrarchan sonnet, a Sapphic Ode, a ballade, a villanelle and a Spenserian stanza, among many other weird and delightful forms; you will be confident with metre, rhyme and much else besides. Whether you choose to write on the stupidity of advertising, the curve of your true love's buttocks, the folly of war or the irritation of not being able to open a pickle jar is unimportant. I will give you the tools, you can finish the job. And once you have got the hang of the forms, you can devise your own. The Robertsonian Sonnet. The Jonesian Ode. The Millerian Stanza.

This is not an academic book. It is unlikely to become part of the core curriculum. It may help you with your English exams because it will certainly allow you to be a smart-arse in Practical Criticism papers (if such things still exist) and demonstrate that you know a trochee from a dactyl, a terza from an ottava rima and assonance from enjambment, in which case I am happy to be of service. It is over a quarter of a century since I did any teaching and I have no idea if such knowledge is considered good or useless these days, for all I know it will count against you.

I have written this book because over the past thirty-five years I have derived enormous private pleasure from writing poetry and like anyone with a passion I am keen to share it. You will be relieved to hear that I will not be burdening you with any of my actual poems (except sample verse specifically designed to help clarify form and metre): I do not write poetry for publication, I write it for the same reason that, according to Wilde, one should write a diary, to have something sensational to read on the train. And as a way of speaking to myself. But most importantly of all *for pleasure*.

This is not the only work on prosody (the art of versification) ever published in English, but it is the one that I should like to have been available to me many years ago. It is technical, yes, inasmuch as it investigates technique, but I hope that does not make it dry, obscure or difficult − after all, 'technique' is just the Greek for 'art'. I have tried to make everything approachable without being loopily matey or absurdly simplistic.

I certainly do not attempt in this book to pick up where those poor teachers left off and instruct you in poetry appreciation. I suspect, however, that once you have started writing a poem of any real shape you will find yourself admiring and appreciating other poets' work a great deal more. If you have never picked up a golf club you will never really know just how remarkable Ernie Els is (substitute tennis racket for Roger Federer, frying pan for Gordon Ramsay, piano for Jools Holland and so on).

But maybe you are too old a dog to learn new tricks? Maybe you have missed the bus? That's hooey. Thomas Hardy (a finer poet than he was a novelist in my view) did not start publishing verse till he was nearly sixty.

> Every child is musical. Unfortunately this natural gift is
> squelched before it has time to develop. From all my life

experience I remember being laughed at because my voice and the words I sang didn't please someone. My second grade teacher, Miss Stone would not let me sing with the rest of the class because she judged my voice as not musical and she said I threw the class off key. I believed her which led to the blockage of my appreciation of music and blocked my ability to write poetry. Fortunately at the age of 57 I had a significant emotional event which unblocked my ability to compose poetry which many people believe has lyrical qualities.

So writes one Sidney Madwed. Mr Madwed may not be Thomas Campion or Cole Porter, but he believes that an understanding of prosody has set him free and now clearly has a whale of a time writing his lyrics and verses. I hope reading this book will take the place for you of a 'significant emotional event' and awaken the poet that has always lain dormant within.

It is never too late. We are all opsimaths.

Opsimath, noun: one who learns late in life.

Let us go forward together now, both opsimathically and optimistically. Nothing can hold us back. The ode beckons.

How to Read this Book

THERE IS no getting away from it: in about five minutes' time, if you keep reading at a steady rate, you will start to find yourself, slowly at first and then with gathering speed and violence, under bombardment from technical words, many of them Greek in origin and many of them perhaps unfamiliar to you. I cannot predict how you will react to this. You might rub your hands in glee, you might throw them up in whatever is the opposite of glee, you might bunch them into an angry fist or use them to hurl the book as far away from you as possible.

It is important for you to realise now, at this initial stage, that – as I mentioned earlier – most activities worth pursuing come with their own jargon, their private language and technical vocabulary. In music you would be learning about fifths and relative majors, in yachting it would be boom-spankers, tacking into the wind and spinnakers. I could attempt to 'translate' words like *iamb* and *caesura* into everyday English, but frankly that would be patronising and silly. It would also be very confusing when, as may well happen, you turn to other books on poetry for further elucidation.

So please, DO NOT BE AFRAID. I have taken every effort to try to make your initiation into the world of prosody as straight-forward, logical and enjoyable as possible. No art worth the striving after is without its complexities, but if you find yourself confused, if words and concepts start to swim meaninglessly in front of you, do not panic. So long as you obey the three golden rules below, nothing can go wrong. You will grow in poetic power and confidence at a splendid rate. You are not expected to remember every metrical device or every rhyme scheme: I have included a glossary at the back. Just about every unusual and technical word I use is there, so if in doubt flip to the back where you should find an explanation given by definition and/or example.

If you already know, or believe you know, a fair amount about *prosody* (usually pronounced prósser-di, but sometimes prose-a-di), that is to say the art of versification, then you may feel an urge to hurry through the early sections of the book. That is up to you, naturally, but I would urge against it. The course is designed for all comers and it is better followed in the order laid out. Now, I am afraid you are not allowed to read any further without attending to the three golden rules below.

The Golden Rules

RULE ONE

In our age one of the glories of poetry is that it remains an art that demonstrates the virtues and pleasures of TAKING YOUR TIME. You can never read a poem too slowly, but you can certainly read one too fast.

Please, and I am on my knees here, *please* read all the sample excerpts and fragments of poetry that I include in this book (usually in indented paragraphs) *as slowly as you possibly can*, constantly rereading them and feeling their rhythm and balance and shape. I'm referring to single lines here as much as to larger selections.

Poems are not read like novels. There is much pleasure to be had in taking the same fourteen-line sonnet to bed with you and reading it many times over for a week. Savour, taste, enjoy. Poetry is not made to be sucked up like a child's milkshake, it is much better sipped like a precious malt whisky. Verse is one of our last stands against the instant and the infantile. Even when it is simple and childlike it is be savoured.

Always try to read verse *out loud*: if you are in a place where such a practice would embarrass you, read out loud inside yourself (if possible, moving your lips). Among the pleasures of poetry is the sheer physical, sensual, textural, tactile pleasure of feeling the words on your lips, tongue, teeth and vocal cords.

It can take weeks to assemble and polish a single line of poetry. Sometimes, it is true, a lightning sketch may produce a wonderful effect too, but as a general rule, poems take time. As with a good painting, they are not there to be greedily taken in at once, they are to be lived with and endlessly revisited: the eye can go back and back and back, investigating new corners, new incidents and the new shapes that seem to emerge. We are perhaps too used to the kind of writing that contains a single message. We absorb the message and move on to the next sentence. Poetry is an entirely different way of using words and I cannot emphasise enough how much more pleasure is to be derived from a slow, luxurious engagement with its language and rhythms.

Rule Two

NEVER WORRY about 'meaning' when you are reading poems, either those I include in the book, or those you choose to read for yourself. Poems are not crossword puzzles: however elusive and 'difficult' the story or argument of a poem may seem to be and however resistant to simple interpretation, it is not a test of your intelligence and learning (or if it is, it is not worth persevering with). Of course some poems are complex and highly wrought and others may contain references that mystify you. Much poetry in the past assumed a familiarity with classical literature, the Christian liturgy and Greek mythology, for example. Some modernist poetry can seem bloody-minded in its dense and forbidding allusion to other poets, to science and to philosophy. It can contain foreign phrases and hieroglyphs. There are literary and critical guides if you wish to acquaint yourself with such works; for the most part we will not concern ourselves with the avant-garde, the experimental and the arcane; their very real pleasures would be for another book.

It is easy to be *shy* when confronting a poem. Poems can be the frightening older children at a party who make us want to cling to our mothers. But remember that poets are people and they have taken the courageous step of sharing their fears, loves, hopes and narratives with us in a rare and crafted form. They have chosen a mode of expression that is concentrated and often intense, they are offering us a music that has taken them a long time to create – many hours in the making, a lifetime in the preparation. They don't mean to frighten or put us off, they long for us to read their works and to enjoy them.

Do not be cross with poetry for failing to deliver meaning and communication in the way that an assemblage of words usually does. Be confident that when encountering a poem you do not have to articulate a response, venture an opinion or make a judgement. Just as the reading of each poem takes time, so a relationship with the whole art of poetry itself takes time. Observation of Rule One will allow meaning to emerge at its own pace.

RULE THREE

Buy a notebook, exercise book or jotter pad and lots of pencils (any writing instrument will do but I find pencils more physically pleasing). This is the only equipment you will need: no cameras, paintbrushes, tuning forks or chopping boards. Poets enjoy their handwriting ('like smelling your own farts,' W. H. Auden claimed) and while computers may have their place, for the time being *write*, don't type.

You may as well invest in a good pocket-sized notebook: the

Moleskin range is becoming very fashionable again and bookshops and stationers have started to produce their own equivalents. Take yours with you *everywhere*. When you are waiting for someone, stuck in an airport, travelling by train, just doodle with words. As you learn new techniques and methods for producing lines of verse, practise them all the time.

Imagine the above-mentioned are the End User Licence Agreement to a piece of computer software. You cannot get any further without clicking 'OK' when the installation wizard asks you if you agree to the terms and conditions. Well, the three rules are *my* terms and conditions, let me restate them in brief:

1. Take your time
2. Don't be afraid
3. Always have a notebook with you

I agree to abide by the terms and conditions of this book

☐ Agree   ☐ Disagree

Now you may begin.

CHAPTER ONE

Metre

Poetry is metrical writing.
If it isn't that I don't know what it is.

J. V. CUNNINGHAM

I

Some very obvious but nonetheless interesting observations about how English is spoken – meet metre – the iamb – the iambic pentameter – Poetry Exercises 1 & 2

YOU HAVE ALREADY achieved the English-language poet's most important goal: you can read, write and speak English well enough to understand this sentence. If this were a book about painting or music there would be a lot more initial spadework to be got through.

Automatic and inborn as language might seem to be, there are still things we need to know about it, elements that are so obvious very few of us ever consider them. Since language for us, as poets in the making, is our paint, our *medium*, we should probably take a little time to consider certain aspects of spoken English, a language whose oral properties are actually very different from those of its more distant ancestors, Anglo-Saxon, Latin and Greek and even from those of its nearer relations, French and German.

Some of what follows may seem so obvious that it will put you in danger of sustaining a nosebleed. Bear with me, nonetheless. We are beginning from first principles.

How We Speak

Each English word is given its own weight or push as we speak it within a sentence. That is to say:

Each English **word** is **giv**en its own **weight** and **push** as
we **speak** it with**in** a **sent**ence.

Only a very badly primitive computer speech programme would give equal stress to all the words in that example. Throughout this chapter I use **bold** type to indicate this weight or push, this 'accent', and I use *italics* for imparting special emphasis and SMALL CAPITALS to introduce new words or concepts for the first time and for drawing attention to an exercise or instruction.

A real English speaker would speak the indented paragraph above much, but certainly not *exactly*, as I (with only the binary choice of **heavy**/light available to me) have tried to indicate. Some words or syllables will be slid over with hardly a breath or a pause accorded to them (light), others will be given more weight (**heavy**).

Surely that's how the whole world speaks?

Well, in the Chinese languages and in Thai, for example, all words are of one syllable (*monosyllabic*) and speech is given colour and meaning by variations in *pitch*, the speaker's voice will go up or down. In English we colour our speech not so much with alterations in pitch as with variations in stress: this is technically known as ACCENTUATION.[1] English, and we shall think about this later – is what is known as a STRESS-TIMED language.

Of course, English does contain a great many monosyllables (many more than most European languages as it happens): some of these are what grammarians call PARTICLES, inoffensive little words like prepositions (*by, from, to, with*), pronouns (*his, my, your, they*),

---

1 Pitch *matters*, of course it does. It matters in speech and in poetry, but for the moment we will concentrate on stress.

articles (*the*, *an*, *a*) and conjunctions (*or*, *and*, *but*). In an average sentence these are *unaccented* in English.

From **time** to **time** and for as **long** as it **takes**.

I must repeat, these are not *special emphases*, these are the **nat**ural **ac**cents im**part**ed. We glide over the particles ('from', 'to', 'and', 'for', 'as', 'it') and give a little push to the important words ('**time**', '**long**', '**takes**').

Also, we tend to accent the *operative* part of monosyllabic words when they are extended, only lightly tripping over the -ing and -ly, of such words as **hop**ing and **quick**ly. This light tripping, this gliding is sometimes called *scudding*.

We always say **Brit**ish, we never say Brit**ish** or Brit-**ish**, always ma**chine**, never **mach**ine or **mach**-ine. The weight we give to the first syllable of **Brit**ish or the second syllable of ma**chine** is called by linguists the TONIC ACCENT. Accent here shouldn't be confused either with the written signs (DIACRITICAL MARKS) that are some-times put over letters, as in café and Führer, or with regional accents – brogues and dialects like Cockney or Glaswegian. Accent for our purposes means the natural push or stress we give to a word or part of a word as we speak. This accent, push or stress is also called *ictus*, but we will stick to the more common English words where possible.

In many-syllabled or POLYSYLLABIC words there will always be *at least one* accent.

Credit. Dis**pose**. Con**tin**ue. De**spair**. **Des**perate.

Sometimes the stress will change according to the meaning or nature of the word. READ THE FOLLOWING PAIRS OUT LOUD:

He in**clines** to pro**ject** bad vibes
A **proj**ect to study the **in**clines.

He pro**ceeds** to re**bel**.
The **reb**el steals the **pro**ceeds.

3

Some words may have two stresses but *one* (marked here with an ´) will always be a little heavier:

ábdicate consiperátion.

Sometimes it is a matter of nationality or preference. READ OUT THESE WORDS:

Chicken-soup. Arm-chair. Sponge-cake. Cigarette.
Magazine.

Those are the more usual accents in *British* English. NOW TRY THE SAME WORDS WITH THESE DIFFERENT STRESSES . . .

Chicken-soup. **Arm**-chair. **Sponge**-cake. **Cig**arette.
Magazine.

That is how they are said in America (and increasingly these days in the UK and Australia too). What about the following?

Lámentable. **Mánd**atory. **Prím**arily. **Yés**terday. Incómparable.

Laméntable. Mandátory. Primárily. **Yes**terdáy. Incompárable.

Whether the tonic should land as those in the first line or the second is a vexed issue and subject to much cóntroversy or contróversy. The pronunciations vary according to circumstances or circumstánces or indeed circum-stahnces too English, class-bound and ticklish to go into here.

You may think, 'Well, now, hang on, surely this is how everyone (the Chinese and Thais aside) talks, pushing one part of the word but not another?' Not so.

The French, for instance, tend towards *equal* stress in a word. They pronounce Canada, **Can-a-da** as opposed to our **Can**ada. We say **Ber**nard, the French say **Ber-nard**. You may have noticed that when Americans pronounce French they tend to go overboard and hurl the emphasis on to the *final* syllable, thinking it sounds more authentic, Ber-**nard** and so on. They are so used to speaking

English with its characteristic *downward* inflection that to American ears French *seems* to go up at the end. With trademark arrogance, we British keep the English inflection. Hence the American pronunciation clich**É**, the English **cli**ché and the authentic French **cli-ché**. Take also the two words 'journal' and 'machine', which English has inherited from French. We pronounce them **jour**nal and ma**chine**. The French give them their characteristic equal stress: **jour-nal** and **ma-chine**. Even words with many syllables are equally stressed in French: we say repe**ti**tion, they say **répétition** (**ray-pay-tee-see-on**).

As you might imagine, this has influenced greatly the different paths that French and English poetry have taken. The rhythms of English poetry are ordered by SYLLABIC ACCENTUATION, those of French more by QUANTITATIVE MEASURE. We won't worry about those terms or what they portend just yet: it should already be clear that if you're planning to write French verse then this is not the book for you.

In a paragraph of written *prose* we pay little attention to how those English accents fall unless, that is, we wish to make an *extra* emphasis, which is usually rendered by *italics*, underscoring or CAPITALISATION. In German an emphasised word is s t r e t c h e d. With prose the *eye* is doing much more than the *ear*. The inner ear *is* at work, however, and we can all recognise the rhythms in any piece of writing. It can be spoken out loud, after all, for recitation or for rhetoric, and if it is designed for that purpose, those rhythms will be all the more important.

But prose, rhythmic as it can be, is not poetry. The rhythm is not *organised*.

Meet Metre

Poetry's rhythm *is* organised.

THE LIFE OF A POEM IS MEASURED IN REGULAR HEARTBEATS.
THE NAME FOR THOSE HEARTBEATS IS *METRE*.

When we want to describe anything technical in English we tend to use Greek. Logic, grammar, physics, mechanics, gynaecology, dynamics, economics, philosophy, therapy, astronomy, politics – Greek gave us all those words. The reservation of Greek for the technical allows us to use those other parts of English, the Latin and especially the Anglo-Saxon, to describe more personal and immediate aspects of life and the world around us. Thus to be *anaesthetised by trauma* has a more technical, medical connotation than to be *numb with shock*, although the two phrases mean much the same. In the same way, *metre* can be reserved precisely to refer to the poetic technique of organising rhythm, while words like 'beat' and 'flow' and 'pulse' can be freed up for less technical, more subjective and personal uses.

PLEASE DO NOT BE PUT OFF by the fact that throughout this section on metre I shall tend to use the conventional Greek names for nearly all the metrical units, devices and techniques that poets employ. In many respects, as I shall explain elsewhere, they are inappropriate to English verse,[2] but English-language poets and prosodists have used them for the last thousand years. It is useful and pleasurable to have a special vocabulary for a special activity.[3] Convention, tradition and precision suggest this in most fields of human endeavour, from music and painting to snooker and snowboarding. It does not make those activities any less rich, individual and varied. So let it be with poetry.

---

2 Unless otherwise stated, I use 'English' here and throughout the book to refer to the English *language*, not the country.
3 'Convenient and innocuous nomenclatorial handles,' as Vladimir Nabokov calls them in his *Notes on Prosody*.

Poetry is a word derived from Greek, as is Ode (from *poein*, to make and *odein*, to sing). The majority of words we use to describe the *anatomy* of a poem are Greek in origin too. Metre (from *metron*) is simply the Greek for measure, as in metronome, kilometre, biometric and so on. The Americans use the older spelling *meter* which I prefer, but which my UK English spellcheck refuses to like.

In the beginning, my old cello teacher used to say, was *rhythm*. Rhythm is simply the Greek for 'flow' (we get our word diarrhoea from the same source as it happens). We know what rhythm is in music, we can clap our hands or tap our feet to its beat. In poetry it is much the same:

> ti-**tum**, ti-**tum**, ti-**tum**, ti-**tum**, ti-**tum**

Say that out loud. Tap your feet, drum your fingers or clap your hands as you say it. It is a meaningless chant, certainly. But it is a meaningless *regular* and *rhythmic* chant.

Ten sounds, alternating in beat or accent. Actually, it is not very helpful to say that the line is made up of *ten* sounds; we'll soon discover that for our prosodic purposes it is more useful to look at it as *five* repeating sets of that ti-**tum** heartbeat. My old cello teacher liked to do it this way, clapping her hands as she did so:

> and **one** and **two** and **three** and **four** and **five**

In music that would be five bars (or five measures if you're American). In poetry such a bar or measure is called a *foot*.

Five *feet* marching in rhythm. If the foot is the heartbeat, the metre can best be described as the readout or cardiogram trace.

1	2	3	4	5
ti **tum**	ti **tum**	ti **tum**	ti **tum**	ti **tum**

Let's give the metre meaning by substituting words.

He **bangs** the **drum** and **makes** a **dread**ful **noise**

That line consists of FIVE ti-**tum** feet:

1	2	3	4	5
He **bangs**	the **drum**	and **makes**	a **dread**	ful **noise**
ti **tum**	ti **tum**	ti **tum**	ti **tum**	ti **tum**

It is a line of TEN syllables (*decasyllabic*):

1 **2** 3 **4** 5 **6** 7 **8** 9 **10**
He **bangs** the **drum** and **makes** a **dread** ful **noise**

Ten syllables where in this metre the accent always falls on the *even-numbered beat*. Notice, though, that there aren't ten *words* in this example, there are only nine. That's because 'dreadful' has two syllables.

Bangs, **drum**, **makes**, **dread** and **noise** are those even-numbered accented words (and syllable) here. You could show the rhythm of the line like this:

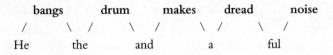

Some metrists would call 'he', 'the', 'and', 'a' and '-ful' DEPRESSIONS. Other words to describe a non-stressed syllable are SLACK, SCUD and WEAK. The line has a rising rhythm, that is the point: from weak to strong, terminating in its fifth stressed beat.

The most usual way to SCAN the line, in other words to demonstrate its metric structure and show the cardiogram trace as it were, is to divide the five feet with this mark | (known as a VIRGULE, the same as the French word for 'comma' or 'slash' that you might remember from school) and use symbols to indicate the accented and the weak syllables. Here I have chosen O to represent the off-beat, the depressed, unaccented syllable, and ● for the beat, stress or accented syllable.

    O   ●   O   ●   O   ●   O   ●   O   ●
    He bangs | the drum | and makes | a dread | ful noise.

    O   ●   O   ●   O   ●   O   ●   O   ●
    If Win | ter comes, | can Spring | be far | behind?
                                    SHELLEY: 'Ode to the West Wind'

There are other accepted ways of marking SCANSION: using – or u or x for an *un*accented beat and / for an *accented* one. If you were taught scansion at school or have a book on the subject you will often see one of the following:

    –   /   –   /   –   /   –   /   –   /
    He bangs | the drum | and makes | a dread | ful noise.

    x   /   x   /   x   /   x   /   x   /
    If Win | ter comes, | can Spring | be far | behind?

    u   /   u   /   u   /   u   /   u   /
    The cur | few tolls | the knell | of part | ing day
                        GRAY: 'Elegy Written in a Country Churchyard'

For the most part I shall be sticking to O and ● however, as I find they represent the ti and the **tum** more naturally. Besides, the other scansion marks derive from classical metre, which was concerned with vowel *length* rather than stress.

The Great Iamb
(and other binary feet)

The word for a rising-rhythm foot with a ti-**tum**, ○●, beat like those above is an iambus, more usually called an IAMB.

I remember this by thinking of Popeye, whose trademark rusty croak went:

I *yam* what I *yam* . . .

○● ○● ○●
Iámb, iámb, iámb

We will concentrate on this foot for the rest of this section, but you should know that there are three other feet in the same BINARY (two unit) family.

The TROCHEE is a backwards iamb, a *falling* rhythm, **tum**-ti:

● ○

trochee

The trochee obeys its own definition and is pronounced to rhyme with **po**ky or **cho**ky.

● ○ ● ○ ● ○ ● ○
Trochee, **tro**chee, **tro**chee, **tro**chee

Thus was **born** my **Hia**watha,
Thus was **born** the **child** of **wond**er;

LONGFELLOW: *The Song of Hiawatha*

As a *falling* rhythm, a **tick**-tock, **tick**-tock, **tick**-tock, it finishes on an unaccented syllable – an 'and' if you're counting and clapping musically:

one and **two** and **three** and **four** and

● ○ ● ○ ● ○ ● ○

The SPONDEE is of equal stressed units: ● ● This also obeys its own definition and is pronounced to rhyme with the name *John Dee*. You may feel that it is almost impossible to give *absolutely equal* stress to two successive words or syllables in English and that there will always be some slight difference in weight. Many metrists (Edgar Allan Poe among them) would argue that the spondee doesn't functionally exist in English verse. Again, we'll think about the ramifications later, for the time being you might as well know it.

●   ●   ●   ●   ●   ●

Spondee, spondee, spondee

The fourth and final permutation is of *unstressed* units OO and is called the PYRRHIC foot. Don't bother to think about the pyrrhic either for the moment, we'll be looking at it later. All the feet possible in English are gathered in a table at the end of the chapter, with examples to demonstrate their stresses.

The *iamb* is the hero of this chapter, so let us take a closer look at it:

Iámb | iámb | iámb | iámb | iámb.

O●   O●   O●   O●   O●

Ten syllables, yes, but a count, or measure, of five feet, five *iambic* feet, culminating (the opposite of the trochaic line) in a *strong* or accented ending. SAY IT OUT LOUD AGAIN:

and **one** and **two** and **three** and **four** and **five**

He **bangs** the **drum** and **makes** a **dread**ful **noise**

It is a measure of five and the prosodic word, from the Greek again, for 'measure of five' is PENTAMETER. That simple line is an example therefore of IAMBIC PENTAMETER.

The Iambic Pentameter

The rising rhythm of the five-beat iambic pentameter has been since the fourteenth century the most widely used metre in English poetry. Chaucer's *Canterbury Tales*, Spenser's *Faerie Queen*, Shakespeare's plays and sonnets, Milton's *Paradise Lost*, the preponderance of verse by Dryden, Pope, Wordsworth, Keats, Browning, Tennyson, Owen, Yeats and Frost, all written in iambic pentameter. It is the very breath of English verse and has earned the title the HEROIC LINE.

Poetry Exercise 1

Try reading the following extracts out loud to yourself, noting the varying pulses, some strong and regularly accented, others gentler and more flowing. Each pair of lines is an example of 'perfect' iambic pentameter, having exactly ten syllables, five iambic feet (five stresses on the *even-numbered* beats) to the line. Once you've read each pair a few times, TAKE A PENCIL AND MARK UP EACH FOOT. Use a ● or a / for the *accented* syllables or words and a O or a – for the *un*accented syllables or word. I have double-spaced each pair to make it easier for you to mark them.

I really would *urge* you to take time over these: savour every line. Remember GOLDEN RULE ONE – reading verse can be like eating chocolate, so much more pleasurable when you allow it slowly to melt inside you, so much less rewarding when you snap off big chunks and bolt them whole, all but untasted.

DON'T LET YOUR EYE FALL FURTHER DOWN THE PAGE THAN THIS LINE until you have taken out your pencil or pen. You may prefer a pencil so that you can rub out your marks and leave this book in pristine condition when you lend it to someone else – naturally the publishers would prefer you to *buy* another copy for your friends – the important thing is to get used to defacing this book in one way or another. Here are the rules of the exercise again:

◆ Read each pair of lines out loud, noting the ti-**tum** rhythms.
◆ Now MARK the weak/strong (accented/unaccented) syllables and the 'bar lines' that separate each foot in this manner:

   ○   ●   ○   ●   ○   ●   ○ ●   ○   ●
He bangs | the drum | and makes | a dread | ful noise.

◆ Or you may find it easier with a pencil to do it like this:

   –   /   –   /   –   /   – /   –   /
He bangs | the drum | and makes | a dread | ful noise.

◆ When you have done this, read each pair of lines OUT LOUD once more, exaggerating the stresses on each beat.

He sit hym up withouten wordes mo,

And with his ax he smoot the corde atwo,[4]
            CHAUCER: *The Canterbury Tales*, The Reeve's Tale

That time of year, thou mayst in me behold

When yellow leaves, or none, or few, do hang
            SHAKESPEARE: Sonnet 73

In sooth I know not why I am so sad:

It wearies me; you say it wearies you;
            SHAKESPEARE: *The Merchant of Venice*, Act I, Scene 1

---

4 He sat up without another word and split the rope in two with his axe.

Their wand'ring course, now high, now low, then hid

Progressive, retrograde, or standing still
MILTON: *Paradise Lost*, Book VIII

Oft has our poet wisht, this happy Seat

Might prove his fading Muse's last retreat.
DRYDEN: 'Epilogue to Oxford'

And, spite of Pride, in erring Reason's spite,

One truth is clear, 'Whatever is, is right.'
POPE: *An Essay on Man*, Epistle 1

And thus they formed a group that's quite antique,

Half naked, loving, natural, and Greek.
BYRON: *Don Juan*, Canto II, CXCIV

Now fades the glimm'ring landscape on the sight

And all the air a solemn stillness holds.
GRAY: 'Elegy Written in a Country Churchyard'

And certain hopes are with me, that to thee

This labour will be welcome, honoured Friend!
WORDSWORTH: *The Prelude*, Book One

St Agnes' Eve – Ah, bitter chill it was!

The owl for all his feathers was a-cold;
KEATS: 'The Eve of St Agnes'

The woods decay, the woods decay and fall,

The vapours weep their burthen to the ground
                              TENNYSON: 'Tithonus'

If you could hear, at every jolt, the blood

Come gargling from the froth-corrupted lungs
                    WILFRED OWEN: 'Dulce et Decorum Est'

When you are old and grey and full of sleep

And nodding by the fire, take down this book
                        W. B. YEATS: 'When You Are Old'

And death is better, as the millions know,

Than dandruff, night-starvation, or B.O.
                    W. H. AUDEN: 'Letter to Lord Byron', II

He's worn out. He's asleep beside the stove.

When I came up from Rowe's I found him here,
                ROBERT FROST: 'The Death of the Hired Man'

Round hayfields, cornfields and potato-drills

We trekked and picked until the cans were full,
                    SEAMUS HEANEY: 'Blackberry Picking'

And praised his wife for every meal she made.

And once, for laughing, punched her in the face.
                              SIMON ARMITAGE: 'Poem'

Nearly seven hundred years of iambic pentameter represented there. Marking the beats is not a supremely challenging exercise, but remains a good way of becoming more familiar with the nature of the line and its five regular accents.

Having marked the couplets up, now GO BACK AND READ THEM, either out loud or to yourself. Simply relish them as if you were tasting wine.

Lines of iambic pentameter are, as I hope you will agree, capable of being formal, strongly accented, flowing, conversational, comic, descriptive, narrative, contemplative, declamatory and any combination of those and many other qualities. I deliberately chose pairs of lines, to show the metre flowing in more than just one line.

For all that the progression of beats is identical in each extract I hope you also saw that there are real differences of bounce and tempo, rise and fall, attack and cadence. Already it should be apparent that a very simple form, constructed from the most basic rules, is capable of strikingly different effects.

Armed with nothing more than the knowledge that an iambic pentameter is a line of five alternating weak-strong beats, it is time to attempt our own!

Poetry Exercise 2

What I want you to do *in a moment* is to put down this book, pick up your notepad and write out at least twenty lines of your *own* iambic pentameter. If you haven't time, or you're in an unsuitable place, then wait until the moment is right or go back and read the samples above again. I don't want you to read *any further* until you've tried this exercise. Before we begin, here are the rules:

♦ Write some SINGLE LINES and some PAIRS OF LINES.
♦ For this exercise, do *not* use rhyme.
♦ Write some lines, or pairs, that are conversational, some that are

simple, some that are more complicated in construction, some that are descriptive, some that are silly, some that are grave.

♦ Write with increasing speed: allow the rhythm and line length to become second nature. You will find yourself *feeling* ten syllables and five accents in an iambic line very quickly. You will hear the feet falling ahead of you to their final stressed syllable.

♦ By all means revise and rewrite your lines but DO NOT polish or strive for any effect beyond the metrical.

♦ This is an *exercise*: even if you already know about enjambment and feminine endings, or trochaic and pyrrhic substitutions *avoid* them. If you don't know about them, don't worry or be put off. You soon will.

♦ Give yourself about thirty seconds a line. That's ten minutes for twenty. No more. This is not about quality, it is about developing a feel for the metre and allowing it to become second nature.

♦ Try to use a variety of word lengths: heed Alexander Pope's warning against monosyllables:

And ten low words oft creep in one dull line[5]

♦ Avoid 'wrenching': a *wrenched* accent is a false stress applied to a word in order for it to fit the metre, thus:

He chose a word to force a wrenched accént

♦ Write in *contemporary* English, avoiding archaic 'poetical' vocabulary, word order inversions, unnecessary ('expletive') filler words like 'did' and 'so' in tortured constructions of this kind:

The swain did stand 'midst yonder sward so green

Then heard I wide the vasty portals ope

I shall do the exercise myself now, adhering to all the conditions, just to give a vague idea of the kind of thing I'm expecting.

5 From *An Essay on Criticism*.

Tock-**tick** tock-**tick** tock-**tick** tock-**tick** tock-**tick** . . .

Right. This is what I have come up with.

> I wonder why the postman hasn't come.
> I looked at eight, I'll look again at nine.
>
> The curtains closed remind me of my death.
>
> You might induce excretion using figs.
>
> Don't worry if the words don't make no sense.
>
> You look at me, your looking turns me on.
>
> I haven't time to take your call right now,
> So leave a message when you hear the tone.
>
> The mind of man can not contain itself.
>
> Some people eat like pigs and some like birds,
> Some eat like horses nosing in a trough.
>
> I write the line and feel the metre flow.
>
> There's nothing you can say to ease my pain.
>
> You can't explain the beauty of a desk –
> That rightness ink and paper seem to breathe.
>
> The needs of many far outweigh our own.
>
> Oh Christ, I hate the way you do your hair,
> Expect you feel the same about my tie.
>
> Your sharpness rips my paper heart in two.
>
> I've been and gone and done a stupid thing.

I hope that gives you the confidence to see that this exercise isn't about quality, poetic vision or verbal mastery.

Your turn now. I'll give you some blank space. It's just in case you've come without a pad. Well, blow me, look at that line 'it's **just in case** you've **come** with**out** a **pad**' – iambic pentameter gets into the system like a germ, as a seasoned Shakespearean actor will tell you.

By all means refer to the samples of iambic pentameter above: mine or those of the Masters . . .

It is time to make your metre . . . now.

How did you do? Did you get any feeling that, crude, elementary, nonsensical and bizarre as some of the lines you've written may be, they nonetheless hint at that thing we call poetry? That nothing more than the simplest use of the simplest metre suggested to you a way of expressing thoughts, stories, reflections, ideas and passions that ordinary speech or prose could never offer? Above all, that writing in strict metre doesn't result in stiff, formal or old-fashioned English?

I would recommend doing that exercise whenever you can. It is like performing scales on your piano or sketching sugar bowls and wineglasses for practice. You just get better and better and better as the extraordinary possibilities of this most basic form begin to open up.

'Nothing more than taking a line for a walk.' That is how the artist Paul Klee described drawing. It can be much the same with poetry.

For the next few days, take lots of iambs for a walk and see where their feet lead you. With notebook in hand and a world of people, nature, thoughts, news and feelings to be compressed into iambic pentameter you are taking your first poetic steps.

II

End-stopping – enjambment – caesura – weak endings – trochaic and pyrrhic substitutions

End-stopping, Enjambment and Caesura

In our first exercise we looked at existing fragments of iambic pentameter:

> The woods decay, the woods decay and fall,
> The vapours weep their burthen to the ground.

And we had a go at producing our own:

> I haven't time to take your call right now,
> So leave a message when you hear the tone.

In both examples each line contains a single thought that *finishes with the line.* This is called *end-stopping*, which we could mark like this.

> The woods decay, the woods decay and fall⊡

> I haven't time to take your call right now⊡

The iambic pentameter would be a dull dog indeed if that were all it could do.

I have already included (in *Poetry Exercise 1*) a couplet from Wilfred Owen where the meaning doesn't stop with the line, but RUNS ON through to the next:

> If you could hear, at every jolt, the blood ↩
> Come gargling from the froth-corrupted lungs

No end-stopping there. The term used to describe such a running on is *enjambment*, from the French *enjamber* to stride, literally to get one's leg over . . .

> His mother was a learned lady, famed ↵
> For every branch of every science known.
>
> BYRON: Don Juan, Canto I, X

> So threatened he, but Satan to no threats ↵
> Gave heed, but waxing more in rage replied:
>
> MILTON: Paradise Lost, Book IV

Look closely at those two examples above. Not only do they feature these run-ons or enjambments, which allow a sense of continual flow, they also contain *pauses* which break up that flow; in the examples above it happens that these pauses are expressed by commas that serve the office of a breath, or change of gear: I shall render them like this ¶.

> His mother was a learned lady ¶ famed ↵
> For every branch of every science known.

> So threatened he ¶ but Satan to no threats ↵
> Gave heed ¶ but waxing more in rage replied:

The name for such a pause or break is a *caesura*[6] (from the Latin caedere, caesum, to cut.[7] You'd pronounce it as in 'he *says* YOU'RE *a* fool').

   Caesuras don't by any means have to lead on to an enjamb-

---

6 Caesuras have a more ordered and specific role to play in French verse, dramatic or otherwise. French poems, like their geometrically planned gardens, were laid out with much greater formality than ours. They are more like regular rests in musical bars. We need not worry about this formal use.

7 Hence too, possibly, caesarean section, though some argue that this is named after Julius Caesar who was delivered that way. Others claim that this was why Julius was called Caesar in the first place, because he was from his mother's womb untimely ripped. We needn't worry about that, either. Incidentally, in America they are spelled 'cesura'.

ment as in the two examples above, however. You can have a caesura in an end-stopped line.

> The woods decay ¶ the woods decay and fall ⊡
>
> St Agnes' Eve ¶ Ah, bitter chill it was! ⊡
>
> And, spite of Pride ¶ in erring Reason's spite ⊡
> One truth is clear ¶'Whatever is, is right.'

Not every comma will signal a caesura, by the way. In Poetry Exercise 1 I included this pair of lines from *Paradise Lost*:

> Their wand'ring course, now high, now low, then hid
> Progressive, retrograde, or standing still.

Only the first comma of the first line is a caesura.

> Their wand'ring course ¶ now high, now low, then hid ⊡
> Progressive, retrograde, or standing still.

Commas in lists (*serial* commas and *Oxford* commas as grammarians would call them – a now archaic usage of commas, placing them before conjunctions like 'and', 'with' and 'or') do not usually herald a caesura; though some readers might argue that the second comma of the second line above *could* betoken the small pause or breath that defines a caesura.

How can a scrutiny of such minuscule nuances possibly help you in your writing of poetry? Well, you wait until Exercise 3: I confidently predict that you will astonish yourself.

The fact is, enjambment and caesura, these two – what shall we call them? techniques, effects, tricks, devices, tools? – however we describe them, are *crucial* liberators of the iambic line. They either *extend* or *break* the flow, allowing the rhythms and hesitations of human breath, thought and speech to enliven and enrich the verse. They are absolutely *not* a failure to obey the rules of pentameter. Let's look at the Byron and the Milton again:

> His mother was a learned lady, famed
> For every branch of every science known.

> So threatened he, but Satan to no threats
> Gave heed, but waxing more in rage replied:

You might be tempted to believe that for the sake of sense the lines *should* be written thus:

> His mother was a learned lady,
> Famed for every branch of every science known.

> So threatened he,
> But Satan to no threats gave heed,
> But waxing more in rage replied:

And Wilfred Owen's two lines could become:

> If you could hear, at every jolt,
> The blood come gargling from the froth-corrupted lungs

This arrangement would enable us to end-stop in our heads or out loud as we read the verse. Surely that's a better way of organising things? That is the *sense* after all, so why not therefore break the lines accordingly? This is the twenty-first century, isn't it?

NO, DAMN YOU, NO! A THOUSAND TIMES NO!
THE ORGANISING PRINCIPLE BEHIND THE VERSE IS NOT THE
SENSE BUT THE *METRE*.

Metre is the *primary rhythm*, the organised background against which the *secondary* rhythms of sense and feeling are played out. This is a *crucial* point. You may think that the idea of feeling and thought being subservient to metre is a loopy one. Why should poets build themselves a prison? If they've got something to say, why don't they get on and say it in the most direct manner possible? Well, painters paint within a canvas and composers within a structure. It is often the feeling of the human spirit trying to break free of constrictions that gives art its power and its correspondence to our lives, hedged in as ours are by laws and restrictions imposed both from within and without. Poets sometimes squeeze their forms to breaking point, this is what energises much verse, but if the forms were not there in the first place the verse would be listless to the point of anomie. Without gravity all would float free: the ballet leaps of the poet's language would lose almost all their power. 'Souls who have felt too much liberty', as Wordsworth said, *welcome* form: 'In truth the prison, into which we doom / Ourselves, no prison is.'[8]

Back to our caesuras and enjambments. We may not consciously be aware as we listen or read on the page, but the five beats, even when paused or run through, predominate in the inner ear. The fact that the *sense* runs through, doesn't mean the lines shouldn't end where they do.

> If you could hear, at every jolt, the blood
> Come gargling from the froth-corrupted lungs

Although there is run-on, consider in your mind and your poet's ear the different value that is given to 'blood' in the example above and in this:

> If you could hear, at every jolt,
> The blood come gargling from the froth-corrupted lungs

READ THEM BOTH ALOUD and note how much more stress is placed on 'blood' in the proper, pentametric layout. I'm sure you agree that Owen knew what he was doing and that the line structure should stay.

There will always be a tiny sense of visual or aural end-stopping at the end of a line no matter how much its sense runs on.

Shakespeare, as you would expect, in the *blank* (unrhymed)

8 Wordsworth, sonnet: 'Nuns fret not at their convent's narrow room.'

verse of his plays, uses caesura and enjambment a great deal. They are keys that unlock the dramatic potential of iambic pentameter. Look at this speech from the first scene of *The Winter's Tale*. Leontes, crazed by jealousy, believes his wife to have cuckolded him (that she's slept with another man). Here he is with their small son, Mamillius. Don't forget to recite or move your lips!

> Go play, boy, play. ¶ Thy mother plays, and I ↩
> Play too; ¶ but so disgraced a part, ¶ whose issue
> Will hiss me to my grave. ¶ Contempt and clamour ↩
> Will be my knell. ¶ Go play, boy, play. ¶ There have been,
> Or I am much deceived, ¶ cuckolds ere now,
> And many a man there is, ¶ even at this present,
> Now, ¶ while I speak this, ¶ holds his wife by th'arm ↩
> That little thinks she has been sluiced in's absence,
> And his pond fished by his next neighbour, ¶ by ↩
> Sir Smile, his neighbour. ¶ Nay there's comfort in't,
> Whiles other men have gates, ¶ and those gates opened,
> As mine, against their will. ¶ Should all despair ↩
> That have revolted wives, ¶ the tenth of mankind ↩
> Would hang themselves. ¶ Physic for't there's none.

Fourteen lines, but sixteen caesuras and seven enjambments: the verse in its stop-start jerking is as pathological and possessed as the mind of the man speaking. Compare it to another fourteen lines, the fourteen lines of the famous Eighteenth sonnet: out loud, please, or as near as dammit:

> Shall I compare thee to a summer's day?
> Thou art more lovely and more temperate.
> Rough winds do shake the darling buds of May,
> And summer's lease hath all too short a date.
> Sometime too hot the eye of heaven shines,
> And often is his gold complexion dimmed,
> And every fair from fair sometime declines,

By chance or nature's changing course untrimmed;
But thy eternal summer shall not fade
Nor lose possession of that fair thou ow'st,
Nor shall death brag thou wander'st in his shade
When in eternal lines to time thou grow'st.

So long as men can breathe or eyes can see,
So long lives this, ¶ and this gives life to thee.

No run-ons at all, and just one caesura,⁹ an absolute killer example, which gives weight to the grand and glorious resolution of the sonnet delivered by those three final feet: 'and **this** gives **life** to **thee**'. The perfectly end-stopped verse, unbroken by caesura up until that point, perfectly reflects a sense of assurance, just as the broken, spasmodic breaks and runs of Leontes's ravings perfectly reflect the opposite: a crazed and unstable state of mind.

Macbeth, considering whether or not to kill Duncan and grasp his destiny, is in something of a dither too. Say this:

> – I have no spur ↵
> To prick the sides of my intent ¶ but only ↵
> Vaulting ambition ¶ which o'erleaps itself
> And falls on th' other ¶ – How now! what news?
>
> *Macbeth*, Act I, Scene 7

How insupportably dull and lifeless dramatic verse would be if made up only of end-stopped lines. How imponderably perfect a poem can be if it *is* all end-stopped.

I should mention here that in performance many Shakespearean actors will give a vocal (and often almost imperceptible) end-stop to a line, even when there is clear run-on in its sense. In the same way that the verse works better to the eye and inner ear when the metric structure is in clear pentameters, so spoken verse

9 There are metrists who would argue that there are more caesuras than that: there may be 'weak' breaks in some of the other lines, but my reading stands, so there.

can work better when the actor represents each line with a faint pause or breath. It is a matter of fashion, context and preference. Some theatre directors hate dramatic end-stopping and are determined that meaning should take precedence over metre, others insist upon it (sometimes at the expense of clarity). An actor friend of mine, unaware of the jargon, was very alarmed on his first day as a member of the Royal Shakespeare Company to hear an old hand ask the director before the first read-through of a new production: 'Are we end-stopping, darling?' Took him three weeks to dare to ask what it meant: he had imagined it was something to do with rehearsal tea breaks.

Robert Browning, some of whose most memorable verse took the form of the *dramatic monologue* (not verse written for the stage, but poems written as if spoken by a first-person narrator), was an absolute master of the interior rhythmic play possible within the wider structures of the metre. Out loud:

> No, friend, you do not beat me: hearken why!
> The common problem, yours, mine, every one's,
> Is not to fancy what were fair in life
> Provided it could be, – but, finding first
> What may be, then find how to make it fair
> Up to our means; a very different thing!
>
> BROWNING: 'Bishop Blougram's Apology'

I'll let you mark that with caesuras and enjambments yourself. It is a marvellously complex and animated series of clauses and subordinate clauses, yet all subservient to the benign tyranny of pure iambic pentameter. Not a syllable out of place, not a 'cheat' (rogue extra syllable or rogue docked one) anywhere. A complicated and disgracefully self-justifying point is being made by the bishop, who is excusing his life of cheating, double-dealing and irreligious selfishness by means of subtle and sophisticated argument. The pauses, inner rhythms and alterations of momentum provided by the use of enjambment and caesura echo this with great wit and precision.

Doubt, assertion, reassurance, second thoughts, affirmation, question and answer, surprise and the unstable rhythms of thought and speech are some of the effects that can be achieved with these two simple devices, caesura and enjambment, within verse that still obeys the 'rules' of iambic pentameter.

I wouldn't want you to believe that they are only for use in dramatic verse like Shakespeare's and Browning's, however. After all, it is unlikely that this is the kind of poetry you will be writing yourself. Verse as reflective and contemplative as that of Wordsworth's *Prelude* makes great use of them too. MARK THE CAESURAS AND ENJAMBMENTS HERE: I shan't let you read on till you've fished out a pencil and begun, saying out loud as you go:

> Thus far, O Friend! did I, not used to make
> A present joy the matter of a song,
> Pour forth that day my soul in measured strains
> That would not be forgotten, and are here
> Recorded: to the open fields I told
> A prophecy: poetic numbers came
> Spontaneously to clothe in priestly robe
> A renovated spirit singled out,

How did it go? You might have found as I did that it was tricky to decide precisely whether or not there were caesuras in the third and seventh lines and whether there was more than one in the first. I have put the doubtful ones in brackets.

> Thus far, O Friend! did I, ¶ not used to make ↵
> A present joy the matter of a song,
> Pour forth that day my soul (¶) in measured strains (↵)
> That would not be forgotten, ¶ and are here ↵
> Recorded: ¶ to the open fields I told ↵
> A prophecy: ¶ poetic numbers came ↵
> Spontaneously (¶) to clothe in priestly robe (↵)
> A renovated spirit singled out,

If you read the poem to yourself I think the bracketed caesuras *do* indicate the faintest of breaths or pauses which would in turn suggest the bracketed run-ons. It is not an exact science despite the claims of some scholiasts and poetasters.[10] Of course, it is only of importance or interest to us here because we are examining the verse as budding poets eager to think about how life and variation is given to an otherwise over-drilled regiment of foot; we are not marking verse up either for performance or for correction by a teacher.

Enjambment and caesura can pack a great comic punch, which Byron demonstrates when he opens his mock epic *Don Juan* with a savage blast aimed precisely at the Wordsworth of the *Prelude* above and his fellow Lake District romantic poets, Coleridge and Southey. Byron *hated* them and what he saw as their pretension and vain belief that theirs was the only Poesy (poetry) worthy of wreaths (prizes and plaudits). Say this out loud:

> You – Gentlemen! ¶ by dint of long seclusion ↵
> From better company, ¶ have kept your own ↵
> At Keswick, and, ¶ through still continued fusion ↵
> Of one another's minds, ¶ at last have grown ↵
> To deem as a most logical conclusion,
> That Poesy has wreaths for you alone:
> There is a narrowness in such a notion,
> Which makes me wish you'd change your lakes for ocean.

I am sure you have now got the point that pausing and running on are an invaluable adjunct to the basic pentametric line. I have taken a long time over this because I think these two devices exemplify the crucial point that ADHERENCE TO METRE DOES NOT MILITATE AGAINST NATURALNESS. Indeed it is one of the paradoxes of art that structure, form and convention *liberate* the artist, whereas openness and complete freedom can be seen as a kind of tyranny.

10 A *scholiast* is an inkhorn or pedantic grammarian and a *poetaster* a tediously bad poet – *not*, as you might think, someone who samples the work of Edgar Allan Poe . . .

Mankind can live free in a society hemmed in by laws, but we have yet to find a historical example of mankind living free in lawless anarchy. As Auden suggested in his analogy of Robinson Crusoe, *some* poets might be able to live outside convention and rules, but most of us make a hash of it.

It is time to try your own. This exercise really is fun: don't be scared off by its conditions: I'll take you through it all myself to show you what is required and how simple it is.

Poetry Exercise 3

♦ Write five pairs of *blank* (non-rhyming) iambic pentameter in which the first line of each pair is end-stopped and there are no caesuras.
♦ Now write five pairs with (give or take) *the same meaning* in which there *is* enjambment.
♦ Make sure that each new pair also contains at least two caesuras.
♦ This may take a little longer than the first writing exercise, but no more than forty-five minutes. Again, it is not about quality.

To make it easier I will give you a specific subject for all five pairs.

1. Precisely what you see and hear outside your window.
2. Precisely what you'd like to eat, right this minute.
3. Precisely what you last remember dreaming about.
4. Precisely what uncompleted chores are niggling at you.
5. Precisely what you hate about your body.

Once again I have had a pitiful go myself to give you an idea of what I mean.

WITHOUT caesura or enjambment:

1 Outside the Window
I hear the traffic passing by my house,
While overhead the blackbirds build their nests.

2 What I'd Like to Eat
I'd really like some biscuits I can dunk,
Unsalted crisps would fill a gap as well.

3 A Recent Dream
I dreamt an airport man had lost my bags
And all my trousers ended up in Spain.

4 Pesky Tasks Overdue
I need to tidy up my papers now
And several ashtrays overflow with butts.

5 My Body
Too many chins and such a crooked nose,
Long flabby legs and rather stupid hair.

With caesura and enjambment:

1 Outside the Window
The song of cars, so like the roar the sea
Can sing, has drowned the nesting blackbirds' call.

2 What I'd Like to Eat
Some biscuits, dunked – but quick in sudden stabs
Like beaks. Oh, crisps as well. Unsalted, please.

3 A Recent Dream
Security buffoons, you sent my strides
To Spain, and all my bags to God knows where.

4 Pesky Tasks Overdue
My papers seethe. Now all my writing desk
Erupts. Volcanic mountains cough their ash.

5 My Body
Three flobbing chins are bad, but worse, a bent
And foolish nose. Long legs, fat thighs, mad hair.

These are only a guide. Go between each Before and After I have composed and see what I did to enforce the rules. Then pick up your pencil and pad and have a go yourself.

Use the same titles for your couplets that I did for mine. The key is to find a way of breaking the line, then running on to make the enjambment. It doesn't have to be elegant, sensible or clever, mine aren't, though I will say that the very nature of the exercise forces you, whether you intend it or not, to *concentrate* the sense and movement of the phrasing in a way that at least gestures towards that distillation and compactness that marks out real poetry. Here's your blank space.

Weak Endings, Trochaic and
Pyrrhic Substitutions

Let us now return to Macbeth, who is still considering whether or
not he should kill Duncan. He says out loud, as indeed do you: 'I
have no spur . . .

> To prick the sides of my intent, but only
> Vaulting ambition, which o'erleaps itself
> And falls on th' other. – How now! what news?

Forgetting caesuras and enjambments this time, have a look at the
three lines as an example of iambic pentameter. Get that pencil out
and try marking each accented and unaccented syllable.

Eleven syllables! There's a rogue extra syllable at the end of line
1, isn't there? An unstressed orphan bringing up the rear. The line
scans like this:

○ ● ○ ● ○ ● ○ ● ○ ● ☐○☐
To **prick** the **sides** of **my** in**tent**, but **on** ly

There is more: the *next* line doesn't start with an iamb at all! Unless
the actor playing Macbeth says 'vaul**ting** ambition' the line goes . . .

☐●○☐   ○ ● ○   ●   ○ ● ○ ●
☐Vaulting☐ ambition **which** o'er **leaps** it**self**

The mighty Shakespeare deviating from metre? He is starting an
iambic line with a **tum**-ti, a *trochee*.

☐tum-ti☐ ti-**tum** ti- **tum**   ti-**tum** ti-**tum**

Actually, in both cases he is employing two *variations* that are so
common and necessary to lively iambic verse that they are not
unusual enough even to call deviations.

We will attend to that *opening trochaic foot* in a moment. Let
us first examine this orphan or 'rogue' unaccented syllable at the

end of the line. It makes the line eleven syllables long or *hendeca-syllabic*.

○ ● ○ ● ○ ● ○● ○ ●○
To prick the sides of my intent, but only

It results in what is called a *weak* or *feminine* ending (I hope my female readers won't be offended by this. Blame the French, we inherited the term from them. I shall try not to use it often). Think of the most famous iambic pentameter of all:

To be or not to be that is the question

Count the syllables and mark the accents. It does the same thing ('question' by the way is *disyllabic*, two syllables, any actor who said **quest**-i-**on** would be laughed off the stage and out of Equity. It is certainly *kwestchən*[11]).

○ ● ○ ● ○ ● ○ ● ○　 ● ○
To be or not to be that is the question

If you think about it, the very nature of the iamb means that if this additional trick were disallowed to the poet then *all* iambic verse would have to terminate in a stressed syllable, a masculine ending . . .

If winter comes can spring be far behind?

. . . would be possible, but

A thing of beauty is a joy for ev(er)

. . . would not. Keats would have had to find a monosyllabic word meaning 'ever' and he would have ended up with something that sounded Scottish, archaic, fey or precious even in his own day (the early nineteenth century).

A thing of beauty is a joy for ay

11　ə is a *schwa*, that slack 'e' sound, the *uh* in *bigger* or *written*.

Words like 'excitement', 'little', 'hoping', 'question', 'idle', 'widest' or 'wonder' could *never* be used to close an iambic line. That would be a ridiculous restriction in English. How absurdly limiting not to be able to end with an -ing, or an -er or a -ly or a -tion or any of the myriad weak endings that naturally occur in our language.

BUT THERE IS MORE TO IT THAN THAT. A huge element of all art is constructed in the form of *question* and *answer*. The word for this is *dialectic*. In music we are very familiar with this call-and-response structure. The opening figure of Beethoven's Fifth is a famous example:

Da-da-da-Dah
Da-da-da-Derr

Beethoven actually went so far as to write the following in the score of the Finale of his String Quartet in F major:

Muss es sein? Must it be?
Es muss sein! It must be!

In poetry this is a familiar structure:

Q: Shall I compare thee to a summer's day?
A: Thou art more lovely and more temperate.

It is common in rhetoric too.

Ask not what your country can do for you
But what you can do for your country.

This is a deep, instinctive property of so much human communication. In the Greek drama and dance it was called *strophe* and *antistrophe*, in the liturgy of the Church it is known as *versicle* and *response*.

One might suggest that this is something to do with the in-and-out pumping of the heart itself (*systole* and *diastole*) and the very breath of life (*inhalation* and *exhalation*). Yin and yang and other binary oppositions in thought and the natural world come to mind. We also reason dialectically, from problem to solution, from proposition to conclusion, from *if* to *then*. It is the copulation of utterance: the means by which thought and expression mimic creation by taking one thing (*thesis*), suggesting another (*antithesis*) and making something new of the coupling (*synthesis*), prosecution, defence, verdict.

The most obvious example of a poem with an *if* ⇨ *then* structure is of course Kipling's poem 'If', regularly voted 'the nation's favourite'. It is written in strict iambic pentameter, but with alternating feminine and masculine line endings throughout. He does this with absolute regularity throughout the poem: switching between lines of weak (eleven syllable) and strong (ten syllable) endings, which gives a characteristic swing to the verse. Try reading out loud each *stanza* (or verse) below, exaggerating the *tenth* syllable in each line as you read, tapping the table (or your thigh) and really emphasising the last beat. Do you see how this metrical alternation precisely suggests a kind of dialectical structure?

> If you can keep your head when all **about** you
> Are losing theirs and blaming it on **you**,
> If you can trust yourself when all men **doubt** you
> But make allowance for their doubting **too**,
>
> If you can dream – and not make dreams your **master**,
> If you can think – and not make thoughts your **aim**;
> If you can meet with Triumph and Dis**aster**
> And meet those two impostors just the **same**;
>
> If you can fill the unforgiving **minute**
> With sixty seconds' worth of distance **run**,
> Yours is the Earth and everything that's **in** it,
> And – which is more – you'll be a Man, my **son**!

What's actually happening is that the wider line structures echo the metrical structure: just as the *feet* go weak-**strong**, so the lines go weak-**strong**.

You might put the thought into iambic pentameters:

The weaker ending forms a kind of question
The stronger ending gives you your reply.

The finality of downstroke achieved by a strong ending seems to answer the lightness of a weak one. After all, the most famous weak ending there is just happens to be the very word 'question' itself . . .

To be, or not to be: that is the question.

It is not a rule, the very phrase 'question-and-answer' is only an approximation of what we mean by 'dialectic' and, naturally, there is a great deal more to it than I have suggested. Through French poetry we have inherited a long tradition of alternating strong-weak line endings, which we will come to when we look at verse forms and rhyme. The point I am anxious to make, however, is that metre is more than just a ti-**tum** ti-**tum**: its very regularity and the consequent variations available within it can yield a structure that EXPRESSES MEANING QUITE AS MUCH AS THE WORDS THEMSELVES DO.

Which is not to say that eleven syllable lines *only* offer questions: sometimes they are simply a variation available to the poet and result in no particular extra meaning or effect. Kipling does demonstrate though, in his hoary old favourite, that when used deliberately and regularly, alternate measures can do more. The metrist Timothy Steele[12] has pointed out how Shakespeare, in his twentieth sonnet 'A woman's face, with Nature's own hand painted' uses *only* weak endings throughout the poem: every line is eleven syllables. Shakespeare's *conceit* in the poem (his image, or overarching concept) is that his beloved, a boy, has all the feminine graces. The proliferation of feminine endings is therefore a kind of metrical pun.

Macbeth's 'Tomorrow and tomorrow and tomorrow' is another

12 T. Steele. *All the Fun's in How You Say a Thing*, Ohio University Press.

celebrated example of iambic pentameter ending with that extra or *hypermetrical* unstressed syllable. Note, incidentally, that while you would not normally choose to emphasise a word like 'and' in a line of poetry, the beauty of Shakespeare's iambs here is that the rhythm calls for the actor playing Macbeth to hit those 'ands' harder than one would in a line like:

I want some jam and tea and toast today

With Shakespeare's line . . .

Tomorrow *and* tomorrow *and* tomorrow

. . . the futility and tedium of the succession of tomorrows is all the more manifest because of the metrical position of those 'ands'. Which of us hasn't stressed them in sentences like 'I've got to mow the lawn *and* pick up the kids from school *and* do the tax returns *and* write a thank you letter *and* cancel the theatre tickets *and* ring the office . . .'?

An eleven-syllable line was more the rule than the exception in Italian poetry, for the obvious reason that an iambic hendeca-syllabic line must have a *weak* ending, like-a almost-a ever-y word-a in Italian-o. Dante's *Inferno* is written in iambic *endecasíllabo*.

Nel mezzo del cammin di nostra vita

An English translation might go, in iambic pentameter:

Midway upon the journey through our life

There would be no special reason to use hendecasyllables in trans-lating the *Inferno*: in fact, it would be rather difficult. English, unlike Italian, is full of words that end with a stressed syllable. The very nature of the iamb is its light-heavy progression, it seems to be a deeply embedded feature of English utterance: to throw that away in the pursuit of imitating the metrics of another language would be foolish.

Lots of food for thought there, much of it beyond the scope of this book. The point is that the eleven-syllable line is open to you in *your* iambic verse.

Why not *nine* syllables, you may be thinking? Why not *dock* a syllable and have a nine-syllable line with a weak ending?

Let's **sit** our**selves** be**side** this **riv**er

Well, this docking, this *catalexis*, results in an iambic *tetrameter* (four accents to a line) with a weak ending, that extra syllable. The point about pentameter is that it must have *five* stresses in it. The above example has only *four*, hence *tetra*meter (pronounced, incidentally, tetrAmeter, as pentameter is pentAmeter).

Writers of iambic pentameter always *add* an unstressed syllable to make eleven syllables with five beats, they don't take off a strong one to make four. They must keep that count of five. If you choose iambic pentameter you stick to it. The heroic line, the five-beat line, speaks in a very particular way, just as a waltz has an entirely different quality from a polka. A four-beat line, a tetrameter, has its individual characteristics too as we shall soon see, but it is rare to mix them up in the same poem. It is no more a *rule* than it is a rule never to use oil paints and watercolours in the same picture, but you *really have to know what you're doing* if you decide to try it. For the purposes of these early exercises, we'll stay purely penta-metric.

Here are a few examples of hendecasyllabic iambic penta-meter, quoting some of the same poets and poems we quoted before. They all go:

And **one** and **two** and **three** and **four** and **five** and

○ ● ○ ● ○ ● ○ ● ○ ● ▢

OUT WITH YOUR PENCIL AND MARK THEM UP: don't forget to SAY THEM OUT LOUD to yourself to become familiar with the *effect* of the weak ending.

So priketh hem nature in hir corages;
Than longen folk to goon on pilgrimages[13]

> CHAUCER: *The Canterbury Tales*, General Prologue

A woman's face with Nature's own hand painted
Hast thou, the master-mistress of my passion;

> SHAKESPEARE: Sonnet 20

That thou shall see the diff'rence of our spirits,
I pardon thee thy life before thou ask it:

> SHAKESPEARE: *The Merchant of Venice*, Act IV, Scene 1

How heinous had the fact been, how deserving
Contempt, and scorn of all to be excluded

> MILTON,[14] *Samson Agonistes*

Our Brethren, are from *Thames* to *Tweed* departed,
And of our Sisters, all the kinder hearted,
To *Edenborough* gone, or Coacht, or Carted.

> DRYDEN: 'Prologue to the University of Oxford'

What can enable sots, or slaves or cowards?
Alas! not all the blood of all the HOWARDS.

> POPE:[15] *Essay on Man*

---

13 'Nature so spurs them on that people long to go on pilgrimages.'

14 Milton, like many seventeenth- and eighteenth-century exponents of iambic pentameter, seemed very reluctant to use feminine endings, going so far as always to mark 'heaven' as the monosyllable 'heav'n' whenever it ended a line. Finding two hendecasyllables in a row in *Paradise Lost* is like looking for a condom machine in the Vatican.

15 Ditto: Pope took great pride in the decasyllabic nature of his rhyming couplets. This is one of only two feminine endings in the whole (over 1,500 line) poem, the other being a rhyme of 'silly' with 'Sir Billy': it seems it was acceptable to Pope so long as the rhyming words were proper names. Maybe here he hears Cowards as Cards and Howards as Hards . . .

It gives to think that our immortal being ...

WORDSWORTH:[16] The Prelude

A thing of beauty is a joy for ever
Its loveliness increases: it will never
Pass into nothingness;

KEATS: *Endymion*, Book One

And like the flowers beside them, chill and shiver,

ROBERT FROST: 'Spring Pools'

With guarded unconcerned acceleration

SEAMUS HEANEY: 'From the Frontier of Writing'

There's far too much encouragement for poets –

WENDY COPE: 'Engineers' Corner'

Substitutions

I hope you can see that the feminine ending is by no means the mark of imperfect iambic pentameter. Let us return to Macbeth, who is *still* unsure whether or not he should stab King Duncan:

To prick the sides of my intent, but only
Vaulting ambition, which o'erleaps itself
And falls on th' other. – How now! what news?

We have cleared up the first variation in this selection of three lines, the weak or unstressed ending. But what about this 'vault**ing**

16 Wordsworth's hero was, poetically and politically, Milton and W shows the same disdain for weak endings. I'm fairly convinced that for him 'being' is actually elided into the monosyllable 'beeng'!

ambition' problem? Keats has done it too, look, at the continuation to his opening to *Endymion*:

A thing of beauty is a joy for ever
Its loveliness increases: it will never
Pass into **nothingness**; but **still** will **keep**
A bower quiet for us, and a sleep
Full of sweet **dreams**, and **health**, and **quiet breath**ing

The first feet of lines 3 and 5 are 'inverted iambs' or *trochees*. What Keats and Shakespeare have employed here is sometimes called *trochaic substitution*, a technique, like weak endings, too common to be considered a deviation from the iambic norm. It is mostly found, as in the above instances and the following, in the *first foot* of a line. You could call it a trochaic substitution, or the *inversion* of an iamb – it amounts to the same thing.

● ○ ○ ●○ ● ○ ● ○ ●
Mix'd in each other's arms, and heart in heart,
> BYRON: *Don Juan*, Canto IV, XXVII

Well have ye judged, well ended long debate,
Synod of gods, and like to what ye are,
> MILTON: *Paradise Lost*, Book II

Far from the madding crowd's ignoble strife
> GRAY: 'Elegy Written in a Country Churchyard'

Shall I compare thee to a summer's day?
> SHAKESPEARE: Sonnet 18

That's an interesting one, the last. Shakespeare's famous sonnet opens in a way that allows different emphases. Is it **Shall** I compare thee, Shall **I** compare thee or **Shall I** compare thee? The last would be a *spondaic substitution*. You remember the spondee, two equally stressed beats?[17] What do you feel? How would you read it out? There's no right or wrong answer.

Trochaic substitution of an *interior* foot is certainly not uncommon either. Let's return to the opening of Hamlet's great soliloquy:

○ ● ○ ● ○ ● | ● ○ | ○ ● ○
To **be**, or **not** to **be**: **that** is the **question**

Here, the fourth foot can certainly be said to be trochaic. It is helped, as most interior trochaic switches are, by the very definite caesura, marked here by the colon. The pause after the opening statement splits the line into two and allows the trochaic substitution to have the effect they usually achieve at the beginning of a line. Without that caesura at the end of the preceding foot, interior trochaic substitutions can be cumbersome.

○ ● ○ ● ○ ● | ● ○ | ○ ●
He bangs the drum and makes terrible sounds

That's not a very successful line, frankly it reads as prose: even with the 'and' where it is, the instinct in reading it as verse is to make the caesural pause after 'makes' – this resolves the rhythm for us. We don't mind starting a phrase with a trochee, but it sounds all wrong inserted into a full flow of iambs.

○ ● ○ ● | ● ○ | ○ ● ○ ●
He bangs the drum: terrible sounds he makes.

That's better: the colon gives a natural caesura with which to split the line allowing us to start the new thought with a trochee.

For this reason, you will find that *initial* trochaic substitution (i.e. that of the first foot) is by far the most common.

---

17 Many prosodists would argue, as I have said earlier, that there is no such thing as a spondee in English verse, partly because no two contiguous syllables can be pronounced with absolute equal stress and partly because a spondee is really a description not of accent, but of *vowel length*, an entirely different concept, and one essentially alien to English prosody.

Milton! Thou shouldst be living at this hour:
England hath need of thee: she is a fen

WORDSWORTH: 'Milton!'

Season of mists and mellow fruitfulness!

KEATS: 'Ode to Autumn'

Just as it would be a pointless limitation to disallow *unstressed endings* to a line, so it would be to forbid *stressed beginnings*. Hence trochaic substitution.

There's one more inversion to look at before our heads burst.

Often in a line of iambic pentameter you might come across a line like this, from Shakespeare's Sonnet 1:

But thou, contracted to thine own bright eyes

How would you scan it?

But **thou,** | contract | ed to | thine **own** | bright **eyes**

'Contracted **to** thine own bright eyes' is rather ugly, don't we think? After all there's no valuable distinction of meaning derived by hitting that innocent little particle. So has Shakespeare, by only the fifth line of his great sonnet sequence already blown it and mucked up his iambic pentameters?

Well no. Let's scan it like this:

But **thou,** | contract | ed to | thine **own** | bright **eyes**[18]

That third foot is now *pyrrhic*, two *unaccented* beats: we've taken the usual stress off its second element, we have 'demoted' the foot, if you like. We have, in metrical jargon, effected *pyrrhic substitution*.

---

18 If you already know your feet and think that this is really an amphibrach, a dactyl and two iambs, I'm afraid I shall have to kill you.

This is most likely to occur in the third or fourth foot of a line, otherwise it disrupts the primary rhythm too much. It is essential too, in order for the metre to keep its pulse, that the pyrrhic foot be followed by a proper iamb. Pyrrhic substitution results, as you can see above, in *three* unaccented beats in a row, which are resolved by the next accent (in this case **own**).

Check what I'm saying by flicking your eyes up and reading out loud. It can all seem a bit bewildering as I bombard you with references to the third foot and the second unit and so on, but so long as you keep checking and reading it out (writing it down yourself too, if it helps) you can keep track of it all and IT IS WORTH DOING.

Incidentally, Vladimir Nabokov in his *Notes on Prosody* is very unkind about calling these effects 'substitutions' – he prefers to call a pyrrhic substitution a 'scud' or 'false pyrrhic' and a trochaic substitution a 'tilted scud' or 'false trochee'. I am not sure this is any clearer, to be honest.

Anyway, you might have spotted that this trick, this trope, this 'downgrading' of one accent, has the effect of drawing extra attention to the following one. The next strong iambic beat, the **own** has *all the more emphasis* for having followed three unstressed syllables.

If the demotion were to take place in the *fourth* foot it would emphasise the *last* beat of the line, as in this pyrrhic substitution in Wilfred Owen's 'Anthem for Doomed Youth', which as it happens also begins with a *trochaic* switch. READ IT OUT LOUD:

1		2		3		4		5
● ○		○ ●		○ ●		○ ○		○ ●
Not in		the **hands**		of **boys**		but in		their **eyes**

Both the excerpts above contain pyrrhic substitution, Shakespeare's in the third foot, Owen's in the fourth. Both end with the word 'eyes', but can you see how Shakespeare's use of it in the *third* foot causes the stress to hammer harder down on the word **own** and

46

how Owen's use of it in the *fourth* really pushes home the emphasis on **eyes**? Which, after all, is the point the line is making, *not* in their hands, but in their *eyes*. (Incidentally, I think the trochaic substitution in the first foot also helps emphasise 'hands'. Thus, when read out, the line contrasts hands and eyes with extra emphasis.)

Owen's next line repeats the pyrrhic substitution in the same, fourth, foot.

Shall shine the holy glimmers of good-byes.

A stressed **of** would be a horrid example of what's called a *wrenched accent*, an unnatural stress forced in order to make the metre work: scudding over the 'of' and making the foot pyrrhic does not sacrifice the metre.

1		2	3		4	5	
○	●	○ ●	○	●	○ ○	○	●

Shall **shine** | the ho | ly **glimm** |ers of |good-**byes**

Owen was a poet who, like Shakespeare, *really knew what he was doing.* These effects are not accidental, the substitutions do not come about by chance or through some carefree inability to adhere to the form and hoping for the best. Owen studied metre and form constantly and obsessively, as did Keats, his hero, as indeed did all the great poets. They would no more be *unaware* of what they were doing than Rubens could be unaware of what he was doing when he applied an impasto dot of white to give shine to an eye, or than Beethoven could be unaware of what happened when he diminished a seventh or syncopated a beat. The freedom and the ease with which a master can do these things belies immense skill derived from practice.

Incidentally, when Rubens was a young man he went round Rome feverishly drawing and sketching antique statues and Old Master paintings, lying on his back, standing on ladders, endlessly varying his viewpoint so as to give himself differing angles and perspectives. He wanted to be able to paint or draw any aspect of the human form from any angle, to master foreshortening and moulding and all the other techniques, spending months on rendering hands alone. All the great poets did the equivalent in their notebooks: busying themselves endlessly with different metres, substitutions, line lengths, poetic forms and techniques. They wanted to master their art as Rubens mastered his. They say that the poet Tennyson knew the *quantity* of every word in the English language except 'scissors'. A word's quantity is essentially the sum of the duration of its vowels. We shall come to that later. The point is this: poetry is all about *concentration*, the concentration of mind and the concentration of thought, feeling and language into words within a rhythmic structure. In normal speech and prose our thoughts and feelings are *diluted* (by stock phrases and round-about approximations); in poetry those thoughts and feelings can be, must be, *concentrated*.

It may seem strange for us to focus in such detail on something as apparently piffling as a pyrrhic substitution, but I am convinced that a sense, an awareness, a familiarity and finally a mastery of this and all the other techniques we have seen and will see allow us a confidence and touch that the uninformed reading and writing of verse could never bestow. It is a little like changing gear in a car: it can seem cumbersome and tricky at first, but it soon becomes second nature. It is all about developing the poetic equivalent of 'muscle memory'. With that in mind, here are some more lines featuring these stress demotions or pyrrhic substitutions. I have boxed the first two examples and explained my thinking. Here is one from the Merchant's Tale:

    ○ ●   ○ ●   ○ ●   &boxed;○   ○&boxed;   ○ ●
And up | he yaf | a ror | yng and | a cry,

You would not say 'a roaring AND a cry' unless the sense demanded it. Chaucer, like Owen, shows that a demotion of the *fourth* beat throws more weight on to the fifth: CRY. Owen demonstrates that it is possible with the second beat too.

○　●　｜○　○｜　○　●　○　●　○　●

Come gargling from the froth-corrupted lungs

'Come gargling **from** the froth-corrupted lungs' seems a bit wrenched. The demotion allows the push here on 'garg' and 'froth' to assume greater power: 'Come **garg**ling from the **froth**-corrupted **lungs**'.

Look at these lines from a poem that every American school-child knows: 'Stopping by Woods on a Snowy Evening', by Robert Frost. It is the literary equivalent of 'The Night Before Christmas', quoted and misquoted every holiday season in the States:

> The **woods** are **lovely**, **dark**, and **deep**,
> But **I** have **prom**ises to **keep**,
> And **miles** to **go** before I **sleep**,

To read the phrase '**prom**isés to **keep**' would be an absurd wrench, wouldn't it? Clearly that's a pyrrhic substitution too.

The opening line of Shakespeare's *Richard III* has a demoted third beat: note that the first line begins with a trochaic substitution:

Now is the **win**ter of our **dis**con**tent**

So here is a summary of the six new techniques we've learned to enrich the iambic pentameter.

1. End-stopping: how the sense, the thought, can end with the line.
2. Enjambment: how it can run *through* the end of a line.
3. Caesura: how a line can have a break, a breath, a pause, a gear change.
4. Weak endings: how you can end the line with an extra, weak syllable.
5. Trochaic substitution: how you can *invert* the iamb to make a trochee.
6. Pyrrhic substitution: how you can *downgrade* the beat of an interior (second, third or fourth) foot to turn it into a doubly weak or *pyrrhic* foot.

Poetry Exercise 4

You can probably guess what I'm going to ask for here. Sixteen unrhymed lines of iambic pentameter. The idea is to use pyrrhic and trochaic substitutions (five points for each), weak endings – that extra syllable at the end (two points for each) but all without going overboard and losing the primary iambic rhythm. You can also award yourself two points for every successful enjambment.

Before you embark upon your own, we are going take a look at and mark my attempt at the exercise. I have sought inspiration, if that is the word, from the headlines on today's BBC news website and would recommend this as preferable to staring out of the window chewing the end of a pencil awaiting the Muse's kiss. Four news stories in all.

> Policemen, in a shocking poll revealed
> They have no time for apprehending felons
> Criminals now at last are free to work.
>
> Why can't the English play the game of cricket?
> Inside a tiny wooden urn are buried
> The Ashes of a great and sporting nation.[19]
>
> Babies are now available in female
> Or male. Hard to decide which sex I'll pick.
> Maybe I'll wait till gender is redundant.
>
> Towards the middle of a mighty ocean
> Squats a forgotten island and its people;
> The sea that laps the margins of the atoll
> Broadcasts no mindless babble on its waves;
> No e-mail pesters the unsullied palm groves
> Newspaper stories pass it quietly by.
> How long before we go there and destroy it?

19 When I wrote this, we had just lost the first Test against Australia and I was pessimistic . . .

I know. Pathetic, isn't it? I hope you are filled with confidence. Once again, I must emphasise, these are no more poems than practise scales are sonatas. They are purely exercises, as yours should be. Work on solving the problems of prosody, but don't get hung up about images, poetic sensibility and word choices. The lines and thoughts should make sense, but beyond that doggerel is acceptable.

GET YOUR PENCIL OUT and mark the metre in each line of my verses. It should be fairly clear when the line starts with a trochee, but pyrrhics can be more subjective. I shall do my marking below: see if you agree with me. **P** for a pyrrhic substitution, **T** for a trochaic. **H** for hendecasyllable (or for hypermetric, I suppose). **E** is for enjambment.

$$- / \quad \boxed{- \ -} - \ / \ - \ / \ - \ / \quad \textbf{P}$$

Policemen, in a shocking poll revealed   5

That's a pretty clear pyrrhic in the second foot: no need to stress the 'in' and I reckon the rest of the line recovers its iambic tread, so five points to me.

$$- \ / \ - \ / \ - \ / \ - \ / \ - \ / \ (-) \quad \textbf{H}$$

They have no time for apprehending felons   2

Straight iambics, just two points for the hypermetric ending.

$$\boxed{/ \ -} - \ / \ - \ / \ - \ / \ - \ / \quad \textbf{T}$$

Criminals now at last are free to work.   5

Five points for the initial trochee.

$$\boxed{/ \ -} \quad - \ / \ - \ / \ - \ / \ - \ / \ (-) \quad \textbf{T} \qquad \textbf{H}$$

Why can't the English learn the game of cricket?   7

Five for the opening trochee (I think you'll agree that it is '**why**
can't', not 'why **can't**') plus two for the weak ending.

$$H$$
$$- \; / \; - \; / \; - \quad / \; - \quad / \quad - \quad / \; (-)$$
Inside a tiny wooden urn are buried   2

Iambics: just two for the ending (it's a bit like scoring for cribbage,
this . . .)

$$\quad\quad\quad\quad P \quad\quad\quad\quad\quad\quad\quad\quad H$$
$$- \quad / \; \boxed{- \; -} - \quad / \quad - \quad\quad / \quad - \quad / \; (-)$$
The Ashes of a great and sporting nation.

Five for the pyrrhic and two for the ending.   7

$$T \quad\quad\quad\quad\quad\quad\quad\quad P \quad\; H$$
$$\boxed{/ \; -} \; - \quad / \quad - \; / \boxed{- \; -} \; - \quad / \; (-)$$
Babies are now available in female ↵   E $14 - 5 = 9$

High-scoring one here: five for the trochaic switch in the first foot,
five for the pyrrhic in the fourth: plus two for the ending and two
for the enjambment. The question is: does it still feel iambic with
all those bells and whistles? My view is that it would if it were in
the midst of more regular iambic lines, but since it is the first line
of a stanza it is hard for the ear to know what is going on. A trochaic
first foot allied to a weak ending gives an overall trochaic effect,
especially when the middle is further vitiated by the slack syllables
of the pyrrhic. Also, the end word 'female' is almost spondaic. So I
shall *deduct* five for bad style.

$$\quad\quad\quad\quad\quad\quad T$$
$$- \quad / \quad \boxed{/ \; -} \; - \; / \quad - \quad / \; - \quad /$$
Or male. Hard to decide which sex I'll pick.   5

A trochaic switch mid line for five points: since it follows a caesura
the rest of the line picks up the iambic pulse adequately.

$$\text{T} \qquad\qquad\qquad \text{P} \qquad \text{H}$$
$$\boxed{/ \ -} \ - \ / \ - \ / \ \boxed{- \ -} \ - \ / \ (-)$$
Maybe I'll wait till gender is redundant. $\qquad 12 - 3 = 9$

Trochaic of the first with pyrrhic of the fourth again. For some reason I don't think this one misses its swing so much as the other, so I'll only deduct three. Then again, perhaps it keeps its swing because it isn't a real pyrrhic: hard not to give a push to the 'is' there, don't we feel?

$$\qquad\qquad\qquad \text{P} \qquad\qquad \text{H}$$
$$- \ / \ - \ / \ \boxed{- \ -} - \ / \ - \ /(-)$$
Towards the middle of a mighty ocean $\qquad\qquad$ 7

$$\quad \text{T} \qquad\qquad\qquad \text{P} \qquad \text{H}$$
$$\boxed{/ \ -} - \ / \ - \ / \ \boxed{- \ -} \ - \ / \ (-)$$
Squats a forgotten island and its people; $\qquad\qquad$ 12

$$\qquad\qquad\qquad\qquad\quad \text{P} \qquad \text{H}$$
$$- \ / \ - \ / \ - \ / \ \boxed{- \ -} \ - \ /(-)$$
The sea that laps the margins of the atoll $\qquad\qquad$ 7

$$\quad \text{T} \qquad\qquad\qquad\qquad\qquad \text{P}$$
$$\boxed{/ \ -} \ - \ / \ - \ / \ \boxed{- \ -} \ - \ /$$
Broadcasts no mindless babble on its waves; $\qquad\qquad$ 10

$$\qquad\qquad \text{P} \qquad\qquad\qquad \text{H}$$
$$- \ / \ - \ / \ \boxed{- \ -} \ - \ / \ - \ / \ (-)$$
No e-mail pesters the unsullied palm groves $\qquad\qquad$ 7

$$\quad \text{T}$$
$$\boxed{/ \ -} - \ / \ - \ / \ - \ / \ - \ /$$
Newspaper stories pass it quietly by. $\qquad\qquad$ 5

$$\qquad\qquad\qquad\qquad \text{P} \qquad\qquad \text{H}$$
$$- \ / \ - \ / \ - \ / \ \boxed{- \ -} \ - \ / \ (-)$$
How long before we go there and destroy it? $\qquad\qquad$ 7

I make my score 106. I'm sure you could do better with your sixteen lines. To recap:

- ◆ 16 lines of iambic pentameter
- ◆ 5 points for trochaic and pyrrhic substitutions
- ◆ 2 points for enjambments
- ◆ 2 points for feminine endings

Be tough on yourself when marking. If, in a bid to make a high score, you have lost the underlying rising tread of the iambic pentameter, then deduct points with honesty. Have fun!

III

More Meters

Why *five* feet to a line, why not four or six? Three or seven? Eight even.

Why not indeed. Here's a list of the most likely possibilities:

1 Beat – Monometer
He **bangs**
The **drum**.

2 Beats – Dimeter
His **drum**ming **noise**
A**wakes** the **boys**.

3 Beats – Trimeter
His **drum**ming **makes** a **noise**,
And **wakes** the **sleep**ing **boys**.

4 Beats – Tetrameter
He **bangs** the **drum** and **makes** a **noise**,
It **shakes** the **roof** and **wakes** the **boys**.

5 Beats – Pentameter
He **bangs** the **drum** and **makes** a **dread**ful **noise**,
It **shakes** the **roof** and **wakes** the **sleep**ing **boys**.

6 Beats – Hexameter
He **bangs** the **drum** and **makes** the **most** ap**pall**ing **noise**,
It **shakes** the **very roof** and **wakes** the **sleep**ing **boys**.

7 Beats – Heptameter

He **bangs** the **wretch**ed **drum** and **makes** the **most**
ap**pall**ing **noise**,
Its **rack**et **shakes** the **very roof** and **wakes** the **sleep**ing
boys.

8 Beats – Octameter

He **starts** to **bang** the **wretch**ed **drum** and **make** the **most**
ap**pall**ing **noise**,
Its **dread**ful **rack**et **shakes** the **very roof** and **wakes** the
sleeping **boys**.

I have hardly given more information in the octameter, heptameter, hexameter or pentameter than there is in the tetrameter – of
course the boys are *sleeping*, you can't wake someone who isn't,
and a *very* roof is still a roof. I have made up my own nonsense
specifically to show the variation in feel when the sense or narrative
is broadly the same and the number of feet marks the only real
difference. Generally speaking, and I do mean very generally, the
pentameter is used for 'serious' poetry, for contemplative, epic, heroic
and dramatic verse. That doesn't mean that the other measures can't
be. We will come to how we choose a particular form or line of
verse later. At the moment we are more interested in discovering
and defining terms than ascribing value or function to them. The
technical difference is what concerns us, the stylistic difference is
for a later section of the book.

Six feet give us a *hexameter*, the line of choice in most classical
verse:

> 1   2   3   4   5   6
> He **bangs** | the **drum** | and **makes** | the **most** | ap**pall** | -ing **noise**.

As a single line it works fine. The experience of writing whole
poems in hexameters, in six footers, is that they turn out to be a bit
cumbersome in English. The pentameter seems to fit the human
breath perfectly (which is why it was used, not just by Shakespeare,

but by just about all English verse dramatists). French poets and playwrights like Racine did use the hexameter or *alexandrine*[20] all the time, in English verse it is rare. What's so different about French, then? I think the most important reason is, as I made clear earlier, that French words tend not to be so varied in their accentuation as English. Why is this relevant? Well, it means that French poetry, since so many words are equally stressed, relies more on what is known as 'quantitative measure' – divisions based on the temporal duration of long and short vowels.[21] This is how classical Greek and Latin poetry was constructed. Most English verse – as I hope we have discovered – is metred by *syllabic accentuation*, the rises and falls of stress.

You can certainly try to write whole English poems composed of iambic hexameter, but I suspect you'll find, in common with English language poets who experimented with it on and off for the best part of a thousand years, that it yields rather clumsy results. Its best use is as a closing line to stanzas, as in Hardy's 'The Convergence of the Twain (Lines on the loss of the *Titanic*)':

And consummation comes and jars two hemispheres.

Keats ends each stanza of 'The Eve of Saint Agnes' with an alexandrine in a style derived from the verse of Edmund Spenser.

She sigh'd for Agnes' dreams, the sweetest of the year.

Alexander Pope in his (otherwise) pentametric *An Essay on Criticism* was harsh on these Spenserian mannerisms and included this self-descriptive hexameter:

A needless Alexandrine ends the song,
That, like a wounded snake, drags its slow length along.

20 Named from a twelfth-century French poem, *Le Roman d'Alexandre*.
21 After all, in French (as opposed to Spanish, say), a *diacritical mark* (a written accent) is not about syllabic emphasis: *école* is evenly stressed, the accent is just there to *modify* the vowel sound, not impart extra stress to it.

There are very few examples of *eight-beat* lines in English verse. Tennyson's 'Locksley Hall' is a rare successful example of a *trochaic octameter*.

●○ ●○ ●○ ●○ ●○ ●○ ●○ ●⊡

In the Spring a fuller crimson comes upon the Robin's breast;
In the Spring the wanton lapwing gets himself another crest;

In the Spring a livelier iris changes on the burnish'd dove;
In the Spring a young man's fancy lightly turns to thoughts
of love.

Another very familiar example is Edgar Allan Poe's 'The Raven':

●○ ●○ ●○ ●○ ●○ ●○ ●○ ●○

Once upon a midnight dreary, while I pondered, weak and
weary,
Over many a quaint and curious volume of forgotten lore,
While I nodded, nearly napping, suddenly there came a
tapping,
As of someone gently rapping, rapping at my chamber door.

You will notice Poe chooses to end the even-numbered lines strongly, docking the final weak syllable, as Tennyson does for every line of 'Locksley Hall'. You might also notice how in reading, one tends to break up these line lengths into two manageable four-stress half-lines: Poe's lines have very clear and unmistakable caesuras, while Tennyson's are less forceful. The four-stress impulse in English verse is very strong, as we shall see. Nabokov, in his *Notes on Prosody*, suggests that the hexameter is a limit 'beyond which the metrical line is no longer felt as a line and breaks in two'.

Heptameters, seven-stress lines, are possible, and certainly do tend to 'break in two'. They are known in the trade as 'fourteeners', referring to the usual syllable count. Here's a line from Hardy's 'The Lacking Sense'.

Assist her where thy creaturely dependence can or may

As you can see, it is perfectly iambic (though one could suggest demoting the fourth foot to a pyrrhic):

1   2   3   4   5   6   7
As**sist** | her **where** | thy **creat** | urely | de**pend** | ence **can** | or **may**

Actually, fourteeners were very popular in the sixteenth century, although Shakespeare disdained their use, a fact which has been adduced by some to damn the claims of Edward de Vere, seventeenth Earl of Oxford, as the real author of the Shakespearean canon, for Oxford loved them:

> My life through lingering long is lodged, in lair of loathsome ways,
> My death delayed to keep from life, the harm of hapless days.

This preposterously over-alliterated couplet hardly seems Shakespearean – in fact, Shakespeare mocked precisely such bombastic nonsense in 'Pyramus and Thisbe', the play-within-a-play performed by Bottom and the other unlettered 'rude mechanicals' in *A Midsummer Night's Dream*, having great fun at the expense of Oxfordian fourteeners and their vulgar alliterations:

> But stay: O spite! But Mark, poor knight, What dreadful dole is here?
> Eyes, do you see? How can it be? O dainty duck, O dear.

You may notice that Hardy's example is a 'true' heptameter, whereas Oxford's lines (and Shakespeare's parody of them) are in effect so broken by the caesuras after the fourth foot that they could be written thus:

> My life through lingering long is lodged,
> In lair of loathsome ways,
> My death delayed to keep from life,
> The harm of hapless days.

But stay: O spite! But Mark, poor knight,
What dreadful dole is here?
Eyes, do you see? How can it be?
O dainty duck, O dear.

We can do the same thing with Kipling's popular 'Tommy', which he laid out in fourteeners:

Yes, makin' mock o' uniforms that guard you while you sleep
Is cheaper than them uniforms, an' they're starvation cheap;
An' hustlin' drunken soldiers when they're goin' large a bit
Is five times better business than paradin' in full kit.

Yes, makin' mock o' uniforms
That guard you while you sleep
Is cheaper than them uniforms,
An' they're starvation cheap;
An' hustlin' drunken soldiers
When they're goin' large a bit
Is five times better business
Than paradin' in full kit.

What we have there are verses in lines footed in alternating fours and threes: *tetrameters* and *trimeters*, a metrical scheme you will see again and again in English poetry. Such four and three beat lines are also common in verse designed for singing which, after all, uses up more breath than speech. It would be rather difficult to sing a whole heptametric line without turning purple.

The long and winding road

and

You are the sunshine of my life

could be called (by an ass) iambic trimeters and tetrameters respectively, while

That's the way I like it

and

I can't get no satisfaction

are trochaic trimeter and tetrameter. Of course, it is fundamentally daffy to scan lyrics (a word derived from the Greek *lyre*, the harp-like instrument used to accompany song) since it is the musical beat that determines emphasis, not the metrical stress. You could never guess the very particular emphasis on 'get no' just by reading the lyrics of 'Satisfaction' unless you knew the tune and rhythm it was written to fit.

FOUR BEATS TO THE LINE

Wordsworth wrote 'Daffodils' in straight four-beat tetrameters.

I **wand**er'd **lone**ly **as** a **cloud**
   That **floats** on **high** o'er **vales** and **hills**
When **all** at **once** I **saw** a **crowd**,
   A **host**, of **gold**en **daff**odils;

Tetrameter, the four-stress line, is immensely popular in English verse. If iambic pentameter, the Heroic Line, may be described as the great joint of beef, then tetrameters are the sandwiches – the everyday form if you like, and no less capable of greatness. If you ask someone to write a poetic ditty on a Valentine's card or something similar, nine times out of ten they will write tetrameters, whether they do so consciously or not: the four-beat instinct is deep within us, much as in music the four/four time signature is so standard as to be the default: you don't have to write it in the score, just a letter C for Common Time.

Four stresses also mark the base length of a form we will meet later called the *ballad*, where they usually alternate with three-stress lines, as in the anonymous seventeenth-century 'Ballad of Sir Patrick Spens':

> And many was the feather-bed
> That fluttered on the foam;
> And many was the good lord's son
> That never more came home.

Coleridge's 'Rime of the Ancient Mariner':

> The fair breeze blew, the white foam flew,
> The furrow followed free:
> We were the first that ever burst
> Into that silent sea.

and Oscar Wilde's 'Ballad of Reading Gaol':

> I never saw a man who looked
> With such a wistful eye
> Upon that little tent of blue
> Which prisoners call the sky.

In each of these ballad verses the first and third lines have four stresses (eight syllables) and the second and fourth lines have three (six syllables):

```
o●   o●   o●   o●
o●   o●   o●
o●   o●   o●   o●
o●   o●   o●
```

It might have struck you that all three extracts could have come from the same poem, despite their each being separated by roughly a hundred years. We will hold that thought until we come to look at the ballad later. You will remember, I hope, that the Earl of Oxford's duff heptameters and Kipling's rather better managed ones seemed to beg to be split into a similar arrangement:

> My life through lingering long is lodged,
> In lair of loathsome ways,

> Yes, makin' mock o' uniforms
> That guard you while you sleep

Tetrameters, even if they follow ballad form and alternate with trimeters, don't *need* to have the swing and narrative drive of a ballad: they can be used in more lyrical and contemplative poetry too, as we have already seen with Wordsworth's use of them for his daffodils. Emily Dickinson (1830-86) is perhaps the poet who most completely mastered the reflective aspect of the four-beat/three-beat measure. Almost none of her poetry is in lines of longer than four feet, yet its atmosphere of depth, privacy and (often sad) thoughtfulness is a world away from lusty narrative ballads.

712[22]

> Because I could not stop for death
> He kindly stopped for me
> The carriage held but just ourselves
> And Immortality.

1612

> The Auctioneer of Parting
> His 'Going, going, gone'
> Shouts even from the Crucifix,
> And brings his Hammer down –
> He only sells the Wilderness,
> The prices of Despair
> Range from a single human Heart
> To Two – not any more –

22 Dickinson's works remain untitled: the numbers refer to their order in the 1955 Harvard variorum edition.

Lord Byron shows that pure four-beat tetrameters can be blissfully lyrical: note the initial trochaic substitution in the last line.

> She walks in beauty like the night
> Of cloudless climes and starry skies
> And all that's best of dark and bright
> Meets in her aspect and her eyes.

While Humbert Wolfe demonstrates here their appropriateness for comic satire:

> You cannot hope to bribe or twist,
> Thank God, the British journalist.
> But seeing what the man will do
> Unbribed, there's no occasion to.

The above examples are of course in *iambic* four-beats.

> ○　●　○　●　○　●　○　●
> She walks in beauty like the night

Mary Sidney Countess of Pembroke's metrical version of Psalm 71 is written in *trochaic* tetrameters:

> ●　○　●　○　●　○　●　○
> **Lord**, on **thee** my **trust** is **ground**ed:
> **Leave** me **not** with **shame** con**found**ed

As is Longfellow's *Song of Hiawatha*:

> ●　○　●　○　●　○　●　○
> **Of**ten **stopped** and **gazed** im**plor**ing
> At the **trembl**ing **Star** of **Eve**ning,
> At the **tend**er **Star** of **Wom**an;
> **And** they **heard** him **mur**mur **soft**ly

Now look at the following two four-stress lines, which reiterate the point I made earlier about question and answer: the obvious but crucial difference in the way each foot as it were distributes its weight.

Trochees **end** their **lines** in **weak**ness

Iambic **lines** re**solve** with **strength**

But as we know, iambic lines don't *have* to end with a stressed syllable: you can add an extra weak syllable (*hypermetric* addition). Similarly, trochaic lines can have their weak ending dropped (*catalectic* subtraction). In both cases you're either adding or subtracting a *weak* syllable: the number of *stresses* stays the same.

Tyger, tyger burning **bright**
In the **forests of** the **night**

Blake's famous opening lines drop the natural weak ending of the fourth trochees, giving a seven syllable count and a strong resolution.

Dum-di, **dum**-di, **dum**-di *dum*

or

Trochee, **tro**chee, **tro**chee *troke*

The full trochaic line 'Tiger, tiger burning brightly' would be rather fatuous, don't we feel? The conclusiveness of a strong ending frames the image so much more pleasingly. Here is the opening to Keats's poem 'Fancy':

Ever let the Fancy roam,
Pleasure never is at home:
At a touch sweet Pleasure melteth,
Like to bubbles when rain pelteth;

Both lines of the first couplet (a *couplet* is a pair of rhyming lines) have their final weak endings docked. The second couplet is of four full trochees. Why?

Well, at the risk of taking us back to English classes, it is worth considering this, for the sake, if not of appreciation, then at least of one's own poetry. The strong endings of the opening give a sense of the epigrammatic and purposeful: they offer a firm opening statement:

> Ever let the Fancy **roam**,
> Pleasure never is at **home**:

The weak endings of 'melteth' and 'pelteth' (after all, in his time Keats could perfectly well have said 'melts' and 'pelts') *echo the meaning of the image* by melting and popping to their end rather than banging to a solid conclusion. Sweet Pleasure's evanescence is evoked by the evanescence of the metre.

> At a touch sweet Pleasure **melt**eth,
> Like to bubbles when rain **pelt**eth;

Did he *consciously* set out to do this and for that reason? Well, I think someone with a sensitive ear for the rhythms and cadences of verse wouldn't need to be taught something like that. To anybody with the slightest instinct such use in metre would come as naturally as finding the right musical phrase for the right emotion comes to a composer. It is true, however, that Keats from an early age completely soaked himself in poetry and (despite being labelled a 'Cockney poet' by literary snobs of the time) experimented all his life with poetic form and constantly wrote about prosody and chewed over its nuances passionately with his friends and fellow poets. A mixture of absorption in poetry, obsession with technique and, of course, natural talent culminates in what you might call 'poetic taste' – a feel for precisely which techniques to reach for.

Incidentally, for some reason Keats's 'Fancy' was one of my favourite poems when I was a mooncalf teenager. Don't ask me why: it is after all a slight work compared to 'Endymion', 'Lamia' and the great Odes.

Mixed Feet

Let us consider the whole issue of *mixing feet* within a poem. The end of writing poetry is not to write 'perfect' metre with every line going da-**dum** or **dum**-da into the distance, it is to use the metre you've chosen to reflect the meaning, mood and emotional colour of your words and images. We've already seen how subtle variations such as pyrrhic and trochaic substitutions stand as perfectly acceptable ways of bringing iambic pentameter to life. What about mixing up whole lines of iambic and trochaic metre in the same verse?

> He **bangs** the **drums** and **makes** a **noise**
> **Scaring girls** and **waking boys**

Nothing necessarily wrong with that either. Don't get hung up on writing perfectly symmetrical parades of consistent rhythm. *Utterance*, sung or spoken, underlies poetry. Human utterance, like its heartbeat and its breathing, quickens, pauses and breaks its patterns according to states of relaxation, excitement, passion, fear and all manner of moods and feelings: this is precisely why I took so long over caesura and enjambment earlier. No one could say that the above two lines are *wrong*, it is surprisingly rare, however, to find two metres mixed in this fashion (in 'literary' verse, as opposed to popular ballad and song lyrics, at least) and you would want to alternate trochaic and iambic lines for a good reason: the 'ear' of the reader would note (however subconsciously) the variation and expect something from it. Perhaps in the above example the alternating trochaic lines could form a kind of chorus or explanatory aside:

> He bangs the drums and makes a noise
> > (Scaring girls and waking boys)
> He makes a row till dawn unfurls
> > (Waking boys and scaring girls)

I never knew a greater pest
   (Even squirrels need a rest)
He drives his wretched family wild
   (Spare the rod and spoil the child)

So long as you are *in control* of the metre, using its swing and balance to fit the mood, motion or story of your poem there is no reason not to use a variety of beats within the same piece. I would only repeat this observation: well-made poems do not mix up their metric scheme *carelessly*. Have you ever seen a parish magazine or some other flyer, newsletter, brochure or poster where the designer has got too excited about the number of fonts available on his computer and created a great crashing mess of different typefaces and sizes? Musical pieces often go into double time or modulate up or down for effect, but generally speaking such techniques are crass and ugly unless there is a good *purpose* behind it all. Most of the paintings we admire use a surprisingly small palette of colours. A profusion of herbs in a dish can cancel out each flavour or drown the main ingredients. You get the idea.

Having said all that, let's look at the *whole* first stanza of Blake's 'The Tyger'.

Tyger, **ty**ger, **bur**ning **bright**
In the **for**ests **of** the **night**
What im**mor**tal **hand** or **eye**
Could **frame** thy **fear**ful **sym**me**try**?

As we observed earlier, these are trochaic four-stress lines (docked of their last weak syllable). That holds true of the first three lines, but what's afoot with the last one? It is a regular *iambic* four-stress line. Here's the third stanza:

And what **shoul**der **and** what **art**
Could **twist** the **sin**ews **of** thy **heart**?
And, **when** thy **heart** be**gan** to **beat**,
What dread **hand** and **what** dread **feet**?

Trochaic first and last lines 'enveloping' two central *iambic* lines; and the poem's penultimate stanza runs:

> When the stars threw down their spears,
> And water'd heaven with their tears,
> Did He smile His work to see?
> Did He who made the lamb make thee?

In this case we alternate between trochaic and iambic tetrameters. The rest of the poem is trochaic. With a little casuistry one could, I suppose, make the argument that Blake's shift between metres 'stripes' the verse as a tiger is striped. I think that is more than a little tenuous: there is no *plan* to the changes between metre, no apparent design at work: certainly, poets in the past and present have employed metre, rhyme and even the shape of the words on a page further to conjoin form with subject matter, but I do not believe this applies here.

Nonetheless, the variations can hardly be said to spoil the poem: the docking of the final trochaic foot matches the standard male endings of the iambic. After all, *one could look at it this way*: are the odd lines out really iambic, or are they trochees with an extra weak syllable at the *beginning*? Trochees are the opposite of iambs: if you can pop a weak syllable at the end of an iambic line, why not shove one on to the beginning of a trochaic one? If you read those stanzas above, missing out the unstressed syllables at the start of each iambic line you will see what I mean. It is finally a matter of nomenclature and one's own ear. For many modern metrists there's no such thing as the iamb or the trochee at all, there are only lines with a set number of beats or stresses to them. Where the *weak* syllables come is, for them, irrelevant. They would have us believe that English verse should be treated as if it is accentual, but not accentual–syllabic. I can't go that far, myself: there is an obvious and to my ear *absolute* difference between the whole nature of *Hiawatha* and that of, say, 'She walks in beauty'. There certainly was to Longfellow and Byron.

Here is a well-known couplet from Blake's 'Auguries of Innocence':

A Robin Red breast in a Cage[23]
Puts all Heaven in a Rage.

That is metrically identical to my made-up hybrid line:

He **bangs** the **drums** and **makes** a **noise**
Scaring girls and **waking boys**

Heartless to quibble with Blake's sentiment, but to most ears, trained or otherwise, it is a bit of a dud, isn't it? This is a naïvety one expects, forgives and indeed celebrates with Blake ('look at his paintings: couldn't draw, couldn't colour in' as Professor Mackenny of Edinburgh University once excellently remarked) and from any poetic sensibility but his one might wrinkle one's nose at such childlike versifying. If the poem went on alternating in regular fashion as I suggested with the drum-banging boy one could understand. In fact the next lines are:

A dove house filled with doves and Pigeons
Shudders Hell thro' all its regions.

That couplet does conform with the plan, the second line is completely trochaic, with weak ending and all, but now Blake continues with:

A dog starv'd at his Master's Gate
Predicts the ruin of the State.

Those are both iambic lines. And the next couplet?

A Horse misus'd upon the Road
Calls to Heaven for Human blood

23 At first attempt I mistyped that as 'A Robin Red breast in a Café', 'Makes Heaven go all daffy', I suppose . . .

Well, I mean I'm sorry, but that's just plain bad. Isn't it? The *syntax* (grammatical construction) for a start: bit wobbly isn't it? Does he really mean that the *horse* is calling to heaven: the other animals don't, surely he means the misuse of horses calls to heaven? But Blake's sentence structure invites us to picture a calling horse. And, my dear, the *scansion*! Presumably Blake means to elide Heaven into the monosyllable Heav'n (a perfectly common elision and one we might remember having to sing in school hymns), but it is odd that he bothers in earlier lines to put apostrophes in 'starv'd' and 'misus'd' and even shortens *through* to *thro'*[24] yet fails to give us an apostrophe here where it really would count: he has already used the word Heaven once *without* elision, as a disyllabic word, six lines earlier: perhaps, one might argue, he felt that as a holy word it shouldn't be altered in any way. I think this unlikely, he tends not to use capitals for God, although he uses them for 'Me' and 'My' and just about every word he can (incidentally, why does Horse deserve majuscules here, but not dog, I wonder? Why Pigeon and not dove?). Well, perhaps the unelided 'Heaven' is a misprint: if so, it is one that all the copies[25] of Blake I have seen repeat. It is fairly obvious that this is how he wrote it in his manuscript.

No, I think we can confidently state that there is no metrical *scheme* in place here: Blake seems to be in such a hurry to list the abominable treatment that animals suffer and the dire consequences attendant upon mankind if this cruelty continues that measured prosody has taken a back seat. Well, maybe that's the point. Any kind of control or cunning in versification would mediate between Blake's righteous indignation and the conscience and compassion of the reader, resulting in 'better' metre perhaps, but less direct and emotionally involving poetry. A more conventional poet might have written something like this:

24 A common but metrically meaningless convention.
25 Including Sir Geoffrey Keynes's definitive 1957 edition.

Robin redbreasts in a cage
Put all heaven in a rage
Dovecotes filled with doves and pigeons
Shudder hell through all its regions
Dogs starved at their masters' gate
Augur ruin for the state.
Horses beaten on the road
Call to Heav'n for human blood.

There *is* a loss there: Blake's point is that *a* robin, one single caged bird, is enough to put heaven in a rage (admittedly that isn't true of the dove house, which has to be filled to cause hell to shudder, but no matter). Pluralising the animals for the sake of trochees does alter the sense, so let us try pure iambs:

A robin redbreast in a cage
Doth put all heaven in a rage.
A dove house filled with doves and pigeons
Will shudder hell through all its regions.
A dog starved at his master's gate
Predicts the ruin of the state.
A horse misused upon the road
Doth call to heav'n for human blood.

Neither, incidentally, solves the curious incident of the dog starved **at** his master's gate: trochaic or iambic, the line's a bitch. Surely it is the *starving* that needs the emphasis? 'A dog that starves at's master's gate' would do it, but it isn't nice.

We have seen two non-hybrid versions of the verse. Let us now remind ourselves of what Blake actually gave us:

A Robin Red breast in a Cage
Puts all Heaven in a Rage.
A dove house filled with doves and Pigeons
Shudders Hell thro' all its regions.
A dog starv'd at his Master's Gate

Predicts the ruin of the State.
A Horse misus'd upon the Road
Calls to Heaven for Human blood.

I have mocked the scansion, syntax and manifold inconsistencies; I have had sport with these lines, but the fact is I love them. They're messy, mongrel and mawkish but such is the spirit of Blake that somehow these things don't matter at all – they only go to convince us of the work's fundamental honesty and authenticity. Am I saying this because Blake is Blake and we all know that he was a Seer, a Visionary and an unique Genius? If I had never seen the lines before and didn't know their author would I forgive them their clumsiness and ill-made infelicities? I don't know and I don't really care. It is a work concerned with innocence after all. And, lest we forget, this is the poem that begins with the *quatrain* (a quatrain is a stanza of four lines) that might usefully be considered the Poet's Credo or Mission Statement.

To see a World in a Grain of Sand
And a Heaven in a Wild Flower,
Hold Infinity in the palm of your hand
And Eternity in an hour.

The metre is shot to hell in every line, but who cares. It is the real thing. I think it was worth spending this much time on those lines because this is what you will do when you write your own verse – constantly make series of judgements about your metre and what 'rules' you can break and with what effect.

Poetry Exercise 5

It is now time, of course, to try writing your own verse of shorter measure. Here is what I want you to do: give yourself forty-five minutes; if you haven't got the time now, come back to the exercise later. I believe it is much simpler if you have a subject, so I have selected *Television*. As usual I have had a go myself. Rhyming seems natural with lines of this length, but if you'd rather not, then don't. I remind you once again that it is the versification that matters here, not any verbal or metaphysical brilliance. This is what I would like, with my attempts included.

♦ Two quatrains of standard, eight-syllable iambic tetrameter:

○● ○● ○● ○●
○● ○● ○● ○●
○● ○● ○● ○●
○● ○● ○● ○●

> They're always chopping bits of meat –
> Forensic surgeons, daytime cooks.
> Extracting bullets, slicing ham
> Detecting flavours, grilling crooks.

> My new TV has got no knobs
> It's sleeker than a marble bowl.
> I'm sure this suits designer snobs,
> But where's the damned remote control?

♦ Two quatrains of alternating iambic tetrameter and trimeter:

○● ○● ○● ○●
○● ○● ○●
○● ○● ○● ○●
○● ○● ○●

Big Brother's on the air again,
Polluting my TV.
Who was it said, 'Mankind can't bear
Too much reality?[26]

Sir Noël Coward drawled, when asked
Which programmes he thought shone:
'TV is not for watching, dear –
It's just for being on.'

♦ Two quatrains of *trochaic* tetrameter: one in 'pure trochee' à la
Hiawatha, and one with docked weak endings in the second and
fourth lines, à la 'Tyger'.

●○ ●○ ●○   ●○
●○ ●○ ●○   ●□
●○ ●○ ●○   ●○
●○ ●○ ●○   ●□

Soap stars seem to do it nightly –
Slap and shag and rape each other.
If I heard the plot-line rightly
Darren's pregnant by his brother.

News of bombs in Central London,
Flesh and blood disintegrate.
Teenage voices screaming proudly,
'Allah akbar! God is great!'

So, your turn. Relax and feel the force.

26 It was T. S. Eliot.

IV

Ternary Feet: we meet the anapaest and the dactyl, the molossus, the tribrach, the amphibrach and the amphimacer

Ternary Feet

Now that you are familiar with four types of two-syllable, binary (or *duple* as a musician might say) foot – the *iamb*, the *trochee*, the *pyrrhic* and the *spondee* – try to work out what is going on metrically in the next line.

> In the dark of the forest so deep
> I can hear all the animals creep.

Did you get the feeling that the only way to make sense of this metre is to think of the line as having feet with *three* elements to them, the third one bearing the beat? A kind of Titty-*tum*, titty-*tum*, titty-*tum* triple rhythm? A *ternary foot* in metric jargon, a *triple measure* in music-speak.

> 1 | 2 | 3
> In the **dark** of the **for** -est so **deep**
> I can **hear** all the **an** -imals **creep**.
>
> ○ ○   ●   ○ ○ ●   ○ ○   ●
> ○ ○   ●   ○ ○ ●   ○ ○   ●

Such a ○○● titty-**tum** foot is called an *anapaest*, to rhyme with 'am a beast', as if the foot is a skiing champion, Anna Piste. It is a ternary version of the iamb, in that it is a *rising* foot, going from weak to strong, but by way of *two* unstressed syllables instead of the iamb's one.

Any purely anapaestic line is either a monometer of three syllables . . .

Uncon**vinced**

. . . a dimeter of six . . .

Uncon**vinced**, at a **loss**

. . . a trimeter of nine . . .

Uncon**vinced**, at a **loss**, discon**tent**

. . . or a tetrameter of twelve . . .

Uncon**vinced**, at a **loss**, discon**tent**, in a **fix**.

And so on. Don't be confused: that line of twelve syllables is not a hexameter, it is a *tetrameter*. It has *four* stressed syllables.

1   2   3   4

Uncon**vinced** | at a **loss** | discon**tent** | in a **fix**.

Remember: it is the number of *stresses*, not the number of *syllables*, that determines whether it is penta- or tetra- or hexa- or any other kind of -meter:

1   2   3   4

Uncon**vinced** | unde**cid** | -ed no **glimpse** | of the **truth**.

Now look at the anapaestic tetrameter above and note one other thing: the first foot is one word, the second foot is two thirds of a single word, foot number three is two and a third words and the fourth foot three whole words. Employing a metre like the anapaest doesn't mean every foot of a line has to be composed of an anapaestic word:

Repre**hend** | uncon**vinced** | under**stand** | dispos**sessed**.

That would be ridiculous, as silly as an iambic pentameter made up of ten words, as mocked by Pope – not to mention fiendishly hard. Nor would an anapaestic tetrameter have to be made up of four pure anapaestic *phrases*:

Is it **true** | that the **world** | has no **chance** | to be **saved**?

The rhythm comes through just as clearly with . . .

Uncon**vinced** | unde**cid** | -ed no **clue** | at a **loss**.

or . . .

In the **dark** | of the **for** | -est so **deep**
I can **hear** | all the **an** | -imals **creep**

. . . where every foot has a different number of words. It is the beats that give the rhythm. Who would have thought poetry would be so arithmetical? It isn't, of course, but prosodic analysis and scansion can be. Not that any of this really matters for our purposes: such calculations are for the academics and students of the future who will be scanning and scrutinising your work.

Poe's 'Annabel Lee' is in anapaestic *ballad* form (four-stress lines alternating with three-stress lines):

○○● ○○● ○○● ○○●
○○● ○○● ○○●
For the **moon** never **beams** without **bring**ing me **dreams**
Of the **beau**tiful **Ann**abel **Lee**.

I suppose the best-known anapaestic poem of all (especially to Americans) is Clement Clarke Moore's tetrametric 'The Night Before Christmas':

○○● ○○● ○○● ○○●
○○● ○○● ○○● ○○●
○● ○○● ○○● ○○●
○● ○○● ○○● ○○●

'Twas the **night** before **Christ**mas, when **all** through the **house**
Not a **crea**ture was **stir**ring, not **even** a **mouse**;
The **stock**ings were **hung** by the **chim**ney with **care**
In **hopes** that St **Nich**olas **soon** would be **there**.

The second couplet has had its initial weak syllable docked in each line. This is called a *clipped* or *acephalous* (literally 'headless') foot. You could just as easily say the anapaest has been substituted for an iamb, it amounts to precisely the same thing.

Both the Poe and the Moore works have a characteristic lilt that begs for the verse to be set to music (which they each have been, of course), but anapaests can be very rhythmic and fast moving too: unsuited perhaps to the generality of contemplative poetry, but wonderful when evoking something like a gallop. Listen to Robert Browning's 'How They Brought the Good News from Ghent to Aix':

> I **sprang** to the **stir**rup and **Jor**is and **he**
> I **gall**oped, Dirk **gall**oped, we **gall**oped all **three**.

It begs to be read out loud. You can really hear the thunder of the hooves here, don't you think? Notice, though, that Browning also dispenses with the first weak syllable in each line. For the verse to be in 'true' anapaestic tetrameters it would have to go something like this (the underline represents an added syllable, not a stress):

> <u>Then</u> I sprang to the stirrup and Joris and he
> <u>And</u> I galloped, Dirk galloped, we galloped all three.

But Browning has given us *clipped* opening feet:

> Da-**dum**, titty-**tum**, titty-**tum**, titty-**tum**
> Da-**dum**, titty-**tum**, titty-**tum**, titty-**tum**.

instead of the full

> Titty-**tum**, titty-**tum**, titty-**tum**, titty-**tum**
> Titty-**tum**, titty-**tum**, titty-**tum**, titty-**tum**

If you tap out the rhythms of each of the above with your fingers on the table, or just mouth them to yourself (quietly if you're on a train or in a café, you don't want to be stared at) I think you will agree that Browning knew what he was about. The straight anapaests are rather dull and predictable. The opening iamb or acephalous foot, Da-**dum**! makes the whole ride so much more dramatic and realistic, mimicking the way horses hooves fall. Which is not to say that, when well done, pure anapaests can't work too. Byron's poem 'The Destruction of Sennacharib' shows them at their best.

TAKE OUT YOUR PENCIL AND MARK THE ANAPAESTS HERE (Assyrian is *three* syllables, by the way, not four):

> The Assyrian came down like the wolf on the fold,
> And his cohorts were gleaming in purple and gold;
> And the sheen on their spears was like stars on the sea,
> And the blue wave rolls nightly on deep Galilee.

Byron doesn't keep this up all the way through, however:

> For the Angel of Death spread his wings on the blast,
> And breathed in the face of the foe as he passed;

He *could* have written the anapaest 'And <u>he</u> breathed . . .' but I think his instinct to use the clipped 'And breathed' instead is exactly right for the conceit. It is a very subtle difference. What do you think? Try saying each alternative aloud. I think the clipping causes us to linger a tiny bit longer on the word 'breathed' than we would in strict anapaestic rhythm and this brings the image to life. Now, back to those standard anapaests beating:

> Titty-**tum**, titty-**tum**, titty-**tum**, titty-**tum**
> Titty-**tum**, titty-**tum**, titty-**tum**, titty-**tum**

Imagine that, instead of doing what Browning and Byron did and clipping off the head like so:

> Da-**dum**, titty-**tum**, titty-**tum**, titty-**tum**
> Da-**dum**, titty-**tum**, titty-**tum**, titty-**tum**

you started with anapaests and ended with a *spondee* which, as I mentioned earlier, is a double-stressed foot: **Hard cheese. Humdrum.**

Ana**paest**, ana**paest**, ana**paest**, **spon**-dee!
Ana**paest**, ana**paest**, ana**paest**, **spon**-dee!

O O ●   OO ●   OO ●   ●   ●
O O ●   OO ●   OO ●   ●   ●

That might remind you of the gallop from Rossini's overture to *William Tell*, famously used for the TV series *The Lone Ranger* and the three-way orgy in Kubrick's *A Clockwork Orange*.

The spondee (inasmuch as it truly exists in English) makes a great **full stop**, either serious like a tolling bell or comic, as in the famous knocking rhythm that Americans express as:

Shave and a **hair cut**, **two bits**!

●   O O   ●   ●   ●   ●

Tum-titty **tum tum**. **Tum tum**!

If you wanted to scan that line, you would say 'haircut' and 'two bits' were both spondaic. But what is 'shave-and-a'? When you think about it, it is an anapaest in reverse. Instead of titty-**tum** (OO●), it is **tum**-titty. (●OO). A new ternary foot for us to meet and its name is *dactyl*.

THE DACTYL

As a matter of fact the earliest and greatest epics in our culture, Homer's *Iliad* and *Odyssey* were written in dactylic hexameters. Remember, though, classical poetry was written in quantitative measure, where those feet were better described as 'long short short', — – – 'wait for it', 'cool, not hot', 'smooth black pig' rather than our sprightly ●OO *tum*-titty. The word dactyl comes from the Greek for 'finger': fingers have one long joint and two short ones. In reality, Greek metrical units are closer to musical notes in that they tell you their duration: a long syllable takes exactly twice as long to utter as a short one, hence you could say a dactyl for Greek-style quantitative verse should be written thus:

Homer's verse didn't swing along in a bouncy rhythmic way, it pulsed in gentle lo-o-o-ng short-short, lo-o-o-ng short-short waves, each line usually ending with a spondee. As I hope I have made pretty clear by now, that sort of metrical arrangement isn't suited to the English tongue. We go, not by duration, but by syllabic accentuation.

Tennyson's dialect poem 'Northern Farmer' shows that, as with Browning's anapaests, a dactyl in English verse, using **stressed-weak-weak** syllables instead of lo-o-o-ng-short-short, has its place, also here imitating the trot of a horse's hooves as it sounds out the word 'property'. (I have stripped it of Tennyson's attempts at phonetic northern brogue – 'paäins', for example.)

> Proputty, proputty, proputty – that's what I 'ears 'em say
> Proputty, proputty, proputty – Sam, thou's an ass for thy pains

The poem ends with the line:

> Proputty proputty, proputty – canter an' canter away.

● ○ ○   ● ○ ○   ● ○ ○   ● ○ ○   ● ○ ○ ●

Five dactyls and a single full stop stress on the 'way' of 'away'. As with anapaests, lines of pure dactyls are rather predictable and uninteresting:

> **Tum**-titty, **tum**-titty, **tum**-titty, **tum**-titty

Just as the anapaest in its rising rhythm, its move from weak to strong, is a ternary version of the iamb, so the dactyl, in its *falling* rhythm, its move from strong to weak, is a ternary version of the trochee. Furthermore, just as it is rewarding to clip the first weak syllable of an anapaestic line, as we saw Browning do (in other words substitute the first foot with an iamb) so dactylic verse can be highly compelling when you dock the *last* weak syllable (in other words substitute the final foot with a trochee).

Tum-titty, **tum**-titty, **tum**-titty, **tum**-ti

Or you could use a single beat as Tennyson does above (a docked trochee, if you like):

Tum-titty, **tum**-titty, **tum**-titty, **tum**.

Browning uses this kind of dactylic metre to great effect in 'The Lost Leader', his savage attack on Wordsworth. Browning regarded him as a sell-out for accepting the post of Poet Laureate:

● ○ ○ ● ○ ○ ● ○ ○ ● ○
● ○ ○ ● ○ ○ ● ○ ○ ●

Just for a handful of silver he left us
Just for a riband to stick in his coat.

This creates verse with great rhythmic dash and drive. Some poets, however, in their admiration for Homer, attempted to construct quantitative English dactylic hexameters, ending them, as is common in classical verse, with spondees. Edgar Allan Poe had this to say about Longfellow's stab at translating the Swedish dactyls of a poet called Tegner:

> In attempting (what never should be attempted) a literal
> version of both the words and the metre of this poem,
> Professor Longfellow has failed to do justice either to his
> author or himself. He has striven to do what no man ever
> did well and what, from the nature of the language itself,
> never can be well done. Unless, for example, we shall come
> to have an influx of spondees in our English tongue, it will
> always be impossible to construct an English hexameter.
> Our spondees, or, we should say, our spondaic words, are rare.
> In the Swedish they are nearly as abundant as in the Latin

and Greek. We have only 'compound', 'context', 'footfall', and a few other similar ones.

Longfellow's *Evangeline* might be considered a more successful attempt to write English dactylic hexameter in the classical style:

> **This** is the **for**est prim**e**val. The **mur**muring **pines** and the
> **hemlocks**.

● ○ ○ ●○ ○●○ ○ ●○○ ● ○ ○ ●●

Poe and modern English metrists might prefer that last foot 'hemlocks' not be called a classical spondee but a trochee. Those last two feet, incidentally, dactyl-spondee, or more commonly dactyl-trochee, are often found as a closing rhythm known as an *Adonic Line* (after Sappho's lament to Adonis: 'O ton Adonin!' 'Oh, for Adonis!'). The contemporary American poet Michael Heller ends his poem 'She' with an excellent Adonic line (or *clausula*, the classical term for a closing phrase):

> And I
> am happy, happier even then when her mouth is on me and I
> gasp at the ceiling.

'Gasp at the ceiling' is an exact 'Oh for Adonis' Adonic clausula. We shall meet it again when we look at Sapphic Odes in Chapter Three.

Robert Southey (Byron's enemy) and Arthur Hugh Clough were about the only significant English poets to experiment with consistent dactylic hexameters: one of Clough's best-known poems 'The Bothie of Tober Na-Vuolich' is in a kind of mixed dactylic hexameter. By happy chance, I heard a fine dactylic tetrameter on the BBC's Shipping Forecast last night:

● ○ ○ ● ○ ○ ● ○ ○ ● ○○

Dogger, **cy**clonic be**com**ing north **east**erly . . .

By all means try writing dactyls, but you will probably discover that they need to end in trochees, iambs or spondees. As a falling rhythm, there is often a pleasingly fugitive quality to dactylics, but they can sound hypnotically dreary without the affirmative closure of stressed beats at line-end.

Bernstein's Latin rhythms in his song 'America' inspired a dactyl–dactyl–spondee combination from his lyricist Stephen Sondheim:

> ● ○ ○ ●○ ○ ●   ●
> I like the city of San Juan
> I know a boat you can get on

And for the chorus:

> I like to be in America
> Everything's free in America.
> ● ○   ○   ● ○ ○ ●●●

You have to wrench the rhythm to make it work when speaking it, but the lines fit the music exactly as I have marked them. Américá, you'll notice, has *three* stressed final syllables, a kind of ternary spondee, **tum-tum-tum**.

THE MOLOSSUS AND TRIBRACH

The **tum-tum-tum** has the splendid name *molossus*, like Colossus, and is a foot of three long syllables — — — or, if we were to use it in English poetry, three *stressed* syllables, ●●●. Molossus was a town in Epirus known for its huge mastiffs, so perhaps the name of the foot derives from the dog's great bow-wow-wow. If a spondee, as Poe remarked, is rare in spoken English, how much rarer still is a molossus. We've seen one from Sondheim, and songwriting, where wrenched rhythms are permissible and even desirable, is precisely where we would most expect to find it. W. S. Gilbert found four triumphant examples for his matchless 'To Sit in Solemn Silence' from *The Mikado*.

To sit in solemn silence in a **dull dark dock**,
In a pestilential prison, with a **life-long lock**,
Awaiting the sensation of a **short, sharp shock**,
From a cheap and chippy chopper on a **big black block**!

The molossus, like its smaller brother the spondee, is clearly impossible for whole lines of poetry, but in combination with a dactyl, for example, it seems to suit not just Gilbert's and Sondheim's lyrics as above, but also call and response chants and playful interludes, like this exchange between Luke Skywalker and Darth Vader.

Why do you **bother me? Go to hell!**
   I am your **destiny. Can't you tell?**
You're not my **father. Eat my shorts.**
   Come to the **dark** side. **Feel the force.**

As you might have guessed, that isn't a poem, but a children's skipping rhyme popular in the eighties. Lines three and four use a trochaic substitution for the dactyl in their second foot, but I wouldn't recommend going on to a playground and pointing this out.

I suppose Tennyson's

Break, break, break
   At the foot of thy crags, O Sea!

could be said to start with a molossus, followed by two anapaests and a spondee.

If a molossus is the ternary equivalent of the spondee, is there a ternary version of the pyrrhic foot too? Well, you bet your boots there is and it is called a *tribrach* (literally three short). A molossus you might use, but a tribrach? Unlikely. Of course, it is very possible that a line of your verse would contain three unstressed syllables in a row, as we know from pyrrhic substitution in lines of binary feet, but no one would call such examples tribrachs. I only mention it for completeness and because I care so deeply for your soul.

The Amphibrach

Another ternary, or triple, foot is the *amphibrach*, though it is immensely doubtful whether you'll have cause to use this one a great deal either. *Amphi* in Greek means 'on both sides' (as in an amphitheatre) and *brachys* means 'short', so an amphibrach is short on both sides. All of which means it is a triplet consisting of two short or unstressed syllables either side of a long or stressed one: - — - or, in English verse: ○ ● ○. 'Romantic' and 'deluded' are both amphibrachic words and believe me, you'd have to be romantic and deluded to try and write consistent amphibrachic poetry.

> Romantic, deluded, a total disaster.
> Don't **do** it I **beg** you, self-**slaugh**ter is **fas**ter

Goethe and later German-language poets like Rilke were fond of it and it can occasionally be found (mixed with other metres) in English verse. Byron experimented with it, but the poet who seemed most taken with the metre was Matthew Prior. This is the opening line of 'Jinny the Just'.

> ○ ● ○ ○ ● ○ ○ ● ○ ○ ● ○
> Re**leas'd** from | the **noise** of | the **butch**er | and **bak**er

And this of 'From my own Monument':

> ○ ● ○ ○ ● ○ ○ ● ○ ○ ● ○
> As **doc**tors give **phys**ic by **way** of pre**ven**tion

You might think amphibrachs (with the weak ending docked) lurk in this old rhyming proverb:

> ○ ● ○ ○ ● ○ ○ ● ○ ○ ●
> If **wish**es were **hors**es then **beg**gars would **ride**
> If **tur**nips were **swords** I'd wear **one** by my **side**.

But that's just plain silly:[27] it is actually more like the metre of Browning's 'Ghent to Aix': anapaests with the opening syllable docked.

> If **wish**es were **horse**s then **begg**ars would **ride**
> I **sprang** to the **sadd**le and **Jor**is and **he**.

Just as *my* amphibrachic doggerel could be called a clipped anapaestic line with a weak ending:

> **Ro**mantic, de**lud**ed, a **tot**al dis**ast**er.
> Don't **do** it I **beg** you, self-**slaught**er is **fast**er

Some metrists claim the amphibrach *can* be found in English poetry. You will see it and hear it in perhaps the most popular of all verse forms extant, they say. I wonder if you can tell what this form is, just by READING OUT THE RHYTHM?

```
○  ●  ○○  ●  ○○  ●  ○
○  ●  ○○  ●  ○○  ●  ○
○  ●  ○○  ●
○  ●  ○○  ●
○  ●  ○○  ●  ○○  ●  ○
```
> Ti-**tum**-ti ti-**tum**-ti ti-**tum**-ti
> Ti-**tum**-ti ti-**tum**-ti ti-**tum**-ti
> Ti-**tum**-ti ti-**tum**
> Ti-**tum**-ti ti-**tum**
> Ti-**tum**-ti ti-**tum**-ti ti-**tum**-ti

It is, of course, the limerick.

> There was a young man from Australia
> Who painted his arse like a dahlia.
> Just tuppence a smell
> Was all very well,
> But fourpence a lick was a failure.

27 'But **that's** just plain **silly**' is amphibrachic: these feet can get into your system.

So, next time someone tells you a limerick you can inform them that it is verse made up of three lines of amphibrachic trimeter with two internal lines of catalectic amphibrachic dimeter. You would be punched very hard in the face for pointing this out, but you could do it. Anyway, the whole thing falls down if your limerick involves a monosyllabic hero:

> There was a young chaplain from King's,
> Who discoursed about God and such things:
>   But his deepest desire
>   Was a boy in the choir
> With a bottom like jelly on springs.

> Ti-**tum** titty-**tum** titty-**tum**
> Titty-**tum** titty-**tum** titty-**tum**
> Titty-**tum** titty-**tum**
> Titty-**tum** titty-**tum**
> Titty-**tum** titty-**tum** titty-**tum**

You don't get much more anapaestic than that. A pederastic anapaestic quintain,[28] in fact. Most people would say that limericks are certainly anapaestic in nature and that amphibrachs belong only in classical quantitative verse. Most people, for once, would be right. The trouble is, if you vary an amphibrachic line even slightly (which you'd certainly want to do whether it was limerick or any other kind of poem), the metre then becomes impossible to distinguish from any anapaestic or dactylic metre or a mixture of all the feet we've already come to know and love. Simpler in verse of triple feet to talk only of rising three-stress rhythms (anapaests) and falling three-stress rhythms (dactyls). But by all means try writing with amphibrachs as an exercise to help flex your metric muscles, much as a piano student rattles out arpeggios or a golfer practises approach shots.

28 A *quintain* or *cinquain* being a five-line verse.

The Amphimacer

It follows that if there is a name for a three-syllable foot with the beat in the middle (ro**man**tic, des**pond**ent, un**yield**ing) there will be a name for a three-syllable foot with a beat either side of an *un*stressed middle (**tamp**erproof, **hand** to **mouth**, **Ox**ford **Road**).[29] Sure enough: the *amphimacer* (*macro*, or long, on both sides) also known as the *cretic foot* (after the Cretan poet Thaletas) goes **tum**-ti-**tum** in answer to the amphibrach's ti-**tum**-ti. Tennyson's 'The Oak', which is short enough to reproduce here in full, is written in amphimacers and is also an example of that rare breed, a poem written in monometer, lines of just one foot. It could also be regarded as a *pattern* or *shaped* poem (of which more later) inasmuch as its layout suggests its subject, an oak tree.

> Live thy life,
> Young and old,
> Like yon oak,
> Bright in spring,
> Living gold;
>
> Summer-rich
> Then; and then
> Autumn-changed,
> Soberer hued
> Gold again.
>
> All his leaves
> Fall'n at length,
> Look, he stands,
> Trunk and bough,
> Naked strength.

29 But not **Ox**ford Street, which would be more of a dactyl, this is an oddity of English utterance.

Alexander Pope a century earlier had written something similar as a tribute to his friend Jonathan Swift's *Gulliver's Travels*:

> In amaze
> Lost I gaze
> Can our eyes
> Reach thy size?

. . . and so on. Tennyson's is more successful, I think. You won't find too many other amphimacers on your poetic travels: once again, English poets, prosodists and metrists don't really believe in them. Maybe you will be the one to change their minds.

QUATERNARY FEET

Can one have metrical units of four syllables? Quaternary feet? Well, in classical poetry they certainly existed, but in English verse they are scarce indeed. Suppose we wrote this:

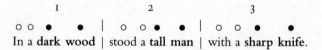

That's a hexameter of alternating pyrrhic and spondaic feet and might make a variant closing or opening line to a verse, but would be hard to keep up for a whole poem. However, you could look at it as a *trimeter*:


```
       I                 2                 3
  o  o  ●     ●   |   o   o ●    ●   |   o   o   ●       ●
In a dark wood | stood a tall man | with a sharp knife.
```

The name for this titty-**tum-tum** foot is a *double iamb*, sometimes called an *ionic minor*. Again, these are incredibly rare in English poetry. One such foot might be used for emphasis, variation or the capturing of a specific speech pattern, but it is never going to form the metrical pattern for a whole poem, save for the purposes of a prosodic equivalent of a Chopin étude, in other words as a kind of training exercise. Whether you call the above line an ionic minor or double iambic trimeter, a pyrrhic spondaic hexameter or any other damned thing really doesn't matter. Rather insanely there is a quaternary foot called a *diamb*, which goes ti-**tum**-ti **tum**, but for our purposes that is not a foot of four, it is simply two standard iambic feet. Frankly my dear, I don't give a diamb. Some people, including a couple of modern practising poets I have come across, like the double iamb, however, and would argue that the Wilfred Owen line I scanned as a pyrrhic earlier:

○　●　　○　●　　○　●　　┌○　○┐　○　　●
Shall **shine**| the **ho** | ly **glimm** |ers of|good-**byes**

Should properly be called a double iamb or ionic minor since 'good-bye' is double-stressed:

○　●　　○　●　　○　●　　┌○　○　●　　●┐
Shall **shine**| the **ho** | ly **glimm** |ers of **good-byes**

Well, hours of lively debate down the pub over that one. We will tiptoe away and leave them to it.

You may have guessed that if a double iamb or ionic *minor* goes titty-**tum-tum**, then an ionic *major* might well do the opposite: **tum-tum**-titty, **tum-tum**-titty: ●●○○ ○○●●: 'make much of it', that sort of rhythm:

Lee Harvey the **lone gun**man, did **cold heart**edly
Shoot fatally **John Kenn**edy: **poor Jac**queline.

You'd be right to think it *ought* to be called a double trochee too, but so far as I am aware this term isn't used for such a foot, just ionic major.

For the record, you'll find the other quaternary feet in the table at the end of this chapter: they include the antispast, the choriamb and the epitrite and paeon families. Again, good for name-dropping at parties, but like the other measures of four, vestiges of Greek poetry that really don't have a useful place in the garden of English verse. Rupert Brooke experimented with accentual versions of choriambs, which go **tum**-titty-**tum**: **Billy** the **Kid**. True classical choriambic verse lines should start with a spondee followed by choriambs and a pyrrhic:

●● | ●○○● | ●○○● | ●○○● |○○

Brooke came up with lines like:

> **Light**-**foot dance** in the **woods, whis**per of **life**, **woo** me to **way**faring

To make the last two syllables a pyrrhic foot you have to read the word as 'wafering', which is not quite what Brooke means. He, of course, was classically educated to a degree unimaginable today and would from his early teens have written Greek and Latin poems scanned according to quantitative vowel length, not stress. The vast bulk of successful English verse is, as we know, accentual-syllabic. Nonetheless, he shows that all the metres lie in readiness, waiting for someone to experiment with them. The problem comes when a form is so specific as to cause you to cast about for what fits the metre rather than what fits the true sense of what you want to say. How far the meaning and feeling drives you and how far, as a poet, you allow form and metre to guide you where you never expected to go is for a later section of the book.

There is another kind of native metre, however, the *accentual*, at which we will take a look when you have completed one more drill.

Poetry Exercise 6

♦ Write some anapaestic hexameters describing how to get to your house.

○○● ○○● ○○● ○○● ○○● ○○●

> Just as **far** as the **mo**torway **takes** you then **straight** past the
> **Lake**nheath **bend**.
> Take a **left** on the **Nar**borough **Road** then a **right** when you
> **come** to the **end**.
> It's the **house** with the **shut**ters all **closed** and a **gar**den that's
> **frank**ly a **slum**.
> When you're **there**, why not **park** round the **back** or just
> **hoot** on your **horn** till I **come**?

♦ And some dactylic pentameter on the subject of cows. For fun these should be in the classical manner: four dactyls and a spondee: try to make the spondee as spondaic as the English tongue will allow – two solid bovine stressed syllables.

●○○ ●○○ ●○○ ●○○ ●●

> **Stan**ding in **ran**domly **cu**rious **hud**dles in **long grass**
> **Pa**tient as **sta**tues, but **twitch**ing and **steam**ing like **stopped**
> **trains**
> **Pen**sively **wait**ing for **some**thing to **hap**pen that **just won't**
> **Prob**ably **think**ing we're **ner**vous and **skitt**ish as **new calves**.

Your turn now. You have forty minutes for your two verses.

V

Anglo-Saxon Attitudes

Accentual verse — alliteration and the two-beat hemistich

English verse sprang, like the English language, from two principal sources, Greco-Roman and Anglo-Saxon. From the Greeks and Romans we took ordered syllabic measures, from the Old English we took *accent*. We put them together to make the native *accentual-syllabic* verse that we have been looking at thus far. It is the classical stream that had the most obvious influence on our poetry and certainly on the technical language we use to describe it, but the Anglo-Saxon tributary has carved its way through our literary landscape too. For hundreds of years it lay isolated, like an old oxbow lake, cut off from the flow, but over the last century or more it has snaked its way back into the mainstream. It is worth dipping our toes in to see if we find it congenial. I suspect that after the syllable counting and footwatching of the foregoing pages, you will find its comparative freedom a great delight.

ANGLO-SAXON and OLD ENGLISH are (more or less) inter-changeable terms used for verse written in England before the Norman Conquest of 1066. MIDDLE ENGLISH or MEDIEVAL applies to a later, post-Norman revival of the Old English style. These are loose ascriptions but will do for our purposes.

With Old English poetry there is NO SYLLABIC COUNT and there is NO RHYME. Is it *free verse*, then, unbounded by rules? By no means. Old English verse is distinctly patterned. Until now we have been looking at metre composed according to rules of *syllabic accentuation*: Anglo-Saxon poetry is composed according to rules of *accent only*: it is a form of *accentual* verse. Accentual-*alliterative* to be precise. Oo-er, sounds a bit scary. It really isn't, I promise you.

Alliteration is the trick of beginning a succession of words with the same consonant.[30] W. S. Gilbert's 'life-long lock', 'short sharp shock' and 'big black block' are examples of alliterative phrases that we have already met. Alliteration is still rife in English – advertisers and magazine sub-editors seem obsessed with it. Next time you find yourself out and about with your notebook, write down examples from advertising hoardings and newspaper headlines. It is an English disease: you won't find it to anything like the same degree in Spanish, French or Italian. It lives on in phrases like 'wit and wisdom', 'parent power', 'feast or famine', 'sweet sixteen', 'dirty dozen', 'buy British', 'prim and proper', 'tiger in your tank', 'you can be sure of Shell' and so on. As we have seen, Shakespeare in *A Midsummer Night's Dream* mocked its overuse when Bottom and his friends attempt dramatic verse. Here is another part of their dreadful 'Pyramus and Thisbe':

> Whereat, with blade, with bloody blameful blade,
> He bravely broach'd his boiling bloody breast;

That is cast in standard Shakespearean iambic pentameter. Old English verse made no such regular, organised use of iambs or any other kind of foot; instead, their verse was based on a much simpler kind of accentuation. The poetic line is *divided in two*. Two parts, each containing two stressed elements, two beats. The Greek for half a line is *hemistich* (pronounced hemmy-stick) and so, Greek being the language even of native English prosody, hemistich is the word commonly used to describe the Anglo-Saxon half-line.

Each hemistich must contain two **stressed** syllables. It doesn't matter where they come or how many unstressed syllables surround them. For now, we will call the stressed syllables **one**, **two**, **three** and

30 'The repetition of the sound of an initial consonant or consonant cluster in stressed syllables close enough to each other for the ear to be affected' is how the *New Princeton Encyclopedia of Poetry and Poetics* puts it, with trademark elegance and concision.

four. One and two are placed in the first hemistich, **three** and **four** in the second. I have left a deliberately wide gap to denote the vital caesura that marks the division into hemistichs.

One comes along with **two**   and **three** is there with **four**
Let old **one** take **two's** hand   while young **three** has a word with **four**
    Here come **one** and **two**   **three** is there with **four**

Although 'comes', 'along', 'there', 'hand', 'young' and 'word' might seem to be words which ought properly to receive some stress, it is only the **numbers** here that take the primary accent. Try reading the three lines aloud, deliberately hitting the numbers hard.

You get the idea. Of course there will always be minor, secondary stresses on the other words, but it is those four stressed elements that matter. You could say, if you love odd words as much as most poets do, that a line of Anglo-Saxon poetry is in reality a syzygy of dipodic hemistichs. A pair of yoked two-foot half-lines, in other words. But I prefer syzygy. It really is a word, I promise you.[31]

Now for the *alliterative* principle, christened by Michael Alexander, Anglo-Saxon scholar and translator of *Beowulf*, the BANG, BANG, BANG – CRASH! rule.

<u>ONE</u>, <u>TWO</u> AND <u>THREE</u> ARE ALLITERATED, <u>FOUR</u> ISN'T

It is as simple as that. No rhyming, so syllable counting. In fact, why bother with the word hemistich at all? The line is divided into two: the first half has **bang** and **bang**, and the second half has **bang** and <u>**crash**</u>. That's all you really need to know. Let us scan this kind of metre with bold for the first three beats and bold-underline for the fourth, to mark its unalliterated difference.

31 Pronounced *scissor-gee*: 'a pair of connected or corresponding things'.

It em**barks** with a **bang**	sucking **breath** from the **lungs**
And **rolls** on di**rect**ly	as **rapid** as **light**ning.
The **speed** and the **splen**dour	come **spilling** like **wine**
Com**pell**ingly **per**fect and	ap**peal**ingly **clear**
The most **ven**erable in**ven**tion	con**ven**iently **sim**ple.

Important to note that it is the stressed *syllables* that matter: 'com**pell**ing' and 'ap**peal**ing' are perfectly legitimate alliteration words, as are 'in**ven**tion' and 'con**ven**ient', '**rolls**' and 'di**rect**ly'. So long as the stress falls heavily enough on the syllable belonging to the alliterating consonant, everything's hotsy-totsy and right as a trivet. And I say again, because it might seem unusual after all the syllabic counting of the previous section of the book, IT DOESN'T MATTER HOW MANY SYLLABLES THERE ARE, ONLY HOW MANY BEATS. Occasionally, in defiance of the b-b-b-crash rule you may see the fourth beat alliterate with the others, but usually it does not.

Although I said that it does not matter where in each half of the line the stressed elements go, it is close enough to a rule to say that the *fourth* stress (the CRASH) is very likely to be in the last word of the line, which may (like 'lightning' and 'simple' above) have a feminine ending.

I could give you some examples of Anglo-Saxon verse, but they involve special letters (*yoghs*, *eths* and *thorns*) and the language is distant enough from our own to be virtually incomprehensible to all but the initiated.

Medieval verse is not so tricky to decipher. Round about the thirteenth and fourteenth centuries English poets began to write once more in the Anglo-Saxon style: this flowering, known as the Alliterative Revival, gave rise to some magnificent works. Here is the opening to William Langland's 'Piers Plowman'.[32]

32 From the C text: shorn of its yoghs and thorns, thanks to Elizabeth Salter and Derek Pearsall's invaluable edition, published by Edward Arnold for York Medieval Texts.

In a somer sesoun, whan softe was the sonne
I shope me into shroudes, as I a shep were,
In habite as an heremite, unholy of werkes,
Wente forth in the world wondres to here,
And saw many selles and sellcouthe thynges.

You hardly need to know what every word means, but a rough translation would be:

One summer, when the sun was gentle
I dressed myself in rough clothes like a shepherd
In the habit of a lazy hermit[33]
Went forth into the world to hear wonders
And saw many marvels and strange things.

You will notice that Langland does open with bang, bang, bang – *bang*. Perhaps it is his way of beginning his poem with special hoopla. *Sir Gawain and the Green Knight*, an anonymous work from the same period (late fourteenth century: contemporary with Chaucer) opens thus:

Sithen the sege and the assaut watz sesed at Troye
The borgh brittened and brent to brondez and askez
The tulk that the trammes of tresoun ther wroght
Watz tried for his tricherie, the trewest on erthe;

My spellcheck has just resigned, but no matter. Here is a basic translation:

Since the siege and the assault ceased at Troy
The town destroyed and burned to brands and ashes
The man that the wiles of treason there wrought
Was tried for his treachery, the veriest on earth;

33 A work-shy monk, not attached to any monastic order. Like Chaucer, Langland was very down on the species.

The Gawain Poet (as he is known in the sexy world of medieval studies – he is considered by some to be the author of three other alliterative works – *Pearl*, *Patience* and *Purity*) occasionally breaks the 'rule' and includes an extra alliterating word, and therefore, one must assume, an extra beat, as he does here in the second line.

Modern poets (by which I mean any from the last hundred years) have tried their hands at this kind of verse with varying degrees of accomplishment. This is a perfect Langlandian four-stress alliterated line in two hemistichs and comes from R. S. Thomas's 'The Welsh Hill Country':

On a bleak background of bald stone.

Ezra Pound's 'The Sea Farer: from the Anglo-Saxon' contains lines like 'Waneth the watch, but the world holdeth' and 'Nor winsome-ness to wife, nor world's delight' but for the most part it does not follow the hemistich b-b-b-c pattern with such exactness. Among the more successful in this manner was that great prosodic experimenter, W. H. Auden. These extracts are from his verse drama *The Age of Anxiety*.

Deep in my dark the dream shines
Yes, of you, you dear always;
My cause to cry, cold but my
Story still, still my music.

Mild rose the moon, moving through our
Naked nights: tonight it rains;
Black umbrellas blossom out;
Gone the gold, my golden ball.

What Auden manages, which other workers in this field often do not, is to imbue the verse with a sense of the modern and the living. He uses enjambment (something very rarely done by Old English and medieval poets) to help create a sense of flow. A grim failing when writing in alliterative four-stress lines is to overdo the

Saxon and produce verse that is the poetic equivalent of morris dancing or Hobbit-speak.[34] When reading such verse out loud you feel the urge to put a finger to your ear and chant nasally like a bad folk singer. This unpleasantness can be aggravated by an over-reliance on a trope known as a *kenning*. Kennings are found in great profusion in Anglo-Saxon, Old German and especially Norse poetry. They are a kind of compound *metonym* (a metaphoric trope, see the glossary) used to represent a single object, person or concept: thus a ship becomes an *oar steed*, the sea is the *whale road* or the *gannet's bath* (*hron-rade* or *ganotes-bæð*) and *din of spears* would stand for 'battle'. My favourite is *brow-stars* for eyes. Eddic and Icelandic bards were very fond of these devices: I suppose modern equivalents would be *iron horse* for train, *chalk face* for the classroom, *fleapit* for cinema, *bunfight* for party, *devil's dandruff* for cocaine and *Hershey highway* for . . . well, ask your mother.

Modern prosodists and teachers (perhaps in a tragic and doomed attempt to get young people interested) have described alliterative-accentual verse of this kind as a sort of Old English fore-runner of hip-hop. There is no doubt that hip-hop will often favour the four-beat line, as the Blazin' Squad remind us . . .

    Me and the **boys**, we'll be **blazin'** it **up**

And certainly MC Hammer's 'Let's Get It Started' can be said to be formed in perfect hemistichs, two beats to each.

    Nobody knows how a **rapper** really **feels**
    A **mind** full of **rhymes**, and a **tongue** of **steel**
    Just **put** on the **Hammer**, and **you** will be **rewarded**
    My **beat** is ever **boomin**, and you **know** I get it **started**

To scan such lyrics in the classical manner would clearly be even more absurd than comparing them to Anglo-Saxon hemistichs,

34 My edition of *Gawain* was edited by Tolkien, who did much to popularise Middle English verse, through his scholarship as much as through his Middle Earth fantasies.

but somewhere between sociology, anthropology, prosody and neurolinguistics there could be found an answer as to why a four-beat line divided in two has continued to have such resonance for well over a millennium. For our purposes, it can do no harm to be familiar with the feel of the Anglo-Saxon split line. To that end, we come to . . .

Poetry Exercise 7

Write a piece of verse following the rules above: each half-line to contain two beats, all four following the bang, bang, bang – crash rule (in other words alliteration on the first three beats).

To make it easier, I would suggest finding something very specific to write about. Poetry comes much more easily when concrete thoughts and images are brought to mind. For the sake of this exercise, since it is getting on for lunchtime and I am hungry, I suggest eighteen or twenty lines on the subject of what you would like, and wouldn't like, to eat right this minute.

Once again, I have scribbled down some drivel to show you that quality is not the point here, just the flexing of your new accentual-alliterative muscles. I have not been able to resist rhyming the last two lines, something entirely unnecessary and, frankly, unacceptable. You will do much better, I know.

Figs are too fussy and fish too dull
I'm quite fond of quince, but I question its point.
Most sushi is salty and somehow too raw
I can't abide bagels and beans make me fart
There's something so sad about salmon and dill
And goose eggs and gherkins are ghastlier still.

But cheese smeared with chutney is cheerful enough
So I'll settle for sandwiches, sliced very thick
The brownest of bread, buttered with love.
A plate of ploughman's will pleasure me well,
I'll lunch like a lord, then labour till four
When teacakes and toast will tempt me once more.

Sprung Rhythm

Stress is the life of it.
GMH – letter to Robert Bridges

One single name rises above all others when considering the influence of Anglo-Saxon modalities on modern poetry. Well – three single names, come to think of it . . .

GERARD MANLEY HOPKINS

It is possible that you came across this mysterious Jesuit priest's verse at school and that someone had the dreadful task of trying to explain to you how *sprung rhythm* worked. Relax: it is like Palmerston and the Schleswig-Holstein Question. Only three people in the world understand it, one is dead, the other has gone mad and the third is me, and I have forgotten.

Hopkins was a nineteenth-century English–Welsh poet who developed his own metrics. Calling the system 'sprung rhythm', he marked his verse with accents, loops and foot divisions to demonstrate how his stresses should fall. Among his prosodic inventions were such devices as 'outriders', 'roving over' and 'hanging stress': these have their counterparts or at least rough equivalents in the *sain* and *lusg* that make up *cynghanedd*, the sound system of ancient Welsh poetry, which Hopkins had studied deeply. I am not going to go into them here for two simple reasons: firstly, they make my head ache and secondly, I think they would only be usefully covered in a much more detailed book than this aspires to be. If you really want to get to grips with what he was up to, I recommend a library. His collected letters are available in academic bookshops and university collections; in these he explains to fellow poets like Robert Bridges and Coventry Patmore what he felt he was doing. Personally I find reading his poems a supreme pleasure *unless* I am trying to figure out their underlying metrical schemes.

Here is one of his best-known works 'Pied Beauty'. YOU ARE STILL READING OUT LOUD AREN'T YOU? GOOD.

GLORY be to God for dappled things –
　　For skies of couple-colour as a brinded cow;
　　　　For rose-moles all in stipple upon trout that swim;
Fresh-firecoal chestnut-falls; finches' wings;
　　Landscape plotted and pieced – fold, fallow, and plough;
　　　　And áll trádes, their gear and tackle and trim.
All things counter, original, spare, strange;
　　Whatever is fickle, freckled (who knows how?)
　　　　With swift, slow; sweet, sour; adazzle, dim;
He fathers-forth whose beauty is past change:
　　　　　　　　　　　　Praise him.

'The achieve of, the mastery of the thing!' as he himself wrote of the windhover. I am sure you have seen that most of the words are Anglo-Saxon in origin, very few Latinate words there at all (*counter*, *original*, *colour* and *trout* are the only ones I am sure of), the alliteration is fierce throughout, though not in the strict bang, bang, bang – crash! form we saw in Langland. You probably don't need to count syllables to be able to tell that there is no standard metric regularity here. His own accents on 'áll trádes' reveal the importance he places on stress and the unusual nature of its disposition.

Now read out the opening of 'That Nature Is a Heraclitean Fire and of the Comfort of the Resurrection'. The endearing title refers to the Greek philosopher Heraclitus, who believed that impermanence, the perpetual flux of all nature, is central to our understanding of existence and that clouds, air, earth and fire constantly transmute one into the other. The language again is almost entirely Anglo-Saxon in derivation. Hopkins uses virgules to mark the long lines for us into hemistichs.

CLOUD PUFFBALL, torn tufts, tossed pillows | flaunt forth,
then chevy on an air-
Built thoroughfare: heaven roisterers, in gay-gangs | they
throng; they glitter in marches,
Down roughcast, down dazzling whitewash, | wherever an
elm arches,
Shivelights and shadowtackle in long | lashes lace, lance, and
pair.

Essentially his technique was all about *compression*: sprung rhythm
squeezes out weak or 'slack' syllables and condenses the strong
stresses, one to each foot. 'Sprung rhythm makes verse stressy,' he
wrote to his brother Everard, 'it purges it to an emphasis as much
brighter, livelier, more lustrous than the regular but commonplace
emphasis of common rhythm, as poetry in general is brighter than
common speech.'

Writing to Bridges of his poem 'The Eurydice' he said this:
'you must not slovenly read it with the eyes but with your ears as
if the paper were declaiming it at you. For instance the line "she had
come from a cruise training seamen" read without stress is mere
Lloyds Shipping Intelligence; properly read it is quite a different
story. *Stress is the life of it.*' My italics, my *stress*.

The manner was designed to create an outward, poetic form
('instress') that mirrored what he saw as the 'inscape' of the world.
He said in a letter to Patmore that stress is 'the making of a thing
more, or making it markedly, what it already is; it is the bringing
out its nature'. His sense of instress and inscape is not unlike the
medieval idea of haecceity or 'thisness'[35] and the later, modernist
obsession with quiddity ('whatness'). If such exquisite words are
leaving you all of a doo-dah, it is worth remembering that for those
of us with a high doctrine of poetry, the art is precisely concerned
with precision, exactly about the exact, fundamentally found in the

35 Derived from the theology of Duns Scots, whom Hopkins revered.

fundamental, concretely concrete, radically rooted in the thisness and whatness of everything. Poets, like painters, look hard for the exact nature of things and feelings, what they really, really are. Just as painters in the late nineteenth and early twentieth century tried to move their form on, tried to find new ways to represent the 'concrete flux of interpenetrating intensities' that T. E. Hulme saw as reality, so Hopkins attempted to create a prosodic scheme that went beyond the calm, regular certainties of iambs and anapaests ('running rhythm' as he called traditional metrics) in order to find a system that mirrored the (for him) overwhelming complexity, density and richness of nature. How they mocked Cézanne and Matisse for their pretension and oddity, yet how truthful to us their representations of nature now seem. The idiosyncrasy of Hopkins is likewise apparent, yet who can argue with such a concrete realisation of the skies? 'Cloud puffball, torn tufts, tossed pillows . . .' The density and relentless energy of his stresses and word-yokings are his way of relaying to us the density and relentless energy of experience. There is nothing 'primitivist', 'folksy' or 'naïve' in Hopkins's appropriation of indigenous, pre-Renaissance poetics, his verse strikes our ear as powerfully modern, complex and tense. 'No doubt my poetry errs on the side of oddness,' he wrote to Bridges in 1879. 'It is the vice of distinctiveness to become queer. This vice I cannot have escaped.'

One more excerpt, this time from 'The Caged Skylark', which, as you will see, refers to *us* more than to the bird:

As a **dare**-gale **sky**lark **scant**ed in a dull **cage**
Man's mounting spirit in his **bone**-house, **mean** house, **dwells**.

How different from Blake's Robin Red breast in *its* cage . . .

Five of those twenty-four syllables are slack and squeezed into the lightest of scudding trips (in order: *a, -ed, a, -it, his*), while the *in* of both lines takes fractionally more push. The others, with varying degrees of weight that you might like to decide upon, are stressed: I have emboldened the words that seem to me to take the primary stress, but I could well be wrong. Incidentally, 'bone-house' to mean 'body' is an example of a kenning: it doesn't take too much to see that the adjectival 'dare-gale' could easily cross over into another kenning too.

All of which demonstrates, I hope, the way in which Hopkins backwards-leapfrogged the Romantics, the Augustans (Pope, Dryden et al.), Shakespeare, Milton and even Chaucer, to forge a distinct poetics of *stress metre* from the ancient verse of the Welsh, Icelandic and Anglo-Saxon traditions. In turn, many British twentieth-century poets looked back the shorter distance to Hopkins, over the shoulders of Eliot, Pound and Yeats. I find it hard to read much of Ted Hughes, for example, without hearing Hopkins's distinct music. Here are two fragments from 'The Sluttiest Sheep in England' for you to recite to yourself.

> They clatter

> Over worthless moraines, tossing
> Their Ancient Briton draggle-tassel sheepskins
> Or pose, in the rain-smoke, like warriors –
> . . .

> This lightning-broken huddle of summits
> This god-of-what-nobody-wants

Or this, from 'Eagle':

> The huddle-shawled lightning-faced warrior
> Stamps his shaggy-trousered dance
> On an altar of blood.

Certainly the sensibility is different: Hopkins is all wonderment, worship, dazzle and delight, where Hughes is often (but certainly not always) in a big mood: filled with disgust, doubt and granite contempt. Nonetheless, the Anglo-Saxon vocabulary, the generally four-stressed split line and use of alliteration and other 'echoic' devices (we'll come to them in a later chapter) reveal much common ground. Many modern British poets show the influence of ancient forms filtered through Hopkins. We've already met this perfect Langlandian line from R. S. Thomas's 'The Welsh Hill Country':

On a bleak background of bald stone.

From the same poem comes this:

the leaves'
Intricate filigree falls, and who shall renew
Its brisk pattern?

We feel a faint echo of Hopkins there, I think, for all that it is more controlled and syntactically conventional. I am not denying the individuality of Hughes or Thomas: the point is that Hopkins cleared a pathway that had long been overgrown, a pathway that in the twentieth century became something of a well-trodden thoroughfare, almost a thronging concourse. Hopkins himself said in a letter to Bridges in 1888 after he had just completed the 'Heraclitean Fire' sonnet, inspired as it was by the distillation 'of a great deal of early philosophical thought':

. . . the liquor of the distillation did not taste very Greek, did it? The effect of studying masterpieces is to make me admire and do otherwise. So it must be on every original artist to some degree, on me to a marked degree.

I have taken a little time over the style, purpose and influence of Hopkins because his oppo, as you might say, Walt Whitman – very different man, but so alike too – was busy in America tearing up the prosodic manuals round about the time Hopkins was experimenting with his sprung rhythms.

Whitman is considered by many to be the father of English language *free verse*[36]: verse without traditional patterning, stanza

36 From the French *vers libre*, coined in Paris in an 1886 edition of *La Vogue*, which included excerpts of Whitman among the Laforgue and Rimbaud.

form, rhyme, metre, syllabic count or regular accentuation. Since such verse is beyond the reach and aim of this book, much of the pleasures of Eliot, Pound, Lawrence, William Carlos Williams, the American 'Open Field' School and Whitman[37] himself (and very real pleasures they are) will not be looked at here. As I have already said, I do not look down on free verse at all: I admire the poet who can master it.

There are two kingdoms of life: Flora and Fauna. In the natural history of poetry there are likewise two kingdoms: there is the kingdom of Accentual-Syllabic Verse and there is the kingdom of Accentual Verse.

Hang on a mo . . .

There are actually *three* kingdoms in the natural world – we have forgotten the kingdom of *Fungi*. And likewise there is a third kingdom of Poetry: the Kingdom of *Syllabic* verse.

---

37 A reading of those poets will of course reveal much in the way of metrics, form and rhyming, but the generality of their work escaped into free verse.

VI

Syllabic Verse

These three then:

A   *accentual-syllabic verse* — the number of syllables and stresses in a line is fixed.

B   *accentual verse* — the number of stresses in a line is fixed, but the number of syllables varies (includes *alliterative-accentual* verse).

C   *syllabic verse* — the number of syllables in a line is fixed, but the number of stresses varies.

A   Meters and feet — iambs, pentameters, trochees, tetrameters and so on.

B   Anglo-Saxon four-stress verse — Hopkins and much song, ballad, folk, hip-hop and nursery rhyme forms.

C   ??

We have spent a fair amount of time looking at categories A and B but C remains unexplored.

Can there really be a form of verse where all that counts is the number of syllables in a line? No patterning of stress *at all*? What is the *point*?

Well, that is a fair and intelligent question and I congratulate myself for asking it. Much syllabic verse is from other linguistic cultures than our own. Perhaps the best known is the Japanese *haiku* which, as you may already know, is a three-line verse of five, seven and five syllables. In Japanese this syllable count is imperative and the form contains other rules which we can examine (as well as seeing whether it is feasible to write haikus in the strict Japanese manner in English) in the chapter on Verse Forms. The Tagalog *tanaga* is another such syllabic measured verse-form. Japanese and Tagalog[38] are syllable-timed languages[39] as are Spanish and many others European and worldwide. English, however, is *stress*-timed. What this means is beyond the scope of this book (or my poor grasp of phono-linguistics) but the upshot is that while verse ordered by syllabic count is popular in many other cultures, and indeed is often the norm, it is a rarity in English, since the lack of equal spacing between syllables in our stress-timed utterance renders such elaborate schemes very different from the foreign mode. They will never carry the *music* that native speakers of syllable-timed languages find in their syllabic verse, the English type involves a mostly visual engagement with the reader, sometimes resulting in a kind of *concrete* or *shaped* poetry. The moment a poet writing in this manner tries to arrange the stress – *voilà!* – we arrive back where we started at accentual-syllabic verse and our good friend the metric foot.

Nonetheless English-language poets have tried to write syllabic verse. The history of it may be stated briefly: with the exception of a few Elizabethan examples the mode did not come into promi-nence until Hopkins's friend Robert Bridges wrote extensively on the subject and in the manner – including his unreadable 'The Testament of Beauty', five thousand lines of twelve-syllable tedium.[40] His daughter Elizabeth Daryush (1887– 1977) took up the standard and wrote many syllabic poems, usually in lines of equal syllabic count, managing artfully to avoid iambic or any other regular stress patterns, as in the decasyllabic 'Still Life', a poem published in 1936:

Through the open French window the warm sun
lights up the polished breakfast table, laid

38 A Filipino language.
39 Technically a *mora*-timed language: morae being phonological units of dura-tion.
40 The longest syllabic verse poem in the language, according to the *Princeton Encyclopedia*. I tried – for your sake, dear reader, I tried – but gave up after line 23.

round a bowl of crimson roses, for one –
a service of Worcester porcelain, arrayed
near it a melon, peaches, figs, small hot
rolls in a napkin, fairy rack of toast,
butter in ice, high silver coffee-pot,
and, heaped, on a salver, the morning's post.

Note that 'porcelain' in true upper-class British would have to be pronounced 'porslin' to make the count work. Some kind of form is offered by the rhyming – one feels otherwise that the heavily run-on lines would be in danger of dissolving the work into prose. It was Daryush's exact contemporary the American poet Marianne Moore (1887–1969) who fully developed the manner. Her style of scrupulous, visually arresting syllabic verse has been highly influential. Here is an extract from her poem 'The Fish' with its syllable count of 1,3,9,6,8 per stanza.

1	All
3	external
9	marks of abuse are present on this
6	defiant edifice
8	all the physical features of
1	ac-
3	cident – lack
9	of cornice, dynamite grooves, burns, and
6	hatchet strokes, these things stand
8	out on it; the chasm-side is
1	dead . . .

As you can see, the count is important enough to sever words in something much fiercer than a usual enjambment. The apparent randomness is held in check by delicate rhyming: *this/edifice, and/stand*.

'I repudiate syllabic verse' Moore herself sniffed to her editor and went further in interview:

I do not know what syllabic verse is, can find no appropriate application for it. To be more precise, to raise to the status of science a mere counting of syllables seems to me frivolous.

As Dr Peter Wilson of London Metropolitan University has pointed out, '. . . since it is clear that many of her finest poems could not have been written in the form they were without the counting of syllables, this comment is somewhat disingenuous.' Other poets who have used syllabics include Dylan Thomas, Thom Gunn and Donald Justice, this from the latter's 'The Tourist from Syracuse':

You would not recognize me.
Mine is the face which blooms in
The dank mirrors of washrooms
As you grope for the light switch.

Between the Daryush and the Moore I hope you can see that there are possibilities in this verse mode. There is form, there is shape. If you like the looser, almost prose-poem approach, then writing in syllabics allows you the best of both worlds: structure to help organise thoughts and feelings into verse, and freedom from what some poets regard as the jackboot march of metrical feet. The beauty of such structures is that they are self-imposed, they are not handed down by our poetic forebears. That is their beauty but also their terror. When writing syllabics you are on your own.

It *must* be time for another exercise.

Poetry Exercise 8

♦ Two stanzas of alternating seven- and five-line syllabic verse: subject *Rain*.
♦ Two stanzas of verse running 3, 6, 1, 4, 8, 4, 1, 6, 3: subject *Hygiene*.

Here are my attempts, vague rhymes in the first, some in the second: you don't have to:

Rain
they say there's a taste before
it comes; a tin tang
like tonguing a battery
or a cola can

I know that I can't smell it
but the animals
glumly lowering their heads
can foretell its fall:

they can remember rains past
as I come closer
their eyewhites flash in fear of
another Noah

Hygiene
I'm filthy
On the outside I stink.
But,
There are people
So cleansed of dirt it makes you think
Unhygienic
Thoughts
Of them. I'd much rather
Stay filthy.

Their lather
Can't reach where they reek,
Suds
Can't soap inside.
All hosed, scrubbed and oilily sleek
They're still deep dyed
They
Can stand all day and drench
They still stench.

We have come to the end of our chapter on metrical modes. It is by no means complete. If you were (heaven forbid) to go no further with my book, I believe you would already be a much stronger and more confident poet for having read thus far. But please don't leave yet, there is much to discover in the next chapters on rhyming and on verse forms: that is where the fun really begins. Firstly, a final little exercise awaits.

Poetry Exercise 9

Coleridge wrote the following verse in 1806 to teach his son Derwent the most commonly used metrical feet. Note that he uses the classical 'long' 'short' appellation where we would now say 'stressed' 'weak'. For your final exercise in this chapter, WHIP OUT YOUR PENCIL and see how in the first stanza he has suited the metre to the description by scanning each line. By all means refer to the 'Table of Metric Feet' below. You are not expected to have learned anything off by heart. I have included the second stanza, which does not contain variations of metre, simply because it is so touching in its fatherly affection.

Lesson for a Boy

Trochee trips from long to short;
From long to long in solemn sort
Slow Spondee stalks, strong foot!, yet ill able
Ever to come up with Dactyl's trisyllable.
Iambics march from short to long; –
With a leap and a bound the swift Anapaests throng;
One syllable long, with one short at each side,
Amphibrachys hastes with a stately stride; –
First and last being long, middle short, Amphimacer
Strikes his thundering hoofs like a proud high-bred Racer.

If Derwent be innocent, steady, and wise,
And delight in the things of earth, water, and skies;
Tender warmth at his heart, with these metres to show it,
With sound sense in his brains, may make Derwent a poet,
May crown him with fame, and must win him the love
Of his father on earth and his Father above.
My dear, dear child!
Could you stand upon Skiddaw, you would not from its whole ridge
See a man who so loves you as your fond S. T. Coleridge . . .

Table of Metric Feet

BINARY

Iamb	○●	da-**dum**	di**vine**, a**lert**, i**nept**, con**fined**
Trochee	●○	**dum**-da	**me**tre, **rhy**thm, **ne**ver, **touch**ing
Spondee	●●	**dum-dum**	**full stop**, **no way**, **get stuffed**
Pyrrhic	○○	da-da:	in the, of a

TERNARY

Anapaest	○○●	titty-**tum**	under**stand**, in a **spin**, mina**ret**, Japa**nese**
Dactyl	●○○	**tum**-titty	**a**gitate, **la**vender, **fan**tasy **sol**emnly, **sig**nature
Amphibrach	○●○	ti-**tum**-ti	im**mor**al, what**ev**er, im**per**fect, de**sir**ing
Amphimacer	●○●	**tum**-ti-**tum**	**mat**ing **game**, **hand** to **mouth**, **up** to **you**
Bacchius	○●●	ti **tum tum**	a **top dog**, your **main man**
Antibacchius	●●○	**tum-tum**-ti	**good morn**ing, **Dick Tur**pin
Molossus	●●●	**dum-dum-dum**	**John Paul Jones**, **short sharp shock**
Tribrach	○○○	ti-ti-ti	and in the, or as a

QUATERNARY

Tetrabrach[41]	○○○○	titty-titty	or isn't it
Dispondee	●●●●	**tum-tum-tum-tum**	**MRSA**, **long time no see**, **fee-fie-fo-fum**
Diamb	○●○●	ti-**tum**-ti-**tum**	the **Queen** of **Hearts**, a**las** a**lack**
Ditrochee	●○●○	**tum**-ti-**tum**-ti	**Hur**dy-**gur**dy, **sil**ly **bil**ly, **Hump**ty **Dump**ty
Ionic minor	○○●●	titty-**tum-tum**	he's a **good man**, in a **mad world**
Ionic major	●●○○	**tum-tum**-titty	**bad pol**icy, **John Ken**nedy
Antispast	○●●○	ti-**tum-tum**-ti	the **big break**fast, Ni**cole Kid**man
Choriamb	●○○●	**tum**-titty-**tum**	**top** of the **world**, **Rich**ard the **Third**, **ov**er to **you**

41 Also sometimes known as a *proceleusmatic* foot.

First Paeon	●○○○	tum-ti-titty	temporary, practically, emissary
Second Paeon	○●○○	ti-tum-titty	ridiculous, preposterous, adorable, pentameter
Third Paeon	○○●○	titty-tum-ti	Jackanory, altogether,
Fourth Paeon	○○○●	titty-ti-tum	is it a boy, give it to me
First epitrite	○●●●	ti-tum-tum-tum	the thin red line, the BBC
Second epitrite	●○●●	tum-ti-tum-tum	mix a stiff drink, have a nice day
Third epitrite	●●○●	tum-tum-ti-tum	give peace a chance, hip hip hurray
Fourth epitrite	●●●○	tum-tum-tum-ti	horse hair sofa, dead man walking

Now about the metrics: the terminology you use – of
amphibrachs, pyrrhics etc. – is obsolete in English. We now
speak of these feet only in analyzing choruses from Greek
plays – because Greek verse is quantitative [. . .] we have
simplified our metrics to five kinds of feet [. . .] trochee,
iambus, anapest, dactyl, spondee. We do not need any more.

Edmund Wilson in a letter to Vladimir Nabokov, 1 September 1942

CHAPTER TWO

Rhyme

It is the one chord we have added to
the Greek lyre.

OSCAR WILDE: 'The Critic as Artist'

I

Rhyme, a few general thoughts

'Do you rhyme?'

This is often the first question a poet is asked. Despite the absence of rhyme in Greece and Rome (hence Wilde's aphorism above), despite the glories of Shakespeare, Milton, Wordsworth, Tennyson and all the blank-verse masterpieces of English literature from the Dark Ages to the present day, despite a hundred years of Modernism, rhyming remains for many an almost defining feature of poetry. *It ain't worth a dime if it don't got that rhyme* is how some poets and poetry lovers would sum it up. For others rhyming is formulaic, commonplace and conventional: a feeble badge of predictability, symmetry and bourgeois obedience.

There are very few poets I can call to mind who *only* used rhyme in their work, but I cannot think of a single one, no matter how free form and experimental, who *never* rhymed. Walt Whitman, Ezra Pound, D. H. Lawrence, Wyndham Lewis, William Carlos Williams, T. S. Eliot, Marianne Moore, e e cummings, Crane, Corso, Ferlinghetti, Ginsberg, Hughes – not an exception do I know.

There are some stanzaic forms, as we shall find in the next chapter, which seem limp and unfinished without the comfort and assurance that rhyme can bring, especially ballads and other forms that derive from, or tend towards, song. In other modes the verse can seem cheapened by rhyme. It is hard to imagine a rhyming version of Wordsworth's 'Tintern Abbey' or Eliot's *Four Quartets*, for example. This may of course be a failure of imagination: once a thing is made and done it is hard to picture it made and done in any other way.

The question 'to rhyme or not to rhyme' is not one I can answer for you, except to say that it would almost certainly be wrong to answer it with 'always' or 'never'.

Rhyme, like alliteration (which is sometimes called *head rhyme*) is thought to have originated in pre-literate times as a way of allowing the words of sung odes, lyrics, epics and sagas more easily to be memorised. Whatever its origin, the expectations it sets up in the mind seem deeply embedded in us. Much of poetry is about 'consonance' in the sense of *correspondence*: the likeness or congruity of one apparently disparate thing to another. Poetry is concerned with the connections between things, seeing the world in a grain of sand as Blake did in 'Auguries of Innocence', or sensing loss of faith in the ebbing of the tide as Arnold did in 'Dover Beach'. You might say poets are always looking for the wider *rhymes* in nature and experience. The Sea 'rhymes' with Time in its relentless flow, its eroding power, its unknowable depth. Hope 'rhymes' with Spring, Death 'rhymes' with Winter. At the level of physical observation, Blood 'rhymes' with Wine, Eyes with Sapphires, Lips with Roses, War with Storms and so on. Those are all stock correspondences which were considered clichés even by Shakespeare's day of course, but the point is this: as pattern-seeking, connection-hungry beings we are always looking for ways in which one thing chimes with another. Metonym, metaphor and simile do this in one way, rhyme, the apparently arbitrary chiming of word sounds, does it in another. Rhyme, as children quickly realise, provides a special kind of satisfaction. It can make us feel, for the space of a poem, that the world is less contingent, less random, more connected, link by link. When used well rhyme can *reify* meaning, it can embody in sound and sight the connections that poets try to make with their wider images and ideas. The Scottish poet and musician Don Paterson puts it this way:

> Rhyme always unifies sense [. . .] it can trick a logic from the shadows where one would not otherwise have existed.

An understanding of rhyme comes to us early in life. One sure way to make young children laugh is to deny them the natural satisfaction of expected end-rhymes, as in this limerick by W. S. Gilbert:

> There was an old man of St Bees
> Who was horribly stung by a wasp
>   When they said: 'Does it hurt?'
>   He replied: 'No it doesn't –
> It's a good job it wasn't a hornet.'

We all know of people who are tone-deaf, colour-blind, dyslexic or have no sense of rhythm, smell or taste, but I have never heard of anyone who cannot distinguish and understand rhyme. There may be those who genuinely think that 'bounce' rhymes with 'freak', but I doubt it. I think we can safely say rhyme is understood by all who have language. All except those who were born without hearing of course, for rhyming is principally a question of *sound*.

The Basic Categories of Rhyme

*End-rhyme*s – *internal rhymes*

While it is possible that before you opened this book you were not too sure about metre, I have no doubt that you have known since childhood exactly what rhyme is. The first poems we meet in life are nursery *rhymes*.

Humpty Dumpty sat on the *wall*
Humpty Dumpty had a great *fall*
All the King's horses and all the King's *men*
Couldn't put Humpty together *again*.

That famous and deeply tragic four-line verse (or *quatrain*) consists of two *rhyming couplets*. Here is an example of a ballady kind of quatrain where only the three-stress (second and fourth) lines bear the rhyme words:

Mary had a little lamb
Its fleece was white as *snow*
And everywhere that Mary went
The lamb was sure to *go*.

In both examples, the rhyme words come at the end of the line: *fall/wall*, *men/again*, *snow/go*. This is called END RHYMING.

Little Bo **Peep** has lost her **sheep**
And doesn't know where to *find them*.
Leave them **alone** and they'll come **home**,
Bringing their tails be*hind them*.

Little Bo **Peep** fell fast **asleep**
And dreamt she heard them *bleating*
But when she **awoke** she found it a *joke*
For they were still *afleeting*.

Here we have end-rhymes as before but INTERNAL RHYMES too, in the four-beat lines: *Peep/sheep*, *alone/home*, *Peep/asleep* and *awoke/joke*. Coleridge used this kind of internal rhyming a great deal in his 'Ancient Mariner':

The fair breeze **blew**, the white foam **flew**,
The furrow followed *free*:
We were the **first** that ever **burst**
Into that silent *sea*.

As did Lewis Caroll in 'The Jabberwocky':

> He left it *dead*, and with its *head*
> He went galumphing back.

A rarer form of internal rhyming is the leonine which derives from medieval Latin verse.[1] This is found in poems of longer measure where the stressed syllable preceding a caesura rhymes with the last stressed syllable of the line. Tennyson experimented with leonine rhymes in his juvenilia as well as using it in his later poem 'The Revenge':

> And the stately Spanish *men* to their flagship bore him
> *then*,
> Where they laid him by the *mast*, old Sir Richard caught
> at *last*,
> And they praised him to his *face* with their courtly foreign
> *grace*.

I suppose the internal rhyming in 'The Raven' might be considered leonine too, though corvine would be more appropriate . . .

> But the raven, sitting *lonely* on that placid bust, spoke *only*
> That one word, as if his soul in that one word he did
> *outpour*.
> Nothing further then he *uttered*; not a feather then he
> *fluttered*;
> Till I scarcely more than *muttered*, 'Other friends have flown
> *before*;
> On the morrow he will leave me, as my hopes have flown
> *before*.'
> Then the bird said, '*Nevermore*.'

Throughout the poem Poe runs a third internal rhyme (here *uttered/fluttered*) into the next line (*muttered*).

1 Named after Leo, the twelfth-century Canon of Saint Victor's in Paris.

Hopkins employed internal rhyme a great deal, but not in such predictable patterns. He used it to yoke together the stresses in such phrases as *dapple-dawn-drawn*, *stirred for a bird*, *he cursed at first*, *fall gall*, *in a flash at a trumpet-crash*, *glean-stream* and so on.

Partial Rhymes

Partial rhymes: assonance and consonance – eye-rhyme and wrenched rhyme

On closer inspection that last internal rhyme from Hopkins is not quite right, is it? *Glean* and *stream* do not share the same final consonant. In the third line of 'Little Bo Beep' the *alone/home* rhyme is imperfect in the same way: this is PARTIAL RHYME, sometimes called SLANT-rhyme or PARA-RHYME.[2] In slant-rhyme of the *alone/home*, *glean/stream* kind, where the vowels match but the consonants do not, the effect is called ASSONANCE: as in *cup/rub*, *beat/feed*, *sob/top*, *craft/mast* and so on. Hopkins uses *plough/down*, *rose/moles*, *breath/bread*, *martyr/master* and many others in *internal* rhymes, but never as end-rhyme. Assonance in end-rhymes is most commonly found in folk ballads, nursery rhymes and other song lyrics, although it was frowned upon (as were all partial rhymes) in Tin Pan Alley and musical theatre. On Broadway it is still considered bad style for a lyricist not to rhyme perfectly. Not so in the world of pop: do you remember the Kim Carnes song 'Bette Davis Eyes'? How's this for assonance?

> She's fer*ocious*
> And she *knows just*
> What it takes to make a *pro blush*

2 *Near* rhyme and *off* rhyme are terms used too.

Yowser! In the sixties the Liverpool School of poets, who were culturally (and indeed personally, through ties of friendship) connected to the Liverpool Sound, were notably fond of assonantal rhyme. Adrian Mitchell, for example, rhymes *size* with *five* in his poem 'Fifteen Million Plastic Bags'. The poets you are most likely to find using assonantal slant-rhymes today work in hip-hop and reggae traditions: Here's 'Talking Turkey' by Benjamin Zephaniah. Have fun reading it out à la B.Z. –

> Be nice to yu turkeys dis christmas
> Cos' turkeys just wanna hav fun
> Turkeys are cool, turkeys are wicked
> An every turkey has a Mum.
> Be nice to yu turkeys dis christmas,
> Don't eat it, keep it alive,
> It could be yu mate, an not on your plate
> Say, 'Yo! Turkey I'm on your side.'
> I got lots of friends who are turkeys
> An all of dem fear christmas time,
> Dey wanna enjoy it,
> dey say humans destroyed it
> n humans are out of dere mind,
> Yeah, I got lots of friends who are turkeys
> Dey all hav a right to a life,
> Not to be caged up an genetically made up
> By any farmer an his wife.

You can see that *fun/Mum*, *alive/side*, *time/mind*, *enjoy it/destroyed it* and perhaps *Christmas/wicked* are all used as rhyming pairs. The final pair *life/wife* constitute the only 'true' rhymes in the poem. Assonantally rhymed poems usually do end best with a full rhyme.

Now let us look at another well-known nursery rhyme:

> Hickory, dickory, *dock*,
> The mouse ran up the *clock*.

The clock struck *one*,
The mouse ran *down*!
Hickory, dickory, *dock*.

The *one*/*down* rhyme is partial too, but here the end consonant is the same but the *vowels* (vowel *sounds*) are different. This is called CONSONANCE: examples would be *off*/*if*, *plum*/*calm*, *mound*/*bond* and so on. Take a look at Philip Larkin's 'Toads':

Why should I let the toad *work*
Squat on my life?
Can't I use my wit as a pitchfork
And drive the brute off?

Six days of the week it soils
With its sickening poison –
Just for paying a few bills!
That's out of proportion.

The whole poem continues for another seven stanzas with loose consonantal para-rhymes of this nature. Emily Dickinson was fond of consonance too. Here is the first stanza of her poem numbered 1179:

Of so divine a Loss
We enter but the Gain,
Indemnity for Loneliness
That such a Bliss has been.

The poet most associated with a systematic mastery of this kind of rhyming is Wilfred Owen, who might be said to be its modern pioneer. Here are the first two stanzas from 'Miners':

There was a whispering in my hearth,
A sigh of the coal,
Grown wistful of a former earth
It might recall.

I listened for a tale of leaves
And smothered ferns;
Frond forests; and the low, sly lives
Before the fawns.

Ferns/fawns, *lives/leaves* and *coal/call* are what you might call *perfect* imperfect rhymes. The different vowels are wrapped in *identical* consonants, unlike Larkin's *soils/bills* and *life/off* or Dickinson's *gain/been* which are much looser.

In his poem 'Exposure', Owen similarly slant-rhymes *war/wire*, *knive us/nervous*, *grow/gray*, *faces/fusses* and many more. His most triumphant achievement with this kind of 'full' partial rhyme is found in the much-loved 'Strange Meeting':

I am the enemy you killed, my friend.
I knew you in this dark: for you so frowned
Yesterday through me as you jabbed and killed.
I parried: but my hands were loath and cold.

Here is the complete list of its slant-rhyme pairs:

escaped/scooped	groined/groaned	bestirred/stared	eyes/bless
hall/Hell	grained/ground	moan/mourn	years/yours
wild/world	hair/hour/here	laughed/left	untold/distilled
spoiled/spilled	tigress/progress	mystery/mastery	world/walled
wheels/wells	taint/stint	war/were	friend/frowned
killed/cold			

All (bar one) are couplets, each pair is different and – perhaps most importantly of all – no *perfect* rhymes at all. A sudden rhyme like 'taint' and 'saint' would stand out like a bum note. Which is not to say that a mixture of pure and slant-rhyme is *always* a bad idea: W. B. Yeats frequently used a mixture of full and partial rhymes. Here is the first stanza of 'Easter 1916', with slant-rhymes in **bold**.

I have met them at close of *day*
Coming with vivid *faces*
From counter or desk among *grey*
Eighteenth century *houses*.
I have passed with a nod of the *head*
Or polite meaningless words,
Or have lingered awhile and *said*
Polite meaningless words,
And thought before I had *done*
Of a mocking tale or a *gibe*
To please a *companion*
Around the fire at the *club*,
Being certain that they and *I*
But lived where motley is *worn*:
All changed, changed **utterly**
A terrible beauty is *born*.

Assonance rhyme is suitable for musical verse, for the vowels (the part the voice sings) stay the same. Consonance rhyme, where the vowels change, clearly works better on the page.

There is a third kind of slant-rhyme which *only* works on the page. Cast your eye up to the list of para-rhyme pairs from Owen's 'Strange Meeting'. I said that all *bar one* were couplets. Do you see the odd group out?

It is the *hair/hour/here* group, a triplet not a couplet, but that's not what makes it stands out for our purposes. *Hair/here* follows the consonance rule, but *hour* does not: it *looks* like a perfect consonance but when read out the 'h' is of course silent. This is a consonantal version of an EYE-RHYME, a rhyme which works visually, but not aurally. Here are two examples of more conventional eye-rhymes from Shakespeare's *As You Like It*:

Blow, blow thou winter *wind*
Thou art not so *unkind* . . .

> Though thou the waters *warp*
> Thy sting is not so *sharp*

It is common to hear 'wind' pronounced 'wined' when the lines are read or sung, but by no means necessary: hard to do the same thing to make the *sharp/warp* rhyme, after all. *Love/prove* is another commonly found eye-rhyme pair, as in Marlowe's 'Passionate Shepherd to his Love'.

> Come live with me and be my *love*
> And we will all the pleasures *prove*.

It is generally held that these may well have been true sound rhymes in Shakespeare's and Marlowe's day. They have certainly been used as eye-rhymes since, however. Larkin used the same pair nearly four hundred years later in 'An Arundel Tomb':

> ... and to prove
> Our almost-instinct almost true:
> What will survive of us is love.

In his poem 'Meiosis' Auden employs another conventional eye-rhyme for that pesky word:

> The hopeful falsehood cannot stem with *love*
> The flood on which all move and wish to *move*.

The same poet's 'Precious Five' shows that eye-rhyme can be used in all kinds of ways:

> Whose oddness may provoke
> To a mind-saving joke
> A mind that would it *were*
> An apathetic *sphere*:

Another imperfect kind is WRENCHED rhyme, which to compound the felony will usually go with a wrenched *accent*.

> He doesn't mind the language being *bent*
> In choosing words to force a wrenched *accént*.
> He has no sense of how the verse should *sing*
> And tries to get away with wrenched rhym*ing*.
> A bad wrenched rhyme won't ever please the *eye:*
> Or find its place in proper poe*try*.

Where 'poetry' would have to be pronounced 'poe-a-try'.[3] You will find this kind of thing a great deal in folk-singing, as I am sure you are aware. However, I can think of at least two fine *elegiac* poems where such potentially wrenched rhymes are given. This from Ben Jonson's heart-rending, 'On My First Son'.

> Rest in soft peace, and asked say, 'Here doth lie
> Ben Jonson his best piece of poetry.'

Auden uses precisely the same rhyme pair in his 'In Memory of W. B. Yeats':

> Let the Irish vessel lie
> Emptied of its poetry.

I think those two examples work superbly, and of course no reader of them in public would wrench those rhymes. However, we should not necessarily assume that since Yeats and Jonson are officially Fine Poets, everything they do must be regarded as unimpeachable. If like me you look at past or present poets to help teach you your craft, do be alive to the fact that they are as capable of being caught napping as the rest of us. *Quandoque bonus dormitat Homerus*, as Horace famously observed: 'sometimes even the great Homer nods'. Here is a couplet from Keats's 'Lamia' by way of example:

> Till she saw him, as once she pass'd him by,
> Where gainst a column he leant thoughtfully

Again, a reader-out-loud of this poem would not be so unkind to

---

3 Presumably this is what a poetaster does: give poe-a-try . . .

poet or listener as to wrench the end-rhyme into 'thoughtful-eye'. Nonetheless, whether wrenched or not the metre can safely be said to suck. The stressed 'he' is unavoidable, no pyrrhic substitutions help it and without wrenching the rhyme or the rhythm the line ends in a lame dactyl.

> Where **gainst** a column **he** leant **thought**fully

Add to this the word order inversion 'gainst a column he leant', the very banality of the word 'thoughtfully' and the archaic aphaeretic[4] damage done to the word 'against' and the keenest Keatsian in the world would be forced to admit that this will never stand as one of the Wunderkind's more enduring monuments to poesy. I have, of course, taken just one couplet from a long (and in my view inestimably fine) poem, so it is rather mean to snipe. Not every line of *Hamlet* is a jewel, nor every square inch of the Sistine Chapel ceiling worthy of admiring gasps. In fact, Keats so disliked being forced into archaic inversions that in a letter he cited their proliferation in his extended poem *Hyperion* as one of the reasons for his abandonment of it.

Wrenching can be more successful when done for comic effect. Here is an example from Arlo Guthrie's 'Motorcycle Song'.

> I don't want a pickle
> Just want to ride on my motorsickle
> And I'm not bein' fickle
> 'Cause I'd rather ride on my motorsickle
> And I don't have fish to fry
> Just want to ride on my motorcy . . . cle

Ogden Nash was the twentieth-century master of the comically wrenched rhyme, often, like Guthrie, wrenching the spelling to aid the reading. These lines are from 'The Sniffle'.

4 *Aphaeresis* means the dropping of a first letter or letters of a word: in poetry it refers to *'neath*, *'twas*, *'mongst* – that kind of thing. It's also something to do with separating plasma from blood cells, but that needn't worry us.

Is spite of her sniffle,
Isabel's chiffle.
Some girls with a sniffle
Would be weepy and tiffle;
They would look awful
Like a rained-on waffle.

. . .

Some girls with a snuffle
Their tempers are uffle,
But when Isabel's snivelly
She's snivelly civilly,
And when she is snuffly
She's perfectly luffly.

Forcing a rhyme can exploit the variations in pronunciation that exist as a result of class, region or nationality. In a dramatic monologue written in the voice of a rather upper-class character *fearfully* could be made to rhyme with *stiffly* for example, or *houses* with *prizes* (although these are rather stale ho-ho attributions in my view). *Foot* rhymes with *but* to some northern ears, but then *foot* in other northern areas (South Yorkshire especially) is pronounced to rhyme with *loot*. *Myth* is a good rhyme for *with* in America where the 'th' is usually *unvoiced*. This thought requires a small explanatory aside: a 'sidebar' as I believe they are called in American courtrooms.

Voiced consonants are exactly that, consonants produced with the use of our vocal chords. We use them for z, b, v and d but not for s, p, f and t, which are their *unvoiced* equivalents. In other words a 'z' sound cannot be made without using the larynx, whereas an 's' can be, and so on: try it by reading out loud the first two sentences of this paragraph. Aside from expressing the consonant sounds, did you notice the two different pronunciations of the word 'use'? 'We *use* them for. . .' and 'without the *use* of . . .' Voiced for the verb, unvoiced for the noun. Some of the changes we make in the voicing or non-voicing of consonants are so subtle that their avoidance is a sure sign of a non-native speaker. Thus in the sentence 'I have two cars' we use the 'v' in *have* in the usual voiced way. But when we say 'I have to do it' we usually un-voice the 'v' into its equivalent, the 'f' – 'I *haff* to do it. 'He *haz* two cars' – 'he *hass* to do it', 'he *had* two cars' – 'he *hat* to do it'. When a regular verb that ends in an unvoiced consonant is put into the past tense then the 'd' of '-ed' usually loses its voice into a 't': thus *missed* rhymes with *list*, *passed* with *fast*, *miffed* with *lift*, *stopped* with *adopt* and so on. But we keep the voiced -ed if the verb has voiced consonants, *fizzed*, *loved*, *stabbed* etc. Combinations of consonants can be voiced or unvoiced too: the 'ch' in *sandwich* has the voiced 'j' sound, but in *rich* it is an unvoiced 'tch'; say the 'th' in *thigh* and it comes out as an unvoiced lisping hiss, say the 'th' in *thy* or *thine* and your larynx buzzes.

To conclude with the pair that started this excursion: in British English there is no rhyme for our voiced *with*, whereas the Americans can happily rhyme it with *pith*, *myth*, *smith* and so on. Weirdly we British *do* voice the 'th' of *with* in 'forth*with*' (but not for some reason in 'herewith'). All of these pronunciations are, of course, natural to us. All we have to do is use our ears: but poets have to use their ears more than anyone else and be alive to all these aural subtleties (or 'anal subtitles' as my computer's auto-correct facility insisted upon when I mistyped both words). Rhyming alerts us to much that others miss.

Feminine and Triple Rhymes

Most words rhyme on their *beat*, on their stressed syllable, a weak ending doesn't have to be rhymed, it can stay the same in both words. We saw this in *Bo Peep* with *find* them/*behind* them. The lightly scudded 'them' is left alone. We wouldn't employ the rhymes *mined gem* or *kind stem*. *Beat*ing rhymes happily with *meet*ing, but you would not rhyme it with *sweet thing* or *feet swing*. Apart from anything else, you would wrench the rhythm. This much is obvious.

Such rhymes, *beating/heating*, *battle/cattle*, *rhyming/chiming*, *station/nation* are called feminine. We saw the *melteth* and *pelteth* in Keats's 'Fancy' and they naturally occur where any metric line has a weak ending, as in Shakespeare's twentieth sonnet:

A woman's face with Nature's own hand *paint*ed
Hast thou, the master-mistress of my *pass*ion;
A woman's gentle heart, but not *acquaint*ed
With shifting change, as is false women's *fash*ion;

And we saw feminine and masculine endings alternate in Kipling's 'If':

If you can dream – and not make dreams your *mast*er,
 If you can think – and not make thoughts your *aim*;
If you can meet with Triumph and Di*sast*er
 And treat those two impostors just the *same*;

It is the stressed syllables that rhyme: there is nothing more you need to know about feminine rhyming – you will have known this instinctively from all the songs and rhymes and poems you have ever heard and seen.

As a rule the more complex and polysyllabic rhymes become, the more comic the result. In a poem mourning the death of a beloved you would be unlikely to rhyme *potato-cake* with *I hate to bake* or *spatula* with *bachelor*[5] for example. Three-syllable rhymes (also known as triple-rhyme or *sdrucciolo*[6]) are almost always ironic, mock-heroic, comic or facetious in effect, in fact I can't think of any that are not. Byron was a master of these. Here are some examples from *Don Juan*:

5 Or 'bachelor' with 'naturaler' as Ogden Nash manages to do . . .
6 From the Italian word meaning 'slippery down-slope' and used for a kind of glib Italian dactylic rhyme. There is a Sdrucciolo dei Pitti in Florence, a sloping lane leading down to the Pitti Palace. I once ate a bun there.

> But – oh! ye lords and ladies intellectual
> Inform us truly, have they not hen pecked you all?

> He learn'd the arts of riding, fencing, gunnery,
> And how to scale a fortress – or a nunnery.

> Since, in a way that's rather of the oddest, he
> Became divested of his modesty

> That there are months which nature grows more merry in,
> March has its hares, and May must have its heroine.

> I've got new mythological machinery
> And very handsome supernatural scenery

He even manages *quadruple* rhyme:

> So that their plan and prosody are eligible,
> Unless, like Wordsworth, they prove unintelligible.

Auden mimics this kind of feminine and triple-rhyming in, appropriately enough, his 'Letter to Lord Byron'.

> Is Brighton still as proud of her pavilion
> And is it safe for girls to travel pillion?

> To those who live in Warrington or Wigan
> It's not a white lie, it's a whacking big 'un.

> Clearer than Scafell Pike, my heart has stamped on
> The view from Birmingham to Wolverhampton.

Such (often annoyingly forced and arch) rhyming is sometimes called *hudibrastic*, after Samuel Butler's *Hudibras* (the seventeenth-century poet Samuel Butler, not the nineteenth-century novelist of the same name), a mock-heroic verse satire on Cromwell and Puritanism which includes a great deal of dreadful rhyming of this kind:

There was an ancient sage philosopher
That had read Alexander Ross over

So lawyers, lest the bear defendant
And plaintiff dog, should make an end on't

Hudibras also offers this stimulating example of *assonance* rhyming:

And though his countrymen, the Huns,
Did stew their meat between their bums.

Rich Rhyme

The last species worthy of attention is *rich rhyme*.[7] I find it rather horrid, but you should know that essentially it is either the rhyming of identical words that are different in meaning (*homonyms*) . . .

Rich rhyme is legal tender and quite sound
When words of different meaning share a sound

When neatly done the technique's fine
When crassly done you'll cop a fine.

. . . or the rhyming of words that *sound* the same but are different in spelling *and* meaning (*homophones*).

Rich rhyming's neither fish nor fowl
The sight is grim, the sound is foul.

John Milton said with solemn weight,
'They also serve who stand and wait.'

Technically there is a third kind, where the words are identical in appearance but the same neither in sound nor meaning, which results in a kind of rich eye-rhyme:

7 From the French *rime riche*.

He took a shot across his bow
From an archer with a bow.

This rhyme is not the best you'll ever read
And surely not the best you've ever read.

Byron rhymes *ours/hours*, *heir/air* and *way/away* fairly successfully, but as a rule *feminine* rich rhymes are less offensive to eye and ear for most of us than full-on monosyllabic rich rhymes like *whole/hole* and *great/grate*. Thus you are likely to find yourself using *produce/induce*, *motion/promotion* and so on much more frequently than the more wince-worthy *maid/made*, *knows/nose* and the like.

A whole poem in rich rhyme? Thomas Hood, a Victorian poet noted for his gamesome use of puns and verbal tricks, wrote this, 'A First Attempt in Rhyme'. It includes a cheeky rich-rhyme triplet on 'burns'.

If I were used to writing verse,
And had a muse not so perverse,
But prompt at Fancy's call to spring
And carol like a bird in Spring;
Or like a Bee, in summer time,
That hums about a bed of thyme,
And gathers honey and delights
From every blossom where it 'lights;
If I, alas! had such a muse,
To touch the Reader or amuse,
And breathe the true poetic vein,
This page should not be fill'd in vain!
But ah! the pow'r was never mine
To dig for gems in Fancy's mine:
Or wander over land and main
To seek the Fairies' old domain –
To watch Apollo while he climbs
His throne in oriental climes;

Or mark the 'gradual dusky veil'
Drawn over Tempe's tuneful vale,
In classic lays remember'd long –
Such flights to bolder wings belong;
To Bards who on that glorious height,
Of sun and song, Parnassus hight,[8]
Partake the divine fire that burns,
In Milton, Pope, and Scottish Burns,
Who sang his native braes and burns.
For me a novice strange and new,
Who ne'er such inspiration knew,
To weave a verse with travail sore,
Ordain'd to creep and not to soar,
A few poor lines alone I write,
Fulfilling thus a lonely rite,
Not meant to meet the Critic's eye,
For oh! to hope from such as I,
For anything that's fit to read,
Were trusting to a broken reed.

8 *Hight* is an archaic word for 'called', as in 'named': 'a poet hight Thomas Hood'.

II

Rhyming Arrangements

The convention used when describing rhyme-schemes is literally as simple as *abc*. The first rhyme of a poem is *a*, the second *b*, the third *c*, and so on:

At the round earth's imagined corners, blow	*a*
Your trumpets, angels; and arise, arise	*b*
From death, your numberless infinities	*b*
Of souls, and to your scattered bodies go;	*a*
All whom the flood did, and fire shall o'erthrow,	*a*
All whom war, dearth, age, agues, tyrannies,	*b*
Despair, law, chance, hath slain, and you whose eyes	*b*
Shall behold God, and never taste death's woe.	*a*
But let them sleep, Lord, and me mourn a space;	*c*
For if, above all these, my sins abound,	*d*
'Tis late to ask abundance of thy grace	*c*
When we are there. Here on this lowly ground,	*d*
Teach me how to repent; for that's as good	*e*
As if thou hadst sealed my pardon with thy blood.	*e*

JOHN DONNE: Sonnet: 'At the round earth's imagined corners'

This particular *abba abba cdcd ee*[9] arrangement is a hybrid of the Petrarchan and Shakespearean sonnets' rhyme-schemes, of which more in Chapter Three.

As to the descriptions of these layouts, well, that is simple enough. There are four very common forms. There is the COUPLET. . .

9 Anthony Burgess wrote a novel *Abba Abba* which imagines a meeting between Keats and the Italian sonneteer Belli: the title is a pun on the Petrarchan rhyme-scheme and the Hebrew for 'father'. Not sure where the Swedish popsters got their name.

> So long as men can breathe and eyes can *see*
> So long lives this, and this gives life to *thee*.

. . . and the TRIPLET:

> What Flocks of Critiques hover here *today*, ⎫
> As vultures wait on Armies for their *Prey*, ⎬
> All gaping for the carcass of a *Play*! ⎭

In the poetry of the Augustan period (Dryden, Johnson, Swift, Pope etc.) you will often find triplets *braced* in one of these long curly brackets, as in the example above from the Prologue to Dryden's tragedy, *All For Love*. Such braced triplets will usually hold a single thought and conclude with a full stop.

Next is CROSS-RHYMING, which rhymes alternating lines, *abab* etc:

> I wandered lonely as a *cloud*
>   That floats on high o'er vales and *hills*,
> When all at once I saw a *crowd*,
>   A host, of golden *daffodils*;

Finally there is ENVELOPE RHYME, where a couplet is 'enveloped' by an outer rhyming pair: *abba*, as in the first eight lines of the Donne poem, or this stanza from Tennyson's *In Memoriam*.

> The yule-log sparkled keen with *frost*,
>   No wing of wind the region *swept*,
>   But over all things brooding *slept*
> The quiet sense of something *lost*.

You might have noticed that in the cross-rhyme and envelope-rhyme examples above, Wordsworth and Tennyson *indent* rhyming pairs, as it were pressing the tab key to shift them to the right: this is by no means obligatory. Larkin does indent with 'Toads', perhaps gently to nudge our attention to the subtle consonance rhyming:

> Lots of folk live up *lanes*
>   With fires in a *bucket*,
> Eat windfalls and tinned *sardines* –
>   They seem to *like it*.

While in his 'truly rhymed' poem 'The Trees' he presents the envelope-rhymed stanzas without indentation:

> The trees are coming into *leaf*
> Like something almost being *said*.
> The recent buds relax and *spread*,
> Their greenness is a kind of *grief*.

Naturally, there are variations on these schemes: Wordsworth ends each cross-rhymed stanza of 'Daffodils' with a couplet, for example (*abbacc*). The world of formal rhyme-schemes awaits our excited inspection in the next chapter, but without delving into neurolinguistics and the deeper waters of academic prosody I really do not believe there is much more we need to know about rhyming in the technical sense. We have met all the types we are likely to meet and seen ways in which they may be arranged. The questions that concern us next are *how* and *why*?

I have already addressed the idea of rhyme as a connective, unifying force in poems, but it is worth considering the obvious point that rhyme uses language. Or is, I should say, *exclusive* to language. Paint can evoke landscape, sculpture the textures of physical form, but neither of these modes of expression has rhyme available to them (save in some metaphorical sense); music, like verse, can do *rhythm* but it is only poetry that can yoke words together in rhyme (sometimes, of course, and aboriginally, at the service of music). Rhyme may not be a defining condition of poetry, but poetry is pretty much a defining condition of rhyme. If poets shun rhyme, they are closing themselves off from one of the few separate and special techniques available to them and that, in my estimation, is foolishly prodigal.

Not all my poetry is in rhyme, but sometimes (and I cannot always be certain at the time why this should be) rhyming seems right and natural for a poem. It is more than likely that this will hold true in your work too.

One of the great faults we 'amateur' poets are prey to is lazy and pointless rhyming. If a poem is not to rhyme then it seems to me very silly indeed arbitrarily to introduce rhymes from time to time with no apparent thought but apparently because a natural rhyme has come up at that moment. So let us look now at good and bad rhyming, or convincing and unconvincing rhyming if you prefer. 'Deferred success rhyming' as those nervous of the word failure would have us say.

III

Good and Bad Rhyme?

There are two issues to consider when rhyming: firstly and most clearly there is the need to avoid *hackneyed* rhyme pairs. For the past seven hundred years poets have been rhyming *love* with *dove*, *moon* with *June*, *girl* with *curl* and *boy* with *joy*. Certain rhymes are so convenient and appropriate that their use had already become stale by the mid 1700s. Alexander Pope was fierce on the subject of bad rhymers in his *An Essay on Criticism*:

> While they ring round the same unvary'd chimes,
> With sure returns of still expected rhymes.
> Where-e'er you find 'the cooling western breeze',
> In the next line, it 'whispers thro' the trees';
> If crystal streams 'with pleasing murmurs creep',
> The reader's threaten'd (not in vain) with 'sleep'.

Night/light/sight, *death/breath* and *cherish/perish* might be included in that list. The poor old word *love*, a natural subject for poetry if ever there was one, offers very few rhyme choices in English. Frances Cornford in 'To a Fat Lady Seen from the Train' did her best:

> O why do you walk through the fields in *gloves*,
>   Missing so much and so much?
> O fat white woman whom nobody *loves*,
> Why do you walk through the fields in gloves,
> When the grass is soft as the breast of *doves*
>   And shivering sweet to the touch?
> O why do you walk through the fields in gloves,
>   Missing so much and so much?

Only the unlikely *shoves* could have been added. When it is a singular *love*, the word *above* becomes available and for the Cockney rhymesters among us, there is, I suppose, *guv*. *Of* is a popular assonance, especially in songs. In written verse you would be forced either to run the word on with an enjambment which is likely to make it overstressed and clumsy or to resort to this kind of stale formulation:

> You're the one I love,
> The one I'm dreaming of.

Hate is so much easier . . .

If there is a rule to rhyming, I suppose it is that (save in comic verse or for some other desired effect) it should usually be – if not invisible – natural, transparent, seamless, discreet and unforced. The reader should not feel that a word has been chosen simply *because* it rhymes. Very often, let us not pretend otherwise, words are chosen for precisely that reason, but *ars est celare artem* – the art lies in the concealment of art. So, two blindingly obvious points:

AVOID THE OBVIOUS PAIRS
STRIVE NOT TO DRAW ATTENTION TO A RHYME

Trying to mint fresh rhymes *and* being transparent and uncontrived in one's rhyming may seem like contradictory aims. Therein lies the art, of course; but if one guideline has to be sacrificed then for my preference it should certainly be the first. Better to go for a traditional rhyme pair than draw unnecessary attention to an unusual one.

Both 'rules', like any, can of course be broken so long as you know what you are doing and why. If you want an ugly rhyme, it is no less legitimate than a dissonance and discord might be in music: horrific in the wrong hands of course, but by no means unconscionable. Talk of the wrong hands leads us to pathology.

It is a deep and important truth that human kind's knowledge advances further when we look not at success but at failure: disease reveals more than health ever can. We would never have understood, for example, how the brain or the liver worked were it not for them going wrong from time to time: they are not, after all, machines whose function is revealed by an intelligent inspection of their mechanisms, they are composed of unrevealing organic spongy matter whose function would be impossible to determine by dissection and examination alone. But when there is injury, disease or congenital defect, you can derive some clue as to their purpose by noticing what goes wrong with the parts of the body they control. A trauma or tumour in an area of the brain that causes the patient to fall over, for example, might suggest to a neurologist that this is the area that controls balance and mobility. In the same way rhyming can be shown to control the balance and mobility of a poem, doing much more than simply providing us with a linked concord of sounds: there is no better way to demonstrate this than by taking a look at some diseased rhyming.

Thus far almost all the excerpts we have scrutinised have been more or less healthy specimens of poetry. We did take a look at a couplet from Keats's 'Lamia':

Till she saw him, as once she pass'd him by,
Where gainst a column he leant thoughtfully.

There was not much doubt in our minds, I think, that this was a triumph neither of rhyme nor metre: in such a long poem we decided (or at least I maintained) this was not a terminal problem. We questioned, too, William Blake's prosodic skill in lines like:

A Robin Red breast in a Cage
Puts all heaven in a Rage.

We forgave him also. It is time now to go further down this path and compare two poems from approximately the same era treating approximately the same themes. One is a healthy specimen, the other very sick indeed.

A Thought Experiment

Your task is to imagine yourself as a Victorian poet, whiskered and wise. You have two poems to write: each will commemorate a disaster.

At approximately seven fifteen on the stormy night of Sunday 28 December 1879, with a howling wind blowing down from the Arctic, the high central navigation girders of the Tay Railway Bridge collapsed into the Firth of Tay at Dundee, taking with them a locomotive, six carriages and seventy-five souls (original estimates projected a death toll of ninety) on their way from Edinburgh to Dundee for Hogmanay. It was a disaster of the first magnitude, the *Titanic* of its day. The bridge had been open for less than twenty months and been pronounced perfectly sound by the Board of Trade, whose subsequent inquiry determined that a lack of buttressing was at fault. As with all such calamities, this one threatened a concomitant collapse in national self-confidence. To this day the event stands as the worst structural failure in British engineering history.

In this poem you, a Victorian poet, are going to tell the story in rhyming verse: the idea is not a contemplative or personal take on the vanity of human enterprise, fate, mankind's littleness when pitted against the might of nature or any other such private rumination, this is to be the verse equivalent of a public memorial. As a public poem it should not be too long, but of appropriate length for recitation. How do you embark upon the creation of such a work?

You get out your notebook and consider some of the words that are likely to be needed. Rhyme words are of great importance since – by definition – they form the last words of each line, the repetition of their sounds will be crucial to the impact of your poem. They need therefore to be words central to the story and its meaning. Let us look at our options.

Well, the River Tay is clearly a chief player in the drama. *Tay*, *say*, *day*, *clay*, *away*, *dismay* and dozens of others available; no real problems there. *Bridge*? Hm, not so easy. *Ridge* is possible, but doesn't seem relevant. Plenty of *midges* in Scotland, but again hardly suitable for our purposes. *Fridges* have not yet been invented. The word *carriage*, marvellously useful as it might be, would have to be wrenched into *carriage* so that is a non-starter too. *Girders* offers *murders*, but that seems a bit unjust. Sir Thomas Bouch, the bridge's chief engineer, may have been incompetent, but he was scarcely homicidal. *Dundee*? *See*, *three*, *be*, *thee*, *wee*, *flee*, *key*, *divorcee*, *employee*, *goatee*, *catastrophe*. The last, while excellently apposite, might lose some of its power with the slight extra push needed on the last syllable for a proper rhyme, *catastrophee*. Ditto *calamitee*. Pity. *Eighteen seventy-nine*? Well, there are rhymes aplenty there: *fine*, *brine*, *wine*, *mine*, *thine* – *railway line* even, now that does suggest possibilities. Other useful rhymes might be *river/quiver/shiver*, *train/strain/rain*, *drown/down/town*, *perhaps/collapse/snaps* and so on.

I hope this gives an idea of the kind of thought processes involved. Of course, I am not suggesting that in praxis any poet will approach a poem quite in this manner: much of these thoughts will come during the trial and error of the poem's development.

I am not going to ask you to write the whole poem, though you might like to do so for your own satisfaction: the idea is to consider the elements that will go into the construction of such a work, paying special attention to the rhyming. We should now try penning a few lines and phrases, as a kind of preliminary sketch:

The bridge that spans the River Tay

For bridges are iron, but man is clay

Icy gale
Would not prevail

The steaming train
The teeming rain
Stress and strain

The girders sigh, the cables quiver

The troubled waters of the river

Locked for ever in the deeps
The mighty broken engine sleeps

The arctic wind's remorseless breath
From laughing life to frozen death

So frail the life of mortal man
How fragile seems the human span

How narrow then, how weak its girth –
The bridge between our death and birth

The cable snaps
All hopes collapse

Nothing very original or startling there: 'human clay' is a very tired old cliché, as is 'stress and strain'; 'girth' and 'birth' don't seem to be going anywhere, but with some tweaking and whittling a poem could perhaps emerge from beneath our toiling fingers. See now if *you* can come up with four or five couplets, rhyming snatches or phrases of a similar nature: do not try and write in modern English – you are a Victorian, remember. When you have done that we can proceed.

How did you do? Well enough to be driven on to complete a few verses? As it happens and as perhaps you already knew from the moment I mentioned the River Tay, a poem *was* written on this very catastrophe by William McGonagall.[10] It remains the work

10 *Sir* William 'Topaz' McGonagall, Knight of the White Elephant, Burma, a title conferred by King Thibaw of Burma and the Andaman Islands in 1894

for which he is best known: his masterpiece, if you will. I am too kind to you and to his memory to reproduce the entire poem:

The Tay Bridge Disaster
Beautiful Railway Bridge of the Silv'ry Tay!
Alas! I am very sorry to say
That ninety lives have been taken away
On the last Sabbath day of 1879,
Which will be remember'd for a very long time.

'Twas about seven o'clock at night,
And the wind it blew with all its might,
And the rain came pouring down,
And the dark clouds seem'd to frown,
And the Demon of the air seem'd to say –
'I'll blow down the Bridge of Tay.'

When the train left Edinburgh
 The passengers' hearts were light and felt no sorrow,
But Boreas blew a terrific gale,
 Which made their hearts for to quail,
And many of the passengers with fear did say –
'I hope God will send us safe across the Bridge of Tay'

So the train sped on with all its might,
And Bonnie Dundee soon hove in sight,
And the passengers' hearts felt light,
Thinking they would enjoy themselves on the New Year,
With their friends at home they lov'd most dear,
And wish them all a happy New Year.

. . .

(Burma's last monarch). Sadly, many believe this was one of many cruel hoaxes perpetrated on the unfortunate poet.

I must now conclude my lay
By telling the world fearlessly without the least dismay,
That your central girders would not have given way,
At least many sensible men do say,
Had they been supported on each side with buttresses,
At least many sensible men confesses,
For the stronger we our houses do build,
The less chance we have of being killed.

Almost everything that can go wrong with a poem has gone wrong here. One might argue that McGonagall has brilliantly memorialised a doomed and structurally flawed bridge in congruently doomed and structurally flawed verse. His poem is a disaster for a disaster: it *is* the Tay Bridge, crashing hopelessly to its destruction and dragging every innocent word with it. It is not buttressed by metre, rhyme, sense or reason and even as we read it we feel it collapse under the weight of its own absurdity and ineptitude.

I will not linger long on why it fails so spectacularly: it must surely be apparent to you. The metre of course is all over the place. Even if this were *accentually* written like a music hall turn, folk ballad or other non-syllabic rhythmic verse, there is no discernible pattern of three-stress, four-stress or five-stress rhythm at work. The poem is arbitrarily laid out in stanzas of five, six, six, five, six, eight, nine and thirteen lines which create no expectations to fulfil or withhold. This in part contributes to its overall narrative slackness.

We have lots of *Tay* rhymes: *say, midway, dismay, lay, bray*. There are *night, might, sight* and *moonlight; known/blown, down/frown, gale/quail* and *build/killed*.

There is, however, excruciating para-rhyme laid on for our pleasure. *Edinburgh/felt no sorrow* forces a rather American *Edin-borrow* pronunciation, or else *surrer* for *sorrow*. *Buttresses/confesses* will never be a happy pair, nor is the repeated *seventy-nine/time* assonance at all successful. If you are going to assonate, much better to do it *within* the verse, not on the last line of a stanza, as we saw with the Zephaniah poem.

The archaic *expletives* (metrical fillers) and inversions: 'did say' and 'do build' for 'said' and 'build' and 'their hearts for to quail' are not pleasant; 'the wind it blew' is a common enough formulation in ballads trying to get round the problem of the lack of a weak syllable between 'wind' and 'blew' ('the rain it raineth every day' and so on), but cannot be considered a satisfactory phrase in a serious poem. Nor do such archaisms as 'hove' (for 'came') and 'lay' (for 'song') please the reader. It is, of course, the sheer *banality* that lives longest in the mind and most contributes to our sense of this being such a *tour de farce*. This banality mostly derives from McGonagall's word choice (what is known as *poetic diction*) and word choice is shown here to be most pitifully at the mercy of *rhyme*. It is not only the rhyming words themselves that are at fault, but the phrases and syntax used in order to reach those rhyme words. Not to mention the accidental and gruesome internal rhyme *Sabbath day* in line 4 of stanza 1. With his rhyming alone McGonagall has already sabotaged his poem. A perfectly fine piece might in other hands have been worked up from the full rhyme pairs he found, *night/might* et cetera, and from the perfectly laudable sentiments he expresses, but a committee comprising Shakespeare, Milton, Tennyson, Frost, Auden and Larkin could do little with those unfortunate para-rhymes.

As it happens Gerard Manley Hopkins had already composed another 'disaster poem', his 'The Wreck of the *Deutschland*' exactly four years earlier: it was written to commemorate the deaths of five Franciscan nuns who lost their lives at sea in 1875.

> Into the snows she sweeps,
> Hurling the haven behind,
> The *Deutschland*, on Sunday; and so the sky keeps,
> For the infinite air is unkind,
> And the sea flint-flake, black-backed in the regular blow

> Sitting Eastnortheast, in cursed quarter, the wind;
> > Wiry and white-fiery and whirlwind-swivellèd snow
> Spins to the widow-making unchilding unfathering deeps.

That splendid last line has spawned the popular kenning 'widow-maker' to describe the sea, and latterly by extension vessels of the deep, as in the Hollywood movie *K-19: The Widowmaker*. *Wiry* and *white-fiery* works well as internal rhyme, together with all the usual head rhymes, assonances and consonances we expect from Hopkins. Otherwise he uses the fairly neutral and simple *sweeps/keeps/deeps*, *blow/snow* and *behind/kind*. He nestles the eye-rhyme *wind* into the *quarter wiry white* alliteration and it doesn't stand out as too ugly. Mind you, there is some less than comfortable rhyming elsewhere in the poem. Stanza 15 contains this unfortunate internal rhyme:

> And frightful the nightfall folded rueful a day

Frightful indeed – to our ears at least: but perhaps 'frightful' was not such a trivial word in 1875. Some three and a half decades later the loss of the *Titanic* inspired Thomas Hardy's 'The Convergence of the Twain':

> ### VIII
> > And as the smart ship grew
> > In stature, grace and hue,
> In shadowy silent distance grew the Iceberg too.
>
> ### IX
> > Alien they seemed to be:
> > No mortal eye could see
> The intimate welding of their later destiny,
>
> ### X
> > Or sign that they were bent
> > By paths coincident
> On being anon twin halves of one august event,

XI

Till the Spinner of the Years
Says 'Now!' And each one hears,
And consummation comes, and jars two hemispheres.

While I yield to none in my admiration of Hardy, I do not believe this to be his finest work. The characteristic obsession with 'the Spinner of the Years' ('The Immanent Will that stirs and urges everything' he calls it in an earlier alexandrine in the same poem, or 'the President of the Immortals' in his deathless phrase from *Tess of the D'Urbervilles*) gives the whole an appropriate sense of imminent, inexorable doom, which is of course its very subject as we know from the title. But 'they were bent/By paths coincident' is not very happy, nor is 'being anon twin halves of one august event'. 'August' seems an almost comically inappropriate word for such a tragedy and 'anon' smells very dated in a poem written just two years before T. S. Eliot's 'The Love Song of J. Alfred Prufrock' and indeed in the very same year that Ezra Pound and others were founding the Imagist movement. All in all it is a surprisingly flawed poem from so fine a poet and it is partly the *rhyming* that makes it so. In stanza VIII the word *hue* is manifestly used only to go with *grew*. The image of the iceberg 'growing' was so important to the central idea of the poem that Hardy could not resist the rhyme. But what was so special about the *hue* of the *Titanic*? Its red funnel? You could argue I suppose that in such a monochrome world as the North Atlantic *anything* man-made would seem colourful, but really it is clear that the word is a dud, chosen primarily for its rhyme. Also unattractively primitive is the internal rhyme in the alexandrine 'In shadowy silent distance *grew* the Iceberg *too*'. In the following stanza the slight wrenching of 'destiny' can hardly be counted a wonderful success either. Infelicitous rhyming triplets in stanzas omitted here include *meant/opulent/indifferent* and *sea/vanity/she*. Nonetheless it is clearly a whole continent better as verse than poor old McGonagall's effort. There is effortless metrical consistency, there is a *scheme*: three-line stanzas (rhyming triplets) the last of which is an alexandrine. The two shorter trimetric lines atop each hexameter look a little like a ship on a wide sea with the roman numeral stanza numbers forming the funnel. That may sound fanciful, but if you squint through half-closed eyes at that last stanza I'm sure you will see what I mean. For all its less than technically superior rhyming (and therefore word choices or *diction*) it is at least memorable, grave and thoroughly thought through.

Now for the second disaster poem that you, the Victorian poet, must write: the year is 1854 and you are Britain's Poet Laureate. Alfred, Lord Tennyson has just unexpectedly resigned the post so it is now *your* patriotic duty to write a poem about a disastrous British cavalry charge that has just taken place on the peninsula that lies between the Ukraine and the Black Sea. Due to some monstrous error, an officer, Captain Nolan, had galloped down from the Causeway Heights above the Balaclava plain pointing with his sabre at the Russian battery in the valley below, yelling 'There are your guns, charge them!' or words to that effect, according at least to the report by W. H. Russell in *The Times* that you, along with the rest of the nation have just read with avid horror. Those were *not* in fact the guns that Lord Cardigan, his commanding officer, had meant at all, the whole thing has been a catastrophic cock-up from start to finish. A cock-up but a gallant one: Disraeli has just told a packed and stunned House of Commons that it was 'a feat of chivalry, fiery with consummate courage, and bright with flashing courage'. Of the 673 mounted officers and men of the 13th Light Dragoons, 17th Lancers and 11th Hussars – a cavalry troop collectively known as the Light Brigade – 157 have lost their lives. Nothing was achieved. A military disaster as traumatic and tragic for the nation as the collapse of the Tay Bridge was to be in twenty-five years' time.

Your mission, then, is to write up the debacle into a poem that will tell the story, sum up the public mood and stand as a worthy memorial to the brave dead.

What do you do? What sort of preparatory scribbles do you make in your poet's notebook?

As for metre, *short* lines, you decide. Falling rhythms of dactyls and trochees would be a good choice, echoing the fierceness and rush of the action and suggesting the cadences of a bugle sounding the charge: **Tum**-da-da, **tum**-da-da, **tum**-da-da **dum**-da! **Tum**-da-da, **tum**-da-da, **tum**-da-da **dum**! That sort of effect. But as for *rhymes* . . .

Hussar is a bummer, only para-rhymes seem to fit: *bizarre, beaux arts, faux pas, disbar, ajar, papa* and *hurrah* might do at a pinch, but they hardly promise suitably solemn material; besides, the plural *Hussars* excludes at least half of them. *Lancers* is OK: *dancers, prancers, answers* – some suggestive possibilities there. *Dragoons* is if anything worse than Hussars: *lagoons* seems to be the only proper rhyme, the slant-rhyme *racoon* is unlikely to come in handy, nor are *jejune, cartoon* and *baboon*, one feels. *Brigade* is better, much better. *Made, invade, fade, raid, dismayed, laid*, all words that might offer some connection with the subject matter. *Russian*? There's *Prussian* which is of no relevance, otherwise there are only bad para-rhymes available, *hushin'*, *cushion*, *pushin'*. *Horses* gives the rather obvious *forces* and *courses*, while *steeds* offers *deeds* . . .

> Off on their galloping steeds
> Praise for their marvellous deeds . . .

Hmmm . . . bit lame. Rhymes for *guns* might come in handy. *Buns, runs, sons, Huns* (shame the enemy are Ruskies), *stuns, shuns*? Hm, come back to that later. *Six hundred and seventy three* is simply too long: a whole three-beat line used up.

> Six hundred and seventy-three
> Charging to victory!

Only it isn't a victory – it is a terrible defeat.

> Six hundred and seventy-three
> Charging for Queen and Country!
> Oh what a wonder to see,
> Marvellous gallantry
> Six hundred and seventy-three!

This is *dreadful*. Six hundred and seventy-three sounds too perky and too literal at the same time. Should we round it up or down? Six hundred or seven hundred? *Hundred* doesn't rhyme with much though – oh, hang on, there are some *good* slant-rhymes here: *thundered, sundered, blundered, wondered, onward*.

> Onward, Light Brigade, Onward
> Onward you splendid six-hundred.
> 'There are the guns to raid,
> Charge them,' brave Nolan said.
> On rode the Light Brigade,
> Not knowing that Nolan had blundered!

It is getting there. The accidental consonance/assonance of knowing/Nolan is inelegant. But a bit of a polish and who knows?

Your turn now. See if you can come up with some phrases with that metre and those rhyme words, or ones close to them.

Well, as you probably know, Tennyson did *not* retire from his laureateship and this is what he came up with to mark the calamity.

> Half a league, half a league,
> Half a league onward,
> All in the valley of Death
> Rode the six hundred.
> 'Forward, the Light Brigade!'
> 'Charge for the guns!' he said:
> Into the valley of Death
> Rode the six hundred.

'Forward, the Light Brigade!'
Was there a man dismay'd?
Not tho' the soldier knew
   Someone had blunder'd:
Their's not to make reply,
Their's not to reason why,
Their's but to do and die:
Into the valley of Death
   Rode the six hundred.

Cannon to right of them,
Cannon to left of them,
Cannon in front of them
   Volley'd and thunder'd;
Storm'd at with shot and shell,
Boldly they rode and well,
Into the jaws of Death,
Into the mouth of Hell
   Rode the six hundred.

. . .

When can their glory fade?
O the wild charge they made!
   All the world wondered.
Honour the charge they made,
Honour the Light Brigade,
   Noble six hundred.

Naturally, I cannot tell how Tennyson embarked upon the preparation and composition of his poem. Quite possibly he charged (as it were) straight in. Maybe the rhythm and some of the phrasing came to him in the bath or while walking. It is possible that he made notes not unlike those we've just made or that the work emerged whole in one immediate and perfect Mozartian stream. We shall never know. What we can agree upon I hope, is that the rhyming is perfect. *Shell/hell*, *brigade/made/dismayed* and the *wondered/blundered*, *thundered/sundered*, *hundred/onward* group work together superbly. A small nucleus of rhyming words like this throughout one poem can set up a pattern of expectation in the listener's or reader's ear. 'Thundered' is close to *onomatopoeic*, it seems somehow more than just descriptive of thunder, it actually seems to mimic it – and those thunderous qualities are in turn passed on to its rhyme-partners, lending a power and force to *wondered* and *hundred* that they would not otherwise possess. The *rhyming*, quite as much as the rhythm, helps generate all the pity, pride and excitement for which the poem is renowned.

We do know that in writing this Tennyson created a rod for the back of all subsequent British Poets Laureate who have struggled in vain to come up with anything that so perfectly captures an important moment in the nation's history. It was perhaps the last great Public Poem written in England, the verse equivalent of 'Land of Hope and Glory'.

It is a hoary old warhorse to our ears now I suppose, as much as a result of social change as literary. Most modern readers, academic, poetic or amateur, would probably feel that Hopkins and Hardy engage our sensibilities more directly than Tennyson, in the same way that – for all their technical mastery – we are less moved by the painters of the mid-Victorian period than by the later impressionists and post-impressionists. Nonetheless, there is always much to be learned from virtuosity and I disbelieve any poet who does not confess that he would give even unto half his wealth to have come up with 'Their's not to reason why, Their's but to do and die'. We should recognise that Tennyson's is a poem written for the nation while the Hopkins and Hardy are essentially inward looking. Indeed, 'The Wreck of the *Deutschland*' is much more an autobiographical contemplation of the poet's religious development than a commemoration of a shipwreck.

Whatever our feelings we can surely acknowledge that Tennyson's versifying is magnificent. It is pleasingly typical, at all events, that this, the best-known poem we have on a military theme, memorialises failure. There are no stirring odes celebrating Agincourt, Waterloo, Trafalgar or the Battle of Britain in our popular anthologies. No English verse equivalent of the *1812 Overture* for us to cheer at and weep over. Earlier on the morning of that same October day in 1854, on the same Crimean battlefield, the Heavy Brigade had fought a supremely *successful* battle during which more men died than in the later disaster, they were just as gallant but *their* heroism goes unremembered.[11] Misfortune, failure and incompetence remain our great themes. It is probable that without the poem the Light Brigade's futile charge would have vanished into history. Among the many books on the subject there are works whose titles and subtitles include: 'Honour the Charge they Made', 'Noble Six Hundred', 'Do or Die', 'Into the Valley of Death', 'The Reason Why', 'The Real Reason Why' and 'Someone Had Blundered'. Not many poems that I can think of can have so completely caught the public attention or for ever defined our understanding of an historical event. Anyway, I hope I have convinced you that in great part, it is the rhyming that has contributed to this immortality. Tennyson's discovery of the *hundred/blundered wondered/thundered* group is the heart of the poem, its engine.

It may strike you as trivial or even unsettling to discuss rhyming options in such detail. I know exactly how you feel and we should address this: we must be honest about the undoubted embarrassment attendant upon the whole business of rhyming. Whatever we may feel about rhymed poetry it is somehow shaming to talk about our search for rhyming words. It is so banal, so mechanistic, so vulgar to catch oneself chanting 'ace, race, chase, space, face, case, grace, base, brace, dace, lace . . .' when surely a proper poet should be thinking high, pure thoughts, nailing objective correlatives, pondering metaphysical insights, observing delicate nuances in nature and the human heart, sifting gold from grit in the

11 Despite Tennyson writing a poem about *their* charge too: 'The charge of the gallant three hundred, the Heavy Brigade!' Don't milk it Alfie, love . . .

swift-running waters of language and soliciting the Muse on the upper slopes of Parnassus. Well, yes. But a rhyme is a rhyme and won't come unless searched for. Wordsworth and Shakespeare, Milton and Yeats, Auden and Chaucer have all been there before us, screwing up their faces as they recite words that only share that sound, that chime, that rhyme. To search for a rhyme is no more demeaning than to search for a harmony at the piano by flattening this note or that and no more vulgar than mixing paints on a palette before applying them to the canvas. It is one of the things we *do*.

Rhyming Practice

Poetry consists in a rhyming dictionary and things.

GERTRUDE STEIN

On that head. Should you use a rhyming dictionary? I must confess that I do, but only as a last resort. They can be frustrating and cumbersome, they can break concentration, they offer no help with assonance or consonance rhymes and are too crammed with irrelevant words like *multicollinearity* and *cordwainer* and *eutectic* (something to do with melting points apparently) or types of Malayan cheese and Albanian nose-flutes which are never going to be of the least use to one's poetry. I prefer first simply to chant the sound to myself in the rhythm the word needs to fit. If that doesn't bear fruit I will write all the letters of the alphabet at the top of a page and then go through the permutations one by one. It is easy enough to find monosyllabic masculine rhymes, they get harder to pop into your mind when you try to think of their compound versions, the various syllables that can precede the word. For *boy*, words like *joy*, *toy*, *soy*, *cloy*, *coy*, *ploy* slip into the mind quite quickly. *Employ, deploy, alloy, annoy, destroy* and *enjoy* might take a little longer. *Decoy* and *convoy* have just occurred to me (although they would need careful use as there is a little more stress on their first syllables) and now I am going to turn to the dictionary. Hm. I've missed *buoy*, but that's a silly rich-rhyme (besides, it doesn't rhyme for Americans, who pronounce it *boo-ey*). *McCoy* is there (as in 'the real' I suppose), *Hanoi, savoy* and *bok choi* (strange to find two different types of cabbage). *Envoy, carboy, borzoi* and *viceroy* are there, though I would argue that they are usually stressed on their first syllable. There are compounds of words we have already found: *redeploy* and *overjoy*. I'm *very* cross that I failed to find *corduroy* for myself and I would like to think that given enough time *saveloy, hobbledehoy* and *hoi polloi* might have come to me unaided. The assonance rhymes *void, Lloyd, Freud, hoik, foil* and so on are naturally not shown. By all means invest in a good rhyming dictionary, there are several available from the usual publishing houses and they are all much the same so far as I can tell. If it is musical lyrics you are thinking of then I would recommend Sammy Cahn's *The Songwriter's Rhyming Dictionary*; the lyricist who gave us 'High Hopes' and 'Come Fly with Me' is full of excellent and affable advice. There is no index, however, so it will take a bit of getting used to. There are also software rhyming dictionaries available either as stand-alone applications or as online resources. Personally I feel that a poet's words are better mumbled out or scribbled on paper. Words have colour, feel, texture, density, shape, weight and person-ality, they are – I have said this before – all we have. Deeply dippy about most things digital I may be, but when it comes to poetry I want the words to have been uttered with my breath and shaped by my hand[12]. I am writing this now on my computer, but even the most frivolous sample lines of verse I have composed for you have

12   Having said which I have invented a poetic method that utilises the provokingly silly incompetence of Voice Recognition Software, allowing its mistakes to furnish interesting poetic ideas. It gave me 'power monkey' for 'poet manqué' recently. Such aleatory assistance can be suggestive.

been sketched on paper first. You may feel differently and no doubt some reader yet unborn who chances upon this book in an antiquarian bookshop of the future will marvel at such distinctions. I send you greetings from the grave: I do trust the sun hasn't exploded yet and that *The Archers* is still running.

Poetry Exercise 10

Your task now is to discover as many rhymes as you can for the word *girl* (my rhyming dictionary offers twenty-four, many of which are absurd dialect words). As many syllables as you like, but obviously it is a masculine rhyme so the 'url' sound will terminate each word you find. When you've done that, you have to do the same for the feminine-rhyming *martyr* (the dictionary offers twenty-eight, many of which are again farcically weird). This is not Scrabble: proper nouns, place names, foreign words and informal language of any description all count. Ten for each would be an excellent score, but don't worry if you can't manage it. Facility and speed in the hunting down of rhyme-words is hardly a sign of poetic genius.

When you have finished, try this as the second part of your rhyming exercise. Take your notebook and wander about the house and garden, if you have one. If you are not reading this at home, then wander around your office, hospital ward, factory floor or prison cell. If you are outside or on a train, plane or bus, in a café, brothel or hotel lobby you can still do this. Simply note down as many things as you can see, hear or smell. They need not be nouns, you can jot down processes, actions, deeds. So, if you are in a café, you might write down: *smoking, steam, raincoat, lover's tiff, cappuccino machine, sipping, flapjacks, cinnamon, jazz music, spilt tea* and so on – whatever strikes the eye, ear or nose. Write a list of *at least* twenty words. When you've done that, settle down and once more see how many rhymes you can come up with for each word. You may find that this simple exercise gets your poetic saliva glands so juiced up that the temptation to turn the words into poetry becomes irresistible. Yield to it. A random, accidental and arbitrary consonance of word sounds can bring inspiration where no amount of pacing, pencil chewing and looking out of the window can help.

Rhyme Categories

1. Masculine rhyme – *box/frocks, spite/tonight, weird/beard, amaze/delays*
2. Feminine rhyme – *breathing/seething, relation/nation, waiter/equator*
3. Triple rhyme – *merrily/verily, merited/inherited, drastically/fantastically*
4. Slant-rhyme:
   a. Assonance – *pit/kiss, mean/dream, stub/rug, slack/shag, hop/dot*
   b. Partial consonance – *coils/gulls, wild/fold, mask/tusk, stump/ramp*
   c. Full consonance – *coils/cools, wild/weld, mask/musk, stump/stamp*
5. Eye-rhyme – *fool/wool, want/pant, heard/beard, mould/could, rove/love*
6. Rich-rhyme – red *rose*/he *rose*, single *file*/nail *file*, *nose/knows, eye/I*

RHYMING COUPLETS

Know then thyself, presume not God to *scan*;
The proper study of mankind is *Man*.

ALEXANDER POPE: *An Essay on Man*

RHYMING TRIPLETS

What Flocks of Critiques hover here *today*,
As vultures wait on Armies for their *Prey*,
All gaping for the carcass of a *Play*!

JOHN DRYDEN: Prologue to *All for Love*

CROSS-RHYME

The boy stood on the burning *deck*
   Whence all but he had *fled*;
The flame that lit the battle's *wreck*
   Shone round him o'er the *dead*.

FELICIA HEMANS: 'Casabianca'

ENVELOPE RHYME

Much have I travell'd in the realms of *gold*
   And many goodly states and kingdoms *seen*;
   Round many western islands have I *been*
Which bards in fealty to Apollo *hold*.

JOHN KEATS: 'On First Looking into Chapman's Homer'

CHAPTER THREE

Form

I

The Stanza

So we can write metrically, in iambs and anapaests, trochees and dactyls. We can choose the length of our measure: hexameter, pentameter, tetrameter. We can write accentually, in three-stress and four-stress lines. We can alliterate and we can rhyme, but thus far our verse has merely been *stichic*, presented in a sequence of lines. Where those lines terminate is determined, as we know, by the measure or, in the case of syllabic verse, by the syllable count. Prose, such as you are reading now, is laid out (or *lineated*) differently – as I write this I have no reason to start a new line (to 'press the return key') until it is time for a new paragraph or a quotation and you certainly won't

find me doing this
or *this*, for that
matter; it would be

highly

odd,

not to mention confusing:
in poetry such a procedure
would not be considered
strange at all, although as
we shall see, how we

> manage the lineation of our poems is not a question of *random* line
>
>> breaks, or it had better not be . . .

Our first clue that the written words on a page might qualify as poetry may indeed be offered by lineation, but an even more obvious indicator is the existence of *stanzas*. The word derives from the Italian for 'stand', which in turn developed into the word for 'room' (*stanza di pranzo* is 'dining room', for example). In everyday speech, in songwriting, hymn singing and many other popular genres a stanza will often be referred to as a *verse* (meaning 'turn', as in 'reverse', 'subvert', 'diversion' and so on). I will be keeping to the word stanza, allowing me to use verse in its looser sense of poetic material generally. Also, I like the image of a poem being a house divided into rooms. Some traditional verse forms have no stanzaic layout, for others it is almost their defining feature. But first we need to go deeper into this whole question of form . . .

What is Form and Why Bother with It?

Stephen gets all cross

By *form*, just so that we are clear, we mean the defining structure of a genre or type. When we say *formal*, the word should not be thought of as bearing any connotations of stiffness, starchiness, coldness or distance – formal for our purposes simply means 'of form', *morphological* if you like.

In music, some examples of form would be sonata, concerto, symphony, fugue and overture. In television, common forms include sit-com, soap, documentary, mini-series, chat show and single drama. Over the years docu-dramas, drama-docs, mocku-mentaries and a host of other variations and sub-categories have emerged: form can be undermined, hybridised and stretched almost to breaking point.

Poetic forms too can be cross-bred, subverted, made sport of, mutilated, sabotaged and rebelled against, but HERE IS THE POINT. If there is no suggestion of an overall scheme at work in the first place, then there is nothing to subvert or undermine: a whole world of possibility is closed off to you. Yes, you can institute your *own* structures, you can devise new forms or create a wholly original poetic manner and approach, but there are at least three major disadvantages to this. First, it is all too often a question of reinventing the wheel (all the trial-and-error discoveries and setbacks that poetic wheelwrights have undergone over two millennia to be caught up with in one short lifetime); second, and this flows from the first point, it is fantastically difficult and lonely; third, it requires the reader to know what you are up to. Since human beings first sang, recited and wrote they have been developing ways of structuring and presenting their verse. Most readers of poetry, whether they are aware of it or not, are instinctively familiar with the elemental forms – for a practising poet to be ignorant of them is foolish at best, perverse and bloody-minded at worst. We can all surely admit without sacrificing any cherished sense of our bold modernity and iconoclastic originality that a painter is in a better position to ignore the 'rules' of composition or perspective if he knows exactly what those rules are. Just because poems are made of our common currency, words, it does not mean that poets should be denied a like grounding and knowledge. Besides, as I have emphasised before, initiation into the technique of poetry is all part of becoming a poet and it is *pleasurable*: one is in the company of one's forebears, one is not alone.

Ezra Pound, generally regarded as the principal founder of modernism, wrote of the need to refresh poetics: 'No good poetry is ever written in a manner twenty years old,' he wrote in 1912, 'for to write in such a manner shows conclusively that the writer thinks from books, convention and cliché, not from real life.' He went further, asserting that extant poetical language and modes were in fact defunct, he declared war on all existing formal structures, metre, rhyme and genre. We should observe that he was a researcher in Romance languages, devoted to medieval troubadour verse, Chinese, Japanese, Sicilian, Greek, Spanish, French and Italian forms and much besides. His call to free verse was not a manifesto for ignorant, self-indulgent maundering and uneducated anarchy. His poems are syntactically and semantically difficult, laden with allusion and steeped in his profound knowledge of classical and oriental forms and culture: they are often laid out in structures that recall or exactly follow ancient forms, cantos, odes and even, as we shall discover later, that most strict and venerable of forms, the *sestina*. Pound was also a Nazi-sympathising, anti-Semitic,[1] antagonistic son of a bitch as it happens: he wasn't trying to open poetry for all, to democratise verse for the kids and create a friendly freeform world in which everyone is equal. But if the old fascist was right in determining that his generation needed to get away from the heavy manner and glutinous clichés of Victorian verse, its archaic words and reflex tricks of poetical language, and all out-dated modes of expression and thought in order to free itself for a new century, is it not equally true that *we* need to escape from the dreary, self-indulgent, randomly lineated drivel that today passes for poetry for precisely the same reasons? After a hundred years of free verse and Open Field poetry the condition of English-language poetics is every bit as tattered and tired as that which Pound and his coevals inherited. 'People find ideas a bore,' Pound wrote, 'because they do not distinguish between live ones and stuffed ones on a shelf.' Unfortunately the tide has turned, and now it is some of Pound's once new ideas that have been stuffed and shelved and become a bore. He wrote in 1910: 'The art of letters will come to an end before AD 2000. I shall survive as a curiosity.' It might be tempting to agree that 'the art of letters' has indeed come to an end,

1 Although, to be fair, he did repent and write: 'the worst mistake I made was that stupid, suburban prejudice of anti-Semitism.'

and to wonder whether a doctrinaire abandonment of healthy, living forms for the sake of a dogma of stillborn originality might not have to shoulder some of the responsibility for such a state of affairs.

Add a feeble-minded kind of political correctness to the mix (something Pound would certainly never have countenanced) and it is a wonder that any considerable poetry at all has been written over the last fifty years. It is as if we have been encouraged to believe that form is a kind of fascism and that to acquire knowledge is to drive a jackboot into the face of those poor souls who are too incurious, dull-witted or idle to find out what poetry can be. Surely better to use another word for such free-form meanderings: 'prose-therapy' about covers it, 'emotional masturbation', perhaps; auto-omphaloscopy might be an acceptable coinage − gazing at one's own navel. Let us reserve the word 'poetry' for something worth fighting for, an ideal we can strive to live up to.

What, then, is the solution? Greeting-card verse? Pastiche? For some the answer lies in the street poetry of rap, hip-hop, reggae and other musically derived discourses: unfortunately this does not suit my upbringing, temperament and talents; I find these modes, admirable as they no doubt are, as alien to my cultural heritage and linguistic tastes as their practitioners no doubt find Browning and Betjeman, Pope, Cope and Heaney. I will try to address this problem at the end of the book, but for now I would urge you to believe that a familiarity with form will not transform you into a reactionary bourgeois, stifle your poetic voice, imprison your emotions, cramp your style, or inhibit your language − on the contrary, it will liberate you from all of these discomforts. Nor need one discourse be adopted at the expense of another, eclecticism is as possible in poetry as in any other art or mode of cultural expression.

There are, to my mind, two aesthetics available when faced by the howling, formless, uncertain, relative and morally contingent winds that buffet us today. One is to provide verse of like formlessness and uncertainty, another is (perhaps with conscious irony) to erect a structured shelter of form. Form is not necessarily a denial of the world's loss of faith and structure, it is by no means of necessity a nostalgic evasion. It can be, as we shall see, a defiant, playful and wholly modern response.

Looking back over the last few paragraphs I am aware that you might think me a dreadful, hidebound old dinosaur. I assure you I am not. I am uncertain why I should feel the need to prove this, but I do want you to understand that I am far from contemptuous of Modernism and free verse, the experimental and the avant-garde or of the poetry of the streets. Whitman, Cummings, O'Hara, Wyndham Lewis, Eliot, Jandl, Olsen, Ginsberg, Pound and Zephaniah are poets that have given me, and continue to give me, immense pleasure. I do not despise free verse. Read this:

> *Post coitum omne animal triste*
> i see you
> !
> you come
> closer
> improvident
> with your coming
> then −
>
>   stretched to scratch
> − is it a trick of the light? −
> i see you
> worlded with pain
> but of
> necessity not
> weeping
>
>   cigaretted and drinked
> loaded against yourself
> you seem so yes bold

irreducible
but nuded and afterloved
you are not so strong
are you
?

after all

There's the problem. The above is precisely the kind of worthless arse-dribble I am forced to read whenever I agree to judge a poetry competition.[2] It took me under a minute and a half to write and while I dare say *you* can see what utter wank it is, there are many who would accept it as poetry. All the clichés are there, pointless lineation, meaningless punctuation and presentation, fatuous creations of new verbs 'cigaretted and drinked', 'worlded', 'nuded', 'afterloved',[3] a posy Latin title – every pathology is presented. Like so much of what passes for poetry today it is also *listless*, utterly drained of energy and drive – a common problem with much contemporary art but an especial problem with poetry that chooses to close itself off from all metrical pattern and form. It is like music without beat or shape or harmony: not music at all, in fact. 'Writing free verse is like playing tennis with the net down,' Robert Frost wrote. Not much of a game at all, really.

My 'poem' is also pretentious, pretentious in exactly the way much hotel cooking is pretentious – aping the modes of seriously innovative culinary artists and trusting that the punters will be fooled. Ooh, it's got a lavender reduction and a sorrel jus: it's a pavane of mullet with an infusion of green tea and papaya. Bollocks, give me steak and kidney pudding. Real haute cuisine is

2 Incidentally, on the off-chance that you have submitted a poem for any competition that I have judged, or plan to in the future, please don't think that I will condemn a poem to the bin because it is in free verse or raise one to the top of the pile because it is formal. A good free verse poem is better than a bad sonnet and *vice versa*.

3 Actually, I have to confess I quite like 'afterloved'. . .

created by those who know what they are doing. Learning metre and form and other such techniques is the equivalent of understanding culinary ingredients, how they are grown, how they are prepared, how they taste, how they combine: then *and only then* is one fit to experiment with new forms. It begins with love, an absolute love of eating and of the grain and particularity of food. It is first expressed in the drudgery of chopping onions and preparing the daily stockpots, in the commitment to work and concentration. They won't let you loose on anything more creative until you have served this apprenticeship. I venerate great chefs like Heston Blumenthal, Richard Corrigan and Gordon Ramsay: they are the real thing, they have done the work – work of an intensity most of us would baulk at. Of course some people think that they, Blumenthal, Corrigan et al., are pretentious, but here such thinking derives from a fundamental ignorance and fear. So much easier to say that everything you fail to understand is pretentious than to learn to discriminate between the authentic and the fraudulent. Between lazy indiscipline and frozen traditionalism there lies a thrilling space where the living, the fresh and the new may be discovered.

Fortunately, practising metre and verse forms is not as laborious, repetitive and frightening as toiling in a kitchen under the eye of a tyrannical chef. But we should never forget that poetry, like cooking, derives from love, an absolute love for the particularity and grain of ingredients – in our case, words.

So, rant over: let us acquaint ourselves with some of the poetic forms that have developed and evolved over the centuries.

The most elemental way in which lineation can be taken forward is through the collection of lines into STANZA FORM: let us look at some options.

II

Stanzaic Variations

OPEN FORMS

Tercets, quatrains and other stanzas — terza rima — ottava rima — rhyme royal — ruba'iyat — the Spenserian stanza

A TERCET is a stanza of three lines, QUATRAINS come in fours, CINQUAINS in fives, SIXAINS in sixes. That much is obvious. There are however specific formal requirements for 'proper' cinquains or sixains written in the French manner. There is, for example, a sixain form more commonly called the *sestina*, which we will examine in a separate section. Forms which follow a set pattern are called *closed forms*: the haiku, limerick and sonnet would be examples of single-stanza closed forms. Forms which leave the overall length of a poem up to the poet are called *open forms*.

Terza Rima

Tercets, three–line stanzas, can be independent entities rhyming *aba cdc* and so on, or they might demand a special kind of interlocking scheme such as can be found in TERZA RIMA, the form in which Dante wrote *Inferno, Purgatorio* and *Paradiso*.

> The TERZA RIMA mode is very fine,
> Great Dante used it for his famous text;
> It rhymes the words in every other line
>
> With each thought drawing you towards the next:
> *A-B-A, B-C-B, C-D-C-D* . . .
> This middle rhyme is sequently annexed

To form the outer rhymes of Stanza Three
And thus we make an interlocking *rhyme*:
This subtle trick explains, at least to me,
    Just why this form has stood the test of *time*.

As you can see, this linked rhyming can go on for ever, the middle line of each stanza forming the outer rhymes of the one that follows it. When you come to the end of a thought, thread or section, you add a fourth line to that stanza and use up the rhyme that would otherwise have gone with the next. I have done this with 'rhyme' and appended the (indented) stop-line 'Just why this form has stood the test of time'. A young Hopkins used a stop-*couplet* to end his early terza rima poem, 'Winter with the Gulf Stream':

I see long reefs of violets
In beryl-covered ferns so dim,
A gold-water Pactolus frets

Its brindled wharves and yellow brim,
The waxen colours weep and run,
And slendering to his burning rim

Into the flat blue mist the sun
Drops out and the day is done.

Chaucer, under Dante's influence, wrote the first English terza rima poem, 'A Complaint to his Lady', but the best-known example in English is probably Shelley's 'Ode to the West Wind':

Drive my dead thoughts over the universe,
Like wither'd leaves, to quicken a new birth;
And, by the incantation of this verse,
Scatter, as from an unextinguish'd hearth
Ashes and sparks, my words among mankind!
Be through my lips to unawaken'd earth
The trumpet of a prophecy! O Wind,
If Winter comes, can Spring be far behind?

It does not matter how you lay out your verse (Shelley used five fourteen-line stanzas) or in what metre (Hopkins wrote in iambic tetrameter and Shelley in pentameter): it is the *rhyme-scheme* that defines the form.

In order of ascending line length, the QUATRAIN comes next.

The Quatrain

> The QUATRAIN is HEROIC and profound
> And glories in the deeds of noble days:
> Pentameters of grave and mighty sound,
> Like rolling cadences of brass, give praise.
>
> Alas! its ELEGIAC counterpart
> Bemoans with baleful woe this world of strife:
> In graveyards and in tears it plies its art
> Lamenting how devoid of hope is life.
>
> In equal form the COMIC QUATRAIN's made,
> But free to say exactly what it thinks;
> It's brave enough to call a spade a spade
> And dig for truth however much it stinks.

There is, of course, no *formal* difference between those three samples, they are merely produced to show you that quatrains in *abab* have been used for all kinds of purposes in English poetry. Gray's 'Elegy Written in a Country Churchyard' is probably the best-known *elegiac* use quatrains have been put to. Its lines have given the world classic book and film titles (*Far from the Madding Crowd* and *Paths of Glory*) as well as providing some memorably stirring phrases:

> Forbade to wade[4] through slaughter to a throne,
> And shut the gates of mercy on mankind;

---

4 You may think 'forbade to wade' is a clumsy internal rhyme – actually 'forbade' was (and still should be, I reckon) pronounced 'for-bad'.

A cross-rhymed quatrain (perhaps obviously) allows for fuller development of an image or conceit than can be achieved with couplets:

> Full many a gem of purest ray *serene*
> The dark unfathomed caves of ocean *bear;*
> Full many a flower is born to blush un*seen,*
> And waste its sweetness on the desert *air.*

(Gray's repetition of 'Full many' is an example of a rhetorical trope called *anaphora*, in case you are interested, in case you care, in case you didn't already know, in case of too much anaphora, break glass. Actually, that was *epanaphora*.)

The Rubai

From Persia comes a quatrain form called the RUBAI (plural *ruba'iat* or *ruba'iyat*), rhyming *aaba*, *ccdc*, *eefe* etc.

> In ancient Persia and Islamic lands,
> The price of heresy was both your hands:
> Indeed the cost could even be your *head*
> (Or burial up to it in the sands).

> The wiser heads would write a RUBAI down
> And pass it quietly round from town to town,
> Anonymous, subversive and direct –
> The best examples garnered great renown.

> Collections of these odes, or RUBA'IYAT
> Showed sultans where progressive thought was at;
> Distributed by dissidents and wits,
> Like early forms of Russian samizdat.

> The Ruba'iyat of Omar, called Khayyam,
> Are quatrains of expansive, boozy charm.
> As found in Horace, Herrick and Marvell,
> The message is: 'Drink! When did wine do harm?

Too soon the sun will set upon our tents,
Don't waste your time with pious, false laments
Drink deep the wine of life, then drink some more'
I never heard a poet make more sense.

The translation of the *Ruba'iat of Omar Khayyam* by Edward Fitzgerald ranks alongside Burton's *Arabian Nights* as one of the great achievements of English orientalism:

A Book of Verses underneath the Bough,
A Jug of Wine, a Loaf of Bread, – and Thou
Beside me singing in the Wilderness –
Oh, Wilderness were Paradise enow!

. . .
'Tis all a Chequer-board of Nights and Days
Where Destiny with Men for Pieces plays:
Hither and thither moves, and mates, and slays,
And one by one back in the Closet lays.

The Ball no Question makes of Ayes and Noes,
But Right or Left, as strikes the Player goes;
And he that toss'd Thee down into the Field,
He knows about it all – He knows – HE knows!

The Moving Finger writes; and, having writ,
Moves on: nor all thy Piety nor Wit
Shall lure it back to cancel half a Line,
Nor all thy Tears wash out a Word of it.

If that kind of poetry doesn't make your bosom heave then I fear we shall never be friends. Open forms in sixain also exist in English verse. Wordsworth in his 'Daffodils' used the stanza form Shakespeare developed in 'Venus and Adonis', essentially a cross-rhymed quatrain closing with a couplet, *abab cc*:

For oft when on my couch I lie
   In vacant or in pensive mood,
They flash upon that inward eye
   Which is the bliss of solitude,
And then my heart with pleasure fills,
And dances with the Daffodils.

Rhyme Royal

RHYME ROYAL has a noble history
   From Geoffrey Chaucer to the present day
Its secret is no hidden mystery:
   Iambic feet, the classic English way
   With *b* and *b* to follow *a b a*.
This closing couplet, like a funeral hearse,
Drives to its end the body of the verse.

RHYME ROYAL (or Rime Royal as it is sometimes rendered) is most associated with Geoffrey Chaucer, whose *Troilus and Criseyde* marks the form's first appearance in English. It was once thought that the name derived from its later use by Henry IV, but this is now, like all pleasing stories (from King Alfred's Cakes to Mr Gere's way with gerbils), disputed by scholars. I suppose by rights a seven-line stanza should be called a heptain or septain, but I have never seen either word used. Auden used the *ababbcc* of rhyme royal in his 'Letter to Lord Byron'. You would think that he would choose *ottava rima*, the form in which the addressee so conspicuously excelled. Auden apologises to his Lordship for not doing so:

Ottava Rima would, I know, be proper
   The proper instrument on which to pay
My compliments, but I should come a cropper;
   Rhyme-royal's difficult enough to play.
   But if no classics as in Chaucer's day,
At least my modern pieces shall be cheery
Like English bishops on the Quantum Theory.

Auden's reluctance to use *ottava rima* stemmed, one suspects, from its demand for an extra rhyme. I have always loved this form, however, as my sample verse makes clear.

Ottava Rima

OTTAVA RIMA is a poet's dream,
    The most congenial of forms by far.
It's quite my favourite prosodic scheme
    And Byron's too, which lends it some éclat.
Much more adaptable than it may seem,
    It plays both classical and rock guitar;
It suits romantic lyric inspiration,
But I prefer Byronic-style deflation.

As you can see, OTTAVA RIMA rhymes *abababcc* and thus presents in eight lines, hence the ottava, as in octave. It is in effect rhyme royal with an extra line, but just as one or more gene in the strand of life can make all the difference, so one or more line in a stanza can quite alter the identity of a form. The origins of ottava rima are to be found in Ariosto's epic *Orlando Furioso* and it entered English in translations of this and other Italian epics. John Hookham Frere saw its potential for mock-heroic use and it was through his 1817 work *Whistlecraft* that Byron came to use the form, first in *Beppo* and then in his masterpiece of subverted epic and scattergun satire, *Don Juan*.

As Auden remarks, 'Rhyme-royal's difficult enough . . .'. Two pairs of three rhymes and a couplet per verse. Perverse indeed.

Some of W. B. Yeats's best loved later poems take the form away from scabrous mock-heroics by mixing true rhyme with the sonorous twentieth-century possibilities opened up by the use of slant-rhyme, finding an unexpected lyricism. This is the celebrated last stanza of 'Among School Children':

Labour is blossoming or dancing where
The body is not bruised to pleasure soul,
Nor beauty born out of its own despair,
Nor blear-eyed wisdom out of midnight oil.
O chestnut-tree, great-rooted blossomer,
Are you the leaf, the blossom or the bole?
O body swayed to music, O brightening glance,
How can we know the dancer from the dance?

I trust you are still *reading out loud* . . .

Spenserian Stanza

Nine lines of verse did **EDMUND SPENSER** take
To forge the style that bears his name divine,
A form that weaves and wanders like a snake
With art all supple, subtle, serpentine,
Constructing verse of intricate design
Whose coils, caressing with sublime conceit,
Engirdle and embrace each separate line:
But Spenser, with an extra final beat,
Unsnakelike ends his verse on hexametric feet.

An open form whose qualities have appealed to few in recent times
is the SPENSERIAN STANZA, which Edmund Spenser developed
from the ottava rima of Tasso and Ariosto for his epic, *The Faerie
Queen*. But you never know, it might be the very structure you have
been looking for all these years. The rhyme-scheme is seen to be
ababbcbcc, and is cast in eight lines of iambic pentameter followed by
an iambic alexandrine. Byron used the form in 'Childe Harold's
Pilgrimage', and Keats in 'The Eve of Saint Agnes':

Saint Agnes' Eve – Ah, bitter chill it was!
The owl, for all his feathers, was a-cold;
The hare limp'd trembling through the frozen grass,
And silent was the flock in woolly fold:
Numb were the Beadsman's fingers, while he told
His rosary, and while his frosted breath,
Like pious incense from a censer old,
Seem'd taking flight for heaven, without a death,
Past the sweet Virgin's picture, while his prayer he saith.

Clive James is one of the few poets I know to have made something new and comic of the Spenserian Stanza: his epistolary verse to friends published in his collection *Other Passports* contains some virtuoso examples, well worth looking at if you are thinking of trying the form: it includes the excellent admonitory alexandrine, 'You can't just arse around for ever having fun.' Martin Amis, to whom the verse was written, certainly took the advice, as we know. I am aware of few modern serious poems in the form, the last significant work appearing to be Tennyson's 'The Lotos-Eaters', although Cambridge University offers an annual[5] Spenserian Stanza Competition open to all comers of any age or fighting weight, which 'fosters and recognizes student excellence in the writing of Spenserian stanzas' and is sponsored by the International Spenser Society, no less. The past winners appear to have written theirs very much in the style of Spenser himself, complete with phalanxes of recondite archaic Spenserian words and syntax, rather than to have exhibited any interest in demonstrating the form's fitness for modern use, which seems a pity.

5 Mind you, at the time of going to print the website advertising these glories had not been updated since 2004. I do hope the competition hasn't been stopped.

Adopting and Adapting

Other stanzaic forms are mentioned in the Glossary, the VENUS AND ADONIS STANZA, for example. Of course it remains your decision as to how you divide your verse: into general quatrains or tercets and so on, or into more formal stanzaic arrangements such as ottava rima or ruba'iat, or any self-invented form you choose. Ted Hughes wrote his poem 'Thistles' in four stanzas of three-line verse. Tercets, if one wishes to call them that, but very much his own form for his own poem.

> Against the rubber tongues of cows and the hoeing hands
> of men
> Thistles spike the summer air
> Or crackle open under a blue-black pressure.
>
> Every one a revengeful burst
> Of resurrection, a grasped fistful
> Of splintered weapons and Icelandic frost thrust up
>
> From the underground stain of a decaying Viking.
> They are like pale hair and the gutturals of dialects.
> Every one manages a plume of blood.
>
> Then they grow grey, like men.
> Mown down, it is a feud. Their sons appear,
> Stiff with weapons, fighting back over the same ground.

You may think that this is arbitrary – enjambment between stanzas two and three shows that each does not wholly contain its own thought. Hughes is following no closed or open form, why then should he bother to set his verse in stanzas at all? Why not one continuous clump of lines? All kinds of neat arguments could be made about the poem itself needing, as the ground does, to fight the random aggression of its thistling, bristling words, to be farmed;

then again, maybe four stanzas reflect the four seasons of the thistles' birth, flourishing, death and rebirth; or one might think the stanzas in their short definitive shape chime with the plainly laid down statements Hughes makes, but I do not think such sophistry, even when it convinces, is necessary. We see, we feel, we know that the layout is just plain *right*. Imagine the same lines in one group: *something* is lost. Perhaps Hughes wrote it as a single stream of lines and then realised that they needed arrangement into four groups of three much as an artist might realise that he needs to regroup his landscape, rubbing out a tree in the background, foregrounding that clump of bushes, moving the church spire to the right and so on. The artist does not consult a book on composition or apply absolutely set rules learned at art school, he just feels, he just *knows*. Experience and openness, instinct and a feel for order, these are not taught, but they are not entirely inborn either. Reading, preparation, concentration and a poetic eye that is every bit as attuned as a poetic ear all contribute to the craftsmanship, the poetic skill that might, in time, make such judgements second nature.

If, then, you wish to use your own stanzas, rhyming or not, organised in traditional or personal ways, allow yourself to feel that same sense of composition and rightness, just as you might when arranging knick-knacks and invitations on a mantelpiece or designing a birthday card. It is not a question of right and wrong, but nor is it a question of anything goes. Incidentally, do allow yourself to enjoy Hughes's use of the word 'fistful' – a fabulous consonantal *and* assonantal play on 'thistle', rhyming back to the first word of the second line. Is it not *divine*?

An open quatrain form whose qualities are *sui generis* enough to deserve a whole section on its own is the *ballad*. It is our next stop – once the following exercise is done.

Poetry Exercise 11

As you can see I have headed each section above with my own attempts to describe each stanza form under discussion in its own dress. Your exercise is to do the same *but better*. I look forward to bumping into you one day in the street or on a train and hearing you recite to me in triumphal tones your self-referential rhymes royal and auto-descriptive Ruba'iyat.

III

The Ballad

In fours and threes and threes and fours
The BALLAD beats its drum:
'The Ancient Mariner' of course
Remains the exemplum.

With manly eights (or female nines)
You are allowed if 'tis your pleasure,
To stretch the length to equal lines
And make a ballad of LONG MEASURE.

Well, what more need a poet know?

In technical prosodic parlance we could say that most ballads present in *quatrains of alternate cross-rhymed iambic tetrameter and trimeter*. However, since the ballad is a swinging, popular form derived from song and folk traditions it is much better described as a form that comes in four-line verses, usually alternating between four and three beats to line. The word comes from *ballare*, the Italian for 'to dance' (same root as ballet, ballerina and ball).

The ballad's irresistible lilt is familiar to us in everything from nursery rhymes to rugby songs. We know it as soon as we hear it, the shape and the rhythm seem inborn:

There's nothing like a ballad song
For lightening the load –
I'll chant the buggers all day long
Until my tits explode.

A sweetly warbled ballad verse
Will never flag or tire
I sing 'em loud for best or worse
Though both my balls catch fire.

I'll roar my ballads loud and gruff,
Like a lion in the zoo
And if I sing 'em loud enough
'Twill tear my arse in two.

Or whatever. Old-fashioned inversions, expletives (both the rude kind *and* the kind that fill out the metre) and other such archaic tricks considered inadmissible or old-fashioned in serious poetry suit the folksy nature of ballad. The ballad is pub poetry, it is naughty and nautical, crude and carefree. Its elbows are always on the table, it never lowers the seat for ladies after it's been or covers its mouth when it burps. It can be macabre, brutal, sinister, preachy, ghostly, doom-laden, lurid, erotic, mock-solemn, facetious, pious or obscene – sometimes it exhibits all of those qualities at once. Its voice is often that of the club bore, the drunken rogue, the music hall entertainer or the campfire strummer. It has little interest in descriptions of landscape or the psychology of the individual. Chief among its virtues is a keen passion to tell you a story: it will grab you by the lapels, stare you in the eyes and plunge right in:

Now gather round and let me tell
The tale of Danny Wise:
And how his sweet wife Annabelle
Did suck out both his eyes.

And if I tell the story true
And if I tell it clear,
There's not a mortal one of you
Won't shriek in mortal fear.

How could we not want to know more? Did she *really* suck them out? Was Danny Wise *asleep*? Was Annabelle a witch? How did it all turn out? Did he get his revenge? Is the teller of the tale poor Danny himself? Sadly, I have no idea because the rest of it hasn't come to me yet.

While the second and fourth lines should rhyme, the first and

third do not need to, it is up to the balladeer to choose, *abab* or *abcb*:
nor is any regularity or consistency in your rhyme-scheme required
throughout, as this popular old ballad demonstrates:

> In Scarlet Town, where I was born,
>   There was a fair maid *dwellin'*
> Made every lad cry wellaway,
>   And her name was Barbara *Allen*.
>
> All in the merry month of *May*,
>   When green buds they were *swellin'*,
> Young Jemmy Grove on his deathbed *lay*,
>   For love of Barbara *Allen*.

A quatrain is by no means compulsory, a six-line stanza is commonly found, rhyming *xbxbxb*, as in Lewis Carroll's 'The Walrus and
the Carpenter' and Wilde's *Ballad of Reading Gaol*.

> The Walrus and the Carpenter
>   Were walking close at *hand*:
> They wept like anything to see
>   Such quantities of *sand*:
> 'If this were only cleared away,'
>   They said, 'it would be *grand*.'
>
> And all men kill the thing they love,
>   By all let this be *heard*,
> Some do it with a bitter look,
>   Some with a flattering *word*,
> The coward does it with a kiss,
>   The brave man with a *sword*!

Although more 'literary' examples may favour a regular accentual-
syllabic measure, ballads are perfect examples of accentual verse: it
doesn't matter how many *syllables* there are, it is the beats that
matter. Here is Marriot Edgar's 'Albert and the Lion', which was
written as a comic monologue to be recited to a background piano

that plunks down its chords on the beats of each four- or three-stress line. Part of the pleasure of this style of ballad is the mad scudding rush of *un*accented syllables, the pausing, the accelerations and decelerations: when Stanley Holloway performed this piece, the audience started to laugh simply at his *timing* of the rhythm. I have marked with underlines the syllables that might receive a little extra push if required: it is usually up to the performer. Recite it as you read.

> There's a **fam**ous seaside <u>place</u> called **Black**pool,
> That's **noted** for **fresh**-<u>air</u> and **fun**,
> And **Mr** and **Mrs** <u>Rams</u>bottom
> **Went** there with young **Al**bert, their **son**.
>
> A **grand** little **lad** was their **Al**bert
> All **dressed** in his **best**; quite a **swell**
> 'E'd a **stick** with an **'orse**'s 'ead '**and**le
> The **fin**est that **Wool**worths could **sell**.

Or there's Wallace Casalingua's 'The Day My Trousers Fell', which has even more syllables to contend with:

> Now I **trust** that your **ears** you'll be **lend**ing,
> To this **tale** of our **dec**adent **times**;
> There's a be**gin**ning, a **mid**dle and an **end**ing
> And for the **most** part there's **rhyth**ms and **ver**ses and
>   **rhymes**.
>
> My **name**, you must **know**, is John **West**on,
> Though to my **friends** I'm **Jack**ie or **Jack**;
> I've a **place** on the **out**skirts of **Pres**ton,
> The tiniest **scrap** of a garden with a **shed** and a **ham**mock
>   round't **back**.
>   . . .
> I was **giv**ing the **fish** girl her **pay**ment,
> The **cod** were **nine**ty a **pound** –
> When, with a **snap** and a rustle of **rai**ment
> My **trous**ers, they **dropped** to the **ground**. <u>Con-ster-nation</u>.

Border ballads, like 'Barbara Allen' and those of Walter Scott, became a popular genre in their own right, often like *broadsheet* ballads expressing political grievances, spreading news and celebrating the exploits of highwaymen and other popular rebels, rogues and heroes: subgenres like the *murder* ballad still exist,[6] often told from the murderer's point of view, full of grim detail and a sardonic acknowledgement of the inevitability of tragedy.

> Frankie and Johnny were lovers,
>   O Lordy, how they could love;
> They swore to be true to each other,
>   Just as true as the stars above.
> *He was her man but he done her wrong.*

Robert Service, the English-born Canadian poet, wrote very popular rough'n'tough ballads mostly set around the Klondike Gold Rush; you will really enjoy reading this out, don't be afraid (if alone) to try a North American accent – and it should be *fast*:

> A bunch of the boys were whooping it up in the Malamute
>   saloon;
> The kid that handles the music-box was hitting a jag-time
>   tune;
> Back of the bar, in a solo game, sat Dangerous Dan McGrew,
> And watching his luck was his light-o'-love, the lady that's
>   known as Lou.
> When out of the night, which was fifty below, and into the
>   din and glare,
> There stumbled a miner fresh from the creeks, dog-dirty, and
>   loaded for bear.
> He looked like a man with a foot in the grave and scarcely
>   the strength of a louse,
> Yet he tilted a poke of dust on the bar, and he called for
>   drinks for the house.

6 Nick Cave and the Bad Seeds produced their album *Murder Ballads* in 1996.

There was none could place the stranger's face, though we
  searched ourselves for a clue;
But we drank his health, and the last to drink was Dangerous
  Dan McGrew.

To observe the regularity of the caesuras in this ballad would be like
complimenting an eagle on its intellectual grasp of the principles of
aerodynamics, but I am sure you can see that 'Dangerous Dan
McGrew' could as easily be laid out with line breaks after 'up' and
'box' in the first two lines, 'drink' in the last and as the commas
indicate elsewhere, to give it a standard four-three structure. We
remember this layout from our examination of Kipling's ballad in
fourteeners, 'Tommy'. A. E. Housman's 'The Colour of his Hair',[7]
a bitter tirade against the trial and imprisonment of Oscar Wilde, is
also cast in fourteeners. I can't resist quoting it in full.

Oh who is that young sinner with the handcuffs on his
  wrists?
And what has he been after, that they groan and shake their
  fists?
And wherefore is he wearing such a conscience-stricken air?
Oh they're taking him to prison for the colour of his hair.

'Tis a shame to human nature, such a head of hair as his;
In the good old time 'twas hanging for the colour that it is;
Though hanging isn't bad enough and flaying would be fair
For the nameless and abominable colour of his hair.

Oh a deal of pains he's taken and a pretty price he's paid
To hide his poll or dye it of a mentionable shade;
But they've pulled the beggar's hat off for the world to see
  and stare,
And they're taking him to justice for the colour of his hair.

7 Written at the time of the trial but published posthumously. Another
wonderful Housman tirade against sexual intolerance is to be found in 'The
Laws of God, the Laws of Man'.

Now 'tis oakum for his fingers and the treadmill for his feet,
And the quarry-gang on portland in the cold and in the heat,
And between his spells of labour in the time he has to spare
He can curse the god that made him for the colour of his
     hair.

There is also a strong tradition of *rural* ballad, one of the best-
known examples being the strangely macabre 'John Barleycorn':

There were three men come out of the West
     Their fortunes for to try,
And these three men made a solemn vow:
     John Barleycorn should die!

They plowed, they sowed, they harrowed him in,
     Threw clods upon his head,
And these three men made a solemn vow:
     John Barleycorn was dead!

They let him lie for a very long time
     'Til the rain from Heaven did fall,
Then Little Sir John sprung up his head,
     And so amazed them all.

After being scythed, threshed, pounded, malted and mashed, John
Barleycorn (not a man of course, but a crop) ends his cycle in
alcoholic form:

Here's Little Sir John in a nut-brown bowl,
     And brandy in a glass!
And Little Sir John in the nut-brown bowl
     Proved the stronger man at last!

For the huntsman he can't hunt the fox
     Nor loudly blow his horn,
And the tinker can't mend kettles nor pots
     Without John Barleycorn!

There are ballad *operas* (John Gay's *The Beggar's Opera* being the best known), *jazz* ballads and pop ballads culminating in that revolting genre, the *power* ballad – but here we are leaking into popular music where the word has come to mean nothing much more than a slow love song, often (in the case of the American diva's power ballad) repulsively vain and self-regarding, all the authentic guts, vibrancy, self-deprecation and lively good humour bleached out and replaced by the fraudulent intensity of grossly artificial climaxing. I acquit country music of these vices. American ballads, *cowboy* ballads, *frontier* ballads and so on, were extensively collected by the Lomax family, much in the same way that Cecil Sharpe had done for rural and border ballads and other native British genres of folk and community music. Shel Silverstein came up with the ever-popular 'A Boy Named Sue' for Johnny Cash, who also wrote and performed his own superb examples, I would especially recommend the 'Ballad of Ira Hayes' if you don't already know it.

One of the great strengths of the ballad in its more *literary* incarnations is that its rousing folk and comic associations can be subverted or ironically countered. Its sense of being somehow traditional, communal and authorless contrasts with that individuality and strong authorial presence we expect from the modern poet, often so alone, angst-ridden and disconnected. Both John Betjeman and W. H. Auden used this contrast to their advantage. The strong ballad structure of Betjeman's 'Death in Leamington' counters the grim, grey hopelessness of suburban lives with a characteristically mournful irony:

> She died in the upstairs bedroom
>   By the light of the evening star
> That shone through the plate glass window
>   From over Leamington Spa.

[...]

Nurse looked at the silent bedstead,
   At the grey, decaying face,
As the calm of a Leamington evening
   Drifted into the place.

She moved the table of bottles
   Away from the bed to the wall;
And tiptoeing gently over the stairs
   Turned down the gas in the hall.

While Auden does much the same with the less genteel 'Miss Gee':

Let me tell you a little story
   About Miss Edith Gee;
She lived in Clevedon Terrace
   At Number 83.

. . .

She bicycled down to the doctor,
   And rang the surgery bell;
'O doctor, I've a pain inside me,
   And I don't feel very well.'

Doctor Thomas looked her over,
   And then he looked some more;
Walked over to his wash-basin,
   Said, 'Why didn't you come before?'

Doctor Thomas sat over his dinner,
   Though his wife was waiting to ring,
Rolling his bread into pellets;
   Said, 'Cancer's a funny thing.'

. . .

They laid her on the table,
   The students began to laugh;
And Mr Rose the surgeon
   He cut Miss Gee in half.

Casting such lost lives as ballad heroes certainly provides an ironic contrast with which to mock the arid futility of much twentieth-century life. To use the rhythms of the greenwood and the yardarm for the cloying refinement of Leamington or the grimness of Miss Gee's forlorn little world can indeed point up the chasm between the sterile present and the rich past, but such a mismatch also works in the *opposite* direction, it raises the lonely spinsters out of their ordinariness and connects them to the tradition and richness of history, it mythologises them, if you like. When an artist paints a prostitute in the manner of a Renaissance Madonna he is simultaneously marking an ironic distinction *and* forging an affirmative connection. The artists Gilbert and George have done much the same with their skinheads in stained-glass. These are strategies that only work because of the nature of form and genre.

Poetry Exercise 12

A poet can be rough and flexible with the ballad, it is the beat and the narrative drive that sustains. Your exercise is to finish the one that I started a few pages ago.

> Now gather round and let me tell
>   The tale of Danny Wise:
> And how his sweet wife Annabelle
>   Did suck out both his eyes.
>
> And if I tell the story true
>   And if I tell it clear
> There's not a mortal one of you
>   Won't shriek in mortal fear.

Don't worry about metre or syllable-count – this is a ballad. I have used an *a* rhyme, by all means drop it from time to time, but do stick to the four-line structure. Enjoy yourself. One thing I can guarantee you: after you have written just one or two stanzas, you'll be chanting ballad lines to yourself as you make coffee, nip to the loo, walk to the shops and brush your teeth. The ballad has a certain flow, a rhythmic swing and a beat; it makes no difference where you go, you're sure to tap your feet – well, hush my mouth . . .

IV

Heroic Verse

HEROIC VERSE has passed the test of time:
Iambic feet in couplets linked by rhyme,
Its non-stanzaic structure simply screams
For well-developed tales and epic themes.
The five-stress line can also neatly fit
Sardonic barbs and aphoristic wit.
Augustan poets marshalled their iambs
To culminate in pithy epigrams.
Pope, Alexander, with pontific skill
Could bend the verse to his satiric will.
John Dryden used the form in diverse ways –
The deft aside, the pert but telling phrase,
Epistles, satires, odes and tragic plays.
   The mode continued in this lofty style
Until – with manic laugh and mocking smile
New modes emerged, a kind of fractured, mad
Enjambment turned up. Pauses. Something had
Gone wrong . . . or right? The stops and starts of human
Speech burst through. Now, once formal lines assume an
Unforced, casual air, but nonetheless
Obey the rigid rules of metre, stress
And rhyming. Gradually another change
Takes place. New poets start to rearrange
The form, unpick the close-knit weave, make room
For looser threads of consonantal rhyme.
   The modern age with all its angst and doubt
Arrives, picks up the tab and pays its debt
To history, precedent and every voice

That did its bit to mould heroic verse.
And still today we grudgingly affirm
There's life in the old dog; our mangy form
Still bites, still barks, still chases cats and birds,
Still wags its tail, still pens and shepherds words,
And, taken off her leash, this bitch on heat
Will walk you off your pentametric feet.

HEROIC VERSE is far from dead. Since its Chaucerian beginnings it has been endlessly revivified: after a playful Elizabethan reshaping it acquired marmoreal elegance in the eighteenth century, only to undergo a complex reworking under John Keats, Robert Browning and Wilfred Owen until it emerged blinking into the light of modern day. At first glance it seems remarkably simple, too simple, perhaps, even to deserve the appellation 'form': it is as open as they come, neither laid out in regular stanzas, nor fixed by any scheme beyond the simple *aabbccdd* of the rhyming couplet. New paragraph presentation is possible either with line breaks or indentation as I have offered above, but in general the verse is presented in one unbroken block. Only the occasional braced triplet will relieve the procession of couplets. To the modern eye this can be forbidding; we like everything in our world to come in handy bite-sized chunks. Yet you might say that handy bite-sized chunks is what heroic verse is best remembered for: Pope's *Essays on Man* and *on Criticism* are veritable vending machines of aphorism.

A little learning is dangerous thing;

Not to go back, is somehow to advance,
And men must walk at least before they dance.

Know then thyself, presume not God to scan,
The proper study of mankind is man.

Hope springs eternal in the human breast.

All are but parts of one stupendous whole.

One truth is clear. Whatever is, is right.

True ease in writing comes from art, not chance,

That last apothegm might be the motto of this book. John Dryden, in my estimation, was the absolute master of the heroic couplet; his use of it seems more natural, more assured, more fluid even than Pope's:

Repentance is the virtue of weak minds.

Either be wholly slaves or wholly free.

For those whom God to ruin hath design'd,
He fits for fate, and first destroys their mind.

Errors, like straw, upon the surface flow;
He who would search for pearls must dive below.

Beware the fury of a patient man

By education most have been misled;
So they believe, because they so were bred.
The priest continues what the nurse began,
And thus the child imposes on the man.

But these were poets from a time when poems, like architecture and garden design, were formal, elegant and assured: this was the Age of Reason, of Certitude, Sense, Wit, Discernment, Judgement, Taste, Harmony – of 'Capital Letter Moralists' as T. E. Hulme called them. The voice and manner of these Augustans can sound altogether too *de haut en bas* for our ears, from lofty to lowly, as if delivered from Olympus.

Their taste and proportion is akin to that of the architecture of the period; by the time of the aftermath of the French Revolution and the publication of Wordsworth's and Coleridge's *Lyrical Ballads* their course seemed run, the profusion of nature and the agony of self seemed to become a more proper study of poets, just as the Gothic and picturesque began to entice the architects. Run your eye down the Index of First Lines in an edition of Pope and then of any Romantic poet and compare the number of entries in each which begin with the word 'I'. The 'egotistical sublime' had landed. It would be a pity if, in our instinctive veneration for all things post-classical, Romantic, post-Romantic, Decadent, Modernist and Postmodernist we overlooked the virtues of late-seventeenth- and eighteenth-century verse. After all, most of us aspire to live in houses of that period, fill them with eclectic fittings and furniture from later eras as we may. The neoclassical harmony and elegance of construction remains our ideal for housing. I think it can be so with verse too. Naturally the discourse and diction, the detail and decor as it were, are of our age, but the rationality and harmony of the Augustans is not to be despised.

Keats did not abandon the form, but contributed to its development with a new freedom of run-ons and syntactical complexity. This extract from 'Lamia' shows how close to dramatic blank verse it becomes, the enjambments almost disguising the rhymes.

> Pale grew her immortality, for woe
> Of all these lovers, and she grieved so
> I took compassion on her, bade her steep
> Her hair in weïrd syrops that would keep
> Her loveliness invisible, yet free
> To wander as she loves, in liberty.

Robert Browning wrestled with the form even more violently. His much anthologised 'My Last Duchess' takes the form of a dramatic monologue in heroic verse. It is 'spoken' by the Renaissance Duke of Ferrara, who is showing around his palace an ambassador who has come to make the arrangements for the Duke's second marriage. We learn, as the monologue proceeds, that the Duke had his first wife killed on account of her displeasing over-friendliness.

Pointing at her portrait on the wall, the Duke explains how polite, compliant and smiling she was, but to *everyone*:

> She had
> A heart – how shall I say? – too soon made glad,
> Too easily impressed; she liked whate'er
> She looked on, and her looks went everywhere.
> Sir, 't was all one! My favour at her breast,
> The dropping of the daylight in the West,
> The bough of cherries some officious fool
> Broke in the orchard for her, the white mule
> She rode with round the terrace – all and each
> Would draw from her alike the approving speech,

In the Duke's view it was 'as if she ranked/My gift of a nine-hundred-years-old name/With anybody's gift'.

> Oh sir, she smiled, no doubt,
> Whene'er I passed her; but who passed without
> Much the same smile? This grew: I gave commands;
> Then all smiles stopped together. There she stands
> As if alive.

In other words, he had her killed. You can see how different this heavily run-on and paused verse is from the restrained fluency of Augustan heroic couplets. But why has Browning not chosen to write in *blank verse*, in the Shakespearean or Jacobean manner, we might wonder? I cannot, of course, second-guess Browning's motives, but the *effect* is to counter the fluency of everyday speech with the formality of a rhymed structure, creating an ironic contrast between the urbane conversational manner, the psychotic darkness of the story and the elegant solidity of a noble form. The heroic verse is the frame out of which character can leap; it is itself the nobly proportioned, exquisitely tasteful palace in which ignobly misproportioned, foully tasteless deeds are done.

Wilfred Owen's use of rhyming couplets in the hell of war

provides another kind of ironic contrast. In the same way that the employment of ballad form for the dreary and mundane makes both a distinction *and* a connection, so the use of heroic couplets both contrasts and unites in Owen's verse: the august and decorous form in such ghastly conditions is a sick joke, but the death agonies, mutilations and horrors of the soldiers' lives are raised to heroic status by their incarnation in heroic couplets. Owen's 'A Terre: (Being the Philosophy of Many Soldiers)' uses Browning-style dramatic monologue in slant-rhymed couplets, casting Owen himself as the visitor to a field hospital where a ruined soldier lies and addresses him.

> Sit on the bed. I'm blind, and three parts shell.
> Be careful; can't shake hands now; never shall.
> Both arms have mutinied against me, – brutes.
> My fingers fidget like ten idle brats.
>
> I tried to peg out soldierly, – no use!
> One dies of war like any old disease.
> This bandage feels like pennies on my eyes.
> I have my medals? – Discs to make eyes close.
> My glorious ribbons? – Ripped from my own back
> In scarlet shreds. (That's for your poetry book.)

Laurence Lerner, Thom Gunn and Tony Harrison have all written with distinction in heroic couplets, as did Seamus Heaney in 'Elegy for a Still-Born Child' and his superb poem 'The Outlaw', which might be regarded as a kind of darkly ironic play on an *eclogue* or *georgic* – Virgilian verse celebrating and philosophically discoursing upon the virtues of agricultural life.

You may find yourself drawn to heroic verse, you may not. Whatever your views, I would recommend practising it: the form has compelling and enduring qualities. Move in: the structure is still sound and spacious enough to accommodate all your contemporary furniture and modern gadgets.

Poetry Exercise 13

Try a short dramatic monologue, à la Browning, in which a young man in police custody, clearly stoned off his head, tries to explain away the half-ounce of cannabis found on his person. Use the natural rhythms of speech, running-on through lines, pausing and running on again, but within rhymed iambic pentameter. You will be amazed what fun you can have with such a simple form. If you don't like my scenario, choose another one, but do try and make it contemporary in tone.

V

The Ode

Sapphic – Pindaric – Horatian – lyric – anacreontic

Deriving from *odein*, the Greek for to chant, the ode is an open form of lyric verse made Public Monument. In English poetry it was once the most grand, ceremonial and high-minded of forms, but for the last hundred years or so it has been all but shorn of that original grandeur, becoming no more than a (frequently jokey) synonym for 'poem'.

Partly this is the due to the popularity of John Keats's four great odes 'To Autumn', 'Ode to a Nightingale', 'Ode on Melancholy' and 'Ode on a Grecian Urn' which, together with the odes of Shelley, Wordsworth, Coleridge, Southey and the rest, turned the form in on itself. Poets today may choose to call their works odes, but rather than suggesting any formal implications this is likely to promise, in the shadow of Keats, a romantic reflection on such themes as nature, beauty, art, the soul and their relationship to the very making of a poem itself.

There are three main genres of classical ode which do have more formal natures or specific functions however – the Sapphic, Pindaric and Horatian, named after the Greeks Sappho and Pindar, and the Latin poet Horace. Of these, the most formally fixed and the most popular today by a dodecametric mile is the SAPPHIC:

Sapphic

Let's hear it for the **Sapphic Ode**
  An oyster bed of gleaming pearls
A finely wrought poetic mode
                Not just for girls.

Lesbian Sappho made this form
  With neat Adonic final line
Her sex life wasn't quite the norm
                And nor is mine.

Three opening lines of just four feet
  Create a style I rather like:
It's closely cropped and strong yet sweet –
                In fact, pure dike.

Actually, the above displays the lineaments of the English *stress-based* imitation as adapted from the classical original, which was made up of four eleven-syllable lines in this metre:

●○ ●□ ●○○ ●○ ●●
●○ ●□ ●○○ ●○ ●●
●○ ●□ ●○○ ●○ ●●
●○○ ●●

The symbol □ stands for an *anceps*, a metrical unit (or *semeion*) which in classical verse can be long *or* short, but for our purposes means can be either stressed or unstressed, according to the poet's wishes. An anceps offers a free choice of trochee or spondee in other words. So, doggerel that makes a *classical* Sapphic Ode might go:

Noble **Sappho** fashioned her odes of high-flown
  Verse in four lines, marked by their classic profile.
Though she's now best remembered for her full-blown
                Lesbian lifestyle.

Not that Ancient Greek Sapphics would be *rhymed,* of course. English verse in this semi-quantitative classical manner does exist, although practitioners (out of Poe-like disbelief in the spondee) usually render the first three lines as trochee-trochee dactyl trochee-trochee. Ezra Pound managed a superb true spondaic line-end in his Sapphic Ode, 'Apparuit':

Green the ways, the breath of the fields is thine there

Dear Algie Swinburne wrote Sapphics too:

All the night sleep came not upon my eyelids,
Shed not dew, nor shook nor unclosed a feather,
Yet with lips shut close and with eyes of iron
                        Stood and beheld me.
. . .
Clothed about with flame and with tears, and singing
Songs that move the heart of the shaken heaven,
Songs that break the heart of the earth with pity,
                       Hearing, to hear them.

The more characteristically English way to adapt the form has been to write in good old iambic tetrameter, as in my first sampler above and Pope's 'Ode on Solitude':

Happy the man, whose wish and care
  A few paternal acres bound,
Content to breathe his native air
                In his own ground

Whose herds with milk, whose fields with bread,
  Whose flocks supply him with attire,
Whose trees in summer yield him shade,
                In winter fire.

The contemporary Canadian poet Anne Carson has used the form (and translated Sappho's own odes). These two stanzas are from her 'Eros the Bittersweet':

no: tongue breaks and thin
fire is racing under skin
and in eyes no sight and drumming
fills ears

and cold sweat holds me and shaking
grips me all, greener than grass
I am and dead – or almost
I seem to me

The Sapphic Ode has generally been used for more personal and contemplative uses. I do recommend you try writing a few: the Adonic ending can serve as conclusion, envoi, sting in the tail, question, denial . . . the form, despite its simplicity, remains surprisingly potent. There is no prescribed number of stanzas. If this kind of verse appeals, you might like to look into another Lesbian form, ALCAICS.

PINDARIC ODE

Strophe / The Turn

We hail thee mighty PINDAR'S ODE
Thou noble and majestic mode!
You trace your roots to far-off ancient times,
Yet still survive in modern English rhymes.
With firm but steady beat,
You march in rhythmic feet
Of varied but symmetric length.
This lends your verse a joyful strength
That suits it well to themes of solemn weight –
Disasters, joys and great affairs of state.

Antistrophe/The Counter-Turn

Yet some suggest that modern life,
Enmeshed in doubt and mired in strife,
Has little use for grandeur, pomp and show,
Preferring inward grief and private woe
To be a poet's theme.
'So, sad as it may seem,
Thy style of verse has had its day
Farewell, God speed!' these doubters say,
'We have no need of thee, Pindaric Ode,
Our future lies along another road.'

Epode/The Stand

Perhaps they speak too soon, such men,
Perhaps the form will rise again.
A nation needs a human public voice
Its griefs to mourn, its triumphs to rejoice.
When life gets mean and hard,
Call out the national bard!
So Pindar, tune thy golden lyre,
Thou hast a people to inspire.
When glory comes, or crisis darkly bodes
We may have need of thine immortal odes!

Yes, well. Quite. But you get the idea. Sappho's fellow Aeolian, Pindar is associated with a form much more suited to ceremonial occasions and public addresses: the PINDARIC ODE. He developed it from choral dance for the purpose of making *encomiums* or praise songs that congratulate athletes or generals on their victories, actors on their performances, philosophers and statesmen on their wisdom and so on. They are written in groups of three stanzas called *triads*, each triad being divided into *strophe* (rhymes with 'trophy'), *antistrophe* (rhymes with 'am pissed today') and *epode* ('ee-pode'). Ben Jonson, who wrote a splendid example, gave them the jolly English names *Turn*, *Counter-Turn* and *Stand*. The choice of stanza length and metre is variable, so long as the poem is in triads and each stanza is identical in scheme: this consistency is called a HOMOSTROPHIC structure. I have followed the scheme Jonson invents for his 'Pindaric Ode to the Immortal Memory and Friendship of that Noble Pair, Sir Lucius Cary and Sir H. Morison'. He begins with a pair of tetrameters, then a pair of pentameters, then trimeters, tetrameters again and finally pentameters, all as rhyming couplets: each stanza must be identically structured, however, that is the key. As I have tried to indicate with mine, the *strophe* states a theme, addresses a hero, king, Muse, athlete, God or other such thing and praises them, celebrating their virtues and importance (Pindaric Odes themselves in my case); the *antistrophe* can express doubt, another point of view or some countervailing theme. The *epode* then tries to unite the two ideas, or comes down in favour of one view or the other. It is thesis, antithesis and synthesis to some extent, a dialectical structure. It derives actually from a Greek choric form in which the dancers would literally *turn* one way and then the other.

Horatian Ode

There are no real formal requirements to observe in a HORATIAN ODE, so I shan't bother to write a sampler for you: they should be, like their Pindaric cousins, homostrophic. The Latin poet Horace adapted Pindar's style to suit Roman requirements. English imitations were popular between the seventeenth and eighteenth centuries, a most notable example being Andrew Marvell's 'An Horatian Ode upon Cromwell's Return from Ireland' (written in rhyming couplets in fours and threes: 'He nothing common did or mean/Upon that memorable scene'). Perhaps the last great two in this manner in our language are Tennyson's 'Ode on the Death of

Wellington' and Auden's 'In Memory of W. B. Yeats'. It is common in the Horatian ode, as in the Pindaric, to include a direct address (APOSTROPHE) as Auden does:

> Earth, receive an honoured guest:
> William Yeats is laid to rest.

The Lyric Ode

Wordsworth apostrophises Nature in his Ode 'Intimations of Immortality from Recollections of Early Childhood':

> And O ye Fountains, Meadows, Hills and Groves!

But here we are looking at a wholly different kind of ode. Although Horace did write public celebratory odes in the Pindaric manner to suit the Roman temper (and especially the short one of his interfering patron, the Emperor Augustus) his real voice is heard in quieter, more contemplative and gently philosophical lyrics. These are the odes with which we associate the great romantics.

These poets created their own forms, varying their stanzaic structure and length, rhyme-scheme and measure for each poem. To call them 'odes' in the classical sense is perhaps inappropriate, but since *they* used the word we can include them in this section. The great Keats foursome emerged more from his development of sonnet structure than out of any debt to Horace or Pindar, yet the *meditative-romantic* or *lyric* ode that he and his fellow poets between them created does still bear the traces of a general tripartite structure. They do not follow the stricter triadic design of the Pindaric form, but usually move from physical description to meditation and finally to some kind of insight, resolution or stasis. An object, phenomenon or image is invoked, addressed or observed by an (often troubled) ode writer; the observation provokes thought which in turn results in some kind of conclusion, decision or realisation. We will meet this structure again when we look at the sonnet. Whether the lyric ode truly descends from the classical ode or from the medieval sonnet is a historical and academic matter which, while of no doubt frantic interest, we shall leave unexplored.

Often the poet, as in grand public odes, opens with direct address: Shelley does so in 'Skylark' and 'Ode to the West Wind':

Hail to thee, blithe spirit!
Bird thou never wert.

O wild west wind, thou breath of Autumn's being –

Or they apostrophise their hero later in the poem as Keats does the Nightingale and Autumn:

Thou wast not born for death, immortal Bird!

Who hath not seen thee oft amid thy store?

But it is *so* usual to open a poem with an invocation, 'O Goddess! hear these tuneless numbers' ('To Psyche'), 'Thou still unravish'd bride of quietness' ('On a Grecian Urn'), that you might almost define the romantic ode as being a meditative poem that commences with a direct address, an address which puts the O! in Ode, as it were.

If you are planning to write an ode yourself, it is unlikely, I suspect, to be Pindaric or Horatian in any classical, ceremonial sense; you may choose to call anything you write an ode, but it is as well to bear in mind the history and associations that go with the appellation.

We will finish with the most pleasant member of the ode family in my estimation. It combines a wholly agreeable nature with a delightfully crunchy name and ought by rights to be far more popular and better known than it is: simple to write, simple to read and easy to agree with, meet –

ANACREONTICS

Syllabically it's seven.
Thematically it's heaven,
Little lines to celebrate
Wine and love and all that's great.
Life is fleeting, death can wait,
Trochees bounce along with zest
Telling us that Pleasure's best.
Dithyrambic[8] measures traipse,
Pressing flesh and pressing grapes.
Fill my glass and squeeze my thighs,
Hedonism takes the prize.
Broach the bottle, time to pour!
Cupid's darts and Bacchus' juice
Use your magic to produce
Something humans can enjoy.
Grab a girl, embrace a boy,
Strum your lyre and hum this tune –
Life's too quick and death's too soon.

Anacreon (pronounced: *Anácreon*) was a sixth-century Greek poet whose name lives on in the style of verse that bears his name ANACREONTICS (*anacreóntics*). Actually, we barely know anything he wrote, his reputation rests on a haul of work called the *Anacreontea*, published in France in the sixteenth century. It was later discovered that these were actually not works by him, but later imitations written in his honour. No matter, Anacreon had been venerated by Horace, who shared his sybaritic, Epicurean philosophy, and by many English-language poets from Herrick and Cowley to the present day.

8 A *dithyramb* is a kind of wild choral hymn (usually to Dionysus, the Greek God of wine – Bacchus to the Romans). It now often refers to any rather overblown, uncontrolled verse style.

There was an Anacreontic Society in the eighteenth century dedicated to 'wit, harmony and the god of wine,' though its real purpose became the convivial celebration of music, hosting evenings for Haydn and other leading musicians of the day, as well as devising their own club song: 'To Anacreon in Heav'n'. A society member, John Stafford Smith, wrote the music for it, a tune which somehow got pinched by those damn Yankees who use it to this day for their national anthem, 'The Star-Spangled Banner' – 'Oh say can you see, by the dawn's early light' and so on. Strange to think that the music now fitting

. . . yet wave

O'er the land of the free and the home of the brave?

was actually written to fit

. . . entwine

The myrtle of Venus with Bacchus's wine!

And this in a country where they prohibited alcohol for the best part of a quarter of a century, a country where they look at you with pitying eyes if you order a weak spritzer at lunchtime. Tsch!

The poet most associated with English anacreontics is the seventeenth-century Abraham Cowley: here he is extolling Epicureanism over Stoicism in 'The Epicure':

Crown me with roses while I live,
Now your wines and ointments give:
After death I nothing crave,
Let me alive my pleasures have:
All are Stoics in the grave.

And a snatch of another, simply called 'Drinking':

Fill up the bowl then, fill it high,
Fill all the glasses there, for why
Should every creature drink but I,
Why, man of morals, tell me why?

Three hundred years later one of my early literary heroes, Norman Douglas, observing a wagtail drinking from a birdbath, came to this conclusion:

> Hark'ee, wagtail: Mend your ways;
> Life is brief, Anacreon says,
> Brief its joys, its ventures toilsome;
> Wine befriends them – water spoils 'em.
> Who's for water? Wagtail, you?
> Give me wine! I'll drink for two.

One of the enduring functions of all art from Anacreon to Francis Bacon, from Horace to Damien Hirst has been, is and always will be to remind us of the transience of existence, to stand as a *memento mori* that will never let us forget Gloria Monday's sick transit. We do, of course, *know* that we are going to die, and all too soon, but we need art to remind us not to spend too much time in the office caring about things that on our deathbeds will mean less than nothing. The particularity of anacreontics (simply writing in seven-syllable trochaic tetrameter as above does not make your verse anacreontic: the verse *must* concern itself with pleasure, wine, erotic love and the fleeting nature of existence) is echoed in the contemplative odes and love poetry of Horace; we find it in Shakespeare, Herrick, Marvell and all poetry between them and the present day. It is also a theme of Middle-Eastern poetry, Hafiz (sometimes called the Anacreon of Persia) and Omar Khayyam most notably.

What of Dylan Thomas's 'In My Craft or Sullen Art'?

> In my craft or sullen art
> Exercised in the still night
> When only the moon rages
> And the lovers lie abed
> With all their griefs in their arms,
> I labour by singing light
> Not for ambition or bread

Or the strut and trade of charms
On the ivory stages
But for the common wages
Of their most secret heart.

Wonderful as the poem is, dedicated to lovers as it is, presented in short sweet lines as it is, it would be bloody-minded to call it anacreontic: a hint of Eros, but no sense of Dionysus or of the need to love or drink as time's winged chariot approaches. However, I would call one of the most beautiful poems in all twentieth-century English verse, Auden's 'Lullaby' (1937), anacreontic, although I have never seen it discussed as such. Here are a few lines from the beginning:

Lay your sleeping head, my love,
Human on my faithless arm;
Time and fevers burn away
Individual beauty from
Thoughtful children, and the grave
Proves the child ephemeral:
But in my arms till break of day
Let the living creature lie,
Mortal, guilty, but to me
The entirely beautiful.

The references to flesh, love and the transience of youth make me feel this does qualify. I have no evidence that Auden thought of it as anacreontic and I may be wrong. Certainly one feels that not since Shakespeare's earlier sonnets has any youth had such gorgeous verse lavished upon him. I dare say both the subjects proved unworthy (the poets knew that, naturally) and both boys are certainly dead – the grave *has* proved the child ephemeral. *Ars longa, vita brevis:*[9] life is short, but art is long.

9 Someone told me they saw a grave to one John Longbottom, who died at the age of ten. His gravestone read *ars longa, vita brevis*: a rude epitaph for a churchyard, but witty. Works especially well if you remember that in Latin the 's' is always *unvoiced* . . .

VI

Closed Forms

Villanelle – sestina – ballade, ballade redoublé

Certain closed forms, such as those we are going to have fun with now, seem demanding enough in their structures and patterning to require some of the qualities needed for so-doku and crosswords. It takes a very special kind of poetic skill to master the form *and* produce verse of a quality that raises the end result above the level of mere cunningly wrought curiosity. They are the poetic equivalent of those intricately carved Chinese étuis that have an inexplicable ivory ball inside them.

THE VILLANELLE

Kitchen Villanelle
How rare it is when things go right
When days go by without a slip
And don't go wrong, as well they might.

The smallest triumphs cause delight –
The kitchen's clean, the taps don't drip,
How rare it is when things go right.

Your ice cream freezes overnight,
Your jellies set, your pancakes flip
And don't go wrong, as well they might

When life's against you, and you fight
To keep a stiffer upper lip.
How rare it is when things go right,

The oven works, the gas rings light,
Gravies thicken, potatoes chip
And don't go wrong as well they might.

Such pleasures don't endure, so bite
The grapes of fortune to the pip.
How rare it is when things go right
And don't go wrong as well they might.

The villanelle is the reason I am writing this book. Not that lame example, but the existence of the form itself.

Let me tell you how it happened. I was in conversation with a friend of mine about six months ago and the talk turned to poetry. I commented on the extraordinary resilience and power of ancient forms, citing the villanelle.[10]

'What's a villanelle?'

'Well, it's a pastoral Italian form from the sixteenth century written in six three-line stanzas where the first line of the first stanza is used as a refrain to end the second and fourth stanzas and the last line of the first stanza is repeated as the last line of the third, fifth and sixth,' I replied with fluent ease.

You have never heard such a snort of derision in your life.

'*What*? You have *got* to be kidding!'

I retreated into a resentful silence, wrapped in my own thoughts, while this friend ranted on about the constraint and absurdity of writing modern poetry in a form dictated by some medieval Italian shepherd. Inspiration suddenly hit me. I vaguely remembered that I had once heard this friend express great admiration for a certain poet.

'Who's your favourite twentieth-century poet?' I asked nonchalantly.

Many were mentioned. Yeats, Eliot, Larkin, Hughes, Heaney, Dylan Thomas.

10 I don't want you to go thinking that this is the usual kind of conversation I have, least of all my friends.

'And your favourite Dylan Thomas poem?'

'It's called "Do not go gentle into that good night".'

'Ah,' I said. 'Does it have any, er, what you might call *form* particularly? Does it rhyme, for instance?'

He scratched his head. 'Well, yeah it does rhyme I think. "Rage, rage against the dying of the light," and all that. But it's like – modern. You know, Dylan Thomas. *Modern.* No crap about it.'

'Would you be surprised to know', I said, trying to keep a note of ringing triumph from my voice, 'that "Do not go gentle into that good night" is a straight-down-the-line, solid gold, one hundred per cent perfect, unadulterated *villanelle*?'

'Bollocks!' he said. 'It's modern. It's free.'

The argument was not settled until we had found a copy of the poem and my friend had been forced to concede that I was right. 'Do not go gentle into that good night' is indeed a perfect villanelle, following all the rules of this venerable form with the greatest precision. That my friend could recall it only as a 'modern' poem with a couple of memorable rhyming refrains is a testament both to Thomas's unforced artistry and to the resilience and adaptability of the form itself: six three-line stanzas or *tercets*,[11] each alternating the refrains introduced in the first stanza and concluding with them in couplet form:

Do not go gentle into that good night,
Old age should burn and rave at close of day;
Rage, rage against the dying of the light.

Though wise men at their end know dark is right,
Because their words had forked no lightning they
Do not go gentle into that good night.

Good men, the last wave by, crying how bright
Their frail deeds might have danced in a green bay,
Rage, rage against the dying of the light.

11 Not *triplets*, which are three-line groups that rhyme with each other *aaa*, *bbb* etc.

Wild men who caught and sang the sun in flight,
And learn, too late, they grieved it on its way,
Do not go gentle into that good night.

Grave men, near death, who see with blinding sight
Blind eyes could blaze like meteors and be gay,
Rage, rage against the dying of the light.

And you, my father, there on the sad height,
Curse, bless me now with your fierce tears, I pray.
Do not go gentle into that good night.
Rage, rage against the dying of the light.

The conventional way to render the villanelle's plan is to call the
first refrain ('Do not go gentle') A1 and the second refrain ('Rage,
rage . . .')A2. These two rhyme with each other (which is why they
share the letter): the second line ('Old age should burn') establishes
the *b* rhyme which is kept up in the middle line of every stanza.

I	2	3	4	5	6
A1*b*A2	*ab*A1	*ab*A2	*ab*A1	*ab*A2	*ab*A1A2

Much easier to grasp in action than in code. I have boxed and shaded
the refrains here in Derek Mahon's villanelle 'Antarctica'. (I have also
numbered the line and stanzas, which of course Mahon did not do):

1

'I am just going outside and may be some time.'	A1
The others nod, pretending not to know.	b
At the heart of the ridiculous, the sublime.	A2

2

He leaves them reading and begins to climb,	a
Goading his ghost into the howling snow;	b
He is just going outside and may be some time.	A1

The tent recedes beneath its crust of rime	*a*
And frostbite is replaced by vertigo:	*b*
At the heart of the ridiculous, the sublime.	A2

Need we consider it some sort of crime,	*a*
This numb self-sacrifice of the weakest? No,	*b*
He is just going outside and may be some time –	A1

In fact, for ever. Solitary enzyme,	*a*
Though the night yield no glimmer, there will glow,	*b*
At the heart of the ridiculous, the sublime.	A2

He takes leave of the earthly pantomime	*a*
Quietly, knowing it is time to go.	*b*
'I am just going outside and may be some time.'	A1
At the heart of the ridiculous, the sublime.	A2

I hope you can see from this layout that the form is actually not as convoluted as it sounds. Describing how a villanelle works is a great deal more linguistically challenging than writing one. Mahon, by the way, as is permissible, has slightly altered the refrain line, in his case turning the direct speech of the first refrain. There are no rules as to metre or length of measure, but the rhyming is important. Slant-rhyme versions exist but for my money the shape, the revolving gavotte of the refrains and their final coupling, is compromised by partial rhyming. The form is thought to have evolved from Sicilian round songs, of the 'London Bridge is falling down' variety.

In the anthologies you will find villanelles culled from the era of their invention, the sixteenth century, especially translations of the work of the man who really got the form going, the French poet Jean Passerat: after these examples there seems to be a notable lacuna until the late nineteenth century. Oscar Wilde wrote 'Theocritus', a rather mannered neo-classical venture – 'O singer of Persephone!/Dost thou remember Sicily?' (I think it best to refer to villanelles by their refrain lines), while Ernest Dowson, Wilde's friend and fellow *Yellow Book* contributor, came up with the 'Villanelle of His Lady's Treasures' which is a much bouncier attempt, very Tudor in flavour: 'I took her dainty eyes as well/And so I made a Villanelle.'

But it is, perhaps surprisingly, during the twentieth century that the villanelle grows in popularity; besides those we have seen by Mahon and Dylan Thomas, there are memorable examples you may like to try to get hold of by Roethke, Auden, Empson, Heaney, Donald Justice, Wendy Cope and a delightful comic one candidly wrestling with the fiendish nature of the form itself entitled 'Villanelle of Ye Young Poet's First Villanelle to his Ladye and Ye Difficulties Thereof' by the playwright Eugene O'Neill: 'To sing the charms of Rosabelle,/I tried to write this villanelle.' But for a reason I cannot quite fathom it is *female* poets who seem to have made the most of the form in the last fifty years or so. Sylvia Plath's 'Mad Girl's Love Song' is especially poignant, given what we know about the poet's unhappy end: 'I shut my eyes and all the world drops dead./(I think I made you up inside my head)'. The American poet Elizabeth Bishop's 'One Art' is as fine a modern villanelle as I know and Marilyn Hacker has also written two superbly ambiguous love villanelles. Carolyn Beard Whitlow's 'Rockin' a Man Stone Blind' shows how a medieval Mediterranean pastoral form can adapt to the twentieth-century African American experience. I like the *Porgy and Bess*-style rhythms:

Cake in the oven, clothes out on the line,
Night wind blowin' against sweet, yellow thighs,
Two-eyed woman rockin' a man stone blind.

Man smell of honey, dark like coffee grind;
Countin' on his fingers since last July.
Cake in the oven, clothes out on the line.

Mister Jacobs say he be colorblind,
But got to tighten belts and loosen ties.
Two-eyed woman rockin' a man stone blind.

Winter becoming angry, rent behind.
Strapping spring sun needed to make mud pies.
Cake in the oven, clothes out on the line.

Looked in the mirror, Bessie's face I find.
I be so down low, my man be so high.
Two-eyed woman rockin' a man stone blind.

Policeman's found him; damn near lost my mind.
Can't afford no flowers; can't even cry.
Cake in the oven, clothes out on the line.
Two-eyed woman rockin' a man stone blind.

A form that seemed so dead in the seventeenth, eighteenth and nineteenth centuries brought back to rude and glistening health in the twentieth and twenty-first. Why? The villanelle has been called 'an acoustic chamber for words' and a structure that lends itself to 'duality, dichotomy, and debate', this last assertion from 'Modern Versions of the Villanelle' by Philip Jason, who goes on to suggest:

> there is even the potential for the two repeating lines to form a paradigm for schizophrenia . . . the mind may not fully know itself or its subject, may not be in full control, and yet it still tries, still festers and broods in a closed room towards a resolution that is at least pretended by the final couplet linking of the refrain lines.

Hm. It is a form that certainly seems to appeal to outsiders, or those who might have cause to consider themselves such. Among the poets we have looked at as authors of villanelles we find an African American lesbian, a Jewish lesbian, a lesbian whose father died when she was four and whose mother was committed into a mental institution four years later, two gay men, two alcoholics who drank themselves to death and a deeply unstable and unhappy neurotic who committed suicide. Perhaps this is coincidence, perhaps not. Once again I am forced to wonder if it is ironic inter-play that might make the most convincing explanation. As I suggested earlier, sometimes the rules of form can be as powerfully modern a response to chaos, moral uncertainty and relativism as open freedom can be. The more marginalised, chaotic, alienated and psychically damaged a life, the greater the impulse to find structure and certainty, surely? The playful artifice of a villanelle, preposter-ous as it may appear at first glance, can embody defiant gestures and attitudes of vengeful endurance. It suits a rueful, ironic reiteration of pain or of fatalism. We mustn't exaggerate that characteristic of the form, however: Heaney's 'Anniversary Villanelle' and some very funny examples by Wendy Cope demonstrate that it need not be always down in the dumps.

Technically the trick of it seems to be to find a refrain pair that is capable of run-ons, ambiguity and ironic reversal. I think you should try one yourself.

Poetry Exercise 14

Any subject, naturally. The skill is to find refrain lines that are open ended enough to create opportunities for enjambment between both lines and stanzas. This is not essential, of course, your refrain line can be closed and contained if you prefer, but you will gain variety, contrast and surprise if run-ons are possible.

Don't hurry the process of chewing over suitable refrains. Naturally the middle lines have to furnish six *b* rhymes, so words like 'plinth' and 'orange' are not going to be very useful . . . enjoy.

The Sestina

Let fair SESTINA start with this first LINE,
So far from pretty, perfect or inSPIRED.
Its six-fold unrhymed structure marks the FORM.
The art is *carefully* to choose your WORDS
Especially those you use at each line's END,
If not you'll find your effort's all in VAIN.

Look up: that final hero word was 'VAIN'
And so it ends this stanza's opening LINE.
We use up all our heroes till the END
And trust that somehow we will be inSPIRED
To find a fitting place for all our WORDS
And satisfy the dictates of the FORM.

It's simple, once you get the hang, to FORM
Your verse in sections like a weather-VANE:
The secret lies in finding six good WORDS
That seem to suit the ending of a LINE.
Your pattern of ideas should be inSPIRED
By heroes who will see you to the END.

Their cyclic repetition to that END
Ensures your poem will at least conFORM
To all the rules. From time to time inSPIRED
Solutions will occur. Write in this VEIN,
Just interweaving neatly line by LINE
Until you've used your stock of six good WORDS.

Composing in this form is *knitting* WORDS:
You cast off, purl and knit and purl to END
Each row, then cast off for another LINE

Until a woolly poem starts to FORM.
You may believe sestinas are a VAIN,
Indulgent, showy, frankly uninSPIRED

Idea. Yet many modern poets have CONSPIRED,
To weave away and knit their scarf of WORDS.
I'll not feel *my* attempt has been in VAIN
If by the time this chapter's reached its END
Just one of you has learned to love this FORM
And taught your hero words to toe the LINE.

Envoi
INSPIRED by fair SESTINA now I END
This run of WORDS. I hope that you will FORM –
And not in VAIN – a poem in this LINE.

This is a *bitch* to explain but a joy to make. There is no set metre to
the modern English sestina, but traditionally it has been cast in
iambics. The form comprises six sixains followed by a three line
envoi, a kind of summation or coda. So, thirty-nine lines in all. We
can best see how it works by concocting a new one together. Let's
begin:

Stanza 1

So take the prize. You're Number ONE.	1
First place is yours, the glory TOO.	2
No charge for smugness, gloating's FREE.	3
It's all you've worked and striven FOR,	4
The losers wilt, the victors THRIVE,	5
So wear the wreath, I hope it STICKS.	6

A silly slab of verse, but never mind. It is just a lash-up, a cardboard
prototype, but it has its uses. You will notice that I have capitalised
and numbered my *end-words*. They are ONE, TOO, FREE, FOR,
THRIVE and STICKS cunningly chosen to sound as much like the

numbers 1–6 as I can contrive. These end-words are the *heroes* of a sestina. Instead of being rhymed, they are reused in a set pattern: this technique is known as *lexical repetition*. So let us compose *Stanza 2*. The method is to shuttle up and down the previous stanza starting at the bottom. The end word there is STICKS. I'll write a line that ends with STICKS, then:

> But you should know that triumph STICKS

Then we go up to the top: ONE.

> Like post-it notes and everyONE

Now we go back to the bottom: we've used up STICKS, so the next free end-word is THRIVE:

> Will soon forget. The kind who THRIVE

The next unused end-word at the top is TOO:

> Are those who show compassion TO

Back down now and the next spare is FOR:

> The slow, who claim their victory FOR

Only one unused end-word left, FREE:

> The weak. I'll tell you this for FREE

So we shuttled from bottom to top, bottom to top, bottom to top taking STICKS, ONE, THRIVE, TO, FOR and FREE. In real digits that would be 6, 1, 5, 2, 4, 3. This string of numbers is our *formula*. *Stanza 2* now looks like this:

> But you should know that triumph STICKS
> Like post-it notes and everyONE
> Will soon forget. The kind who THRIVE
> Are those who show compassion TO
> The slow, who claim their victory FOR
> The weak. I'll tell you this for FREE,

Now *Stanza 3* will take the sixth line from *Stanza 2*, then the first, then the fifth and so on, according to that formula, and build itself accordingly. The sixth line of *Stanza 3* is now FREE:

You think that winning sets you FREE?

The topmost free end-line is STICKS:

No, it's a poison pill that STICKS

Then FOR, WON, TO and THRIVE: The homophone WON is perfectly acceptable for ONE.

In victory's throat. Worth striving FOR?
The golden plaudits you have WON
Are valueless and hollow TOO
The victor's laurels never THRIVE,

Now we do the same to *Stanzas 4*, *5* and *6*, shuttling between lines 6, 1, 5, 2, 4, in formula order.

The weeds of self-delusion THRIVE
On pride: they flourish, thick and FREE,
To choke your glory. Thickly TOO
The burr of disappointment STICKS
To tarnish all the gold you've WON.
Is victory worth the fighting FOR

When friendship's hand is only FOR
The weak, whose ventures never THRIVE?
I'd so much rather be the ONE
Who's always second. I am FREE
To lose. I know how much it STICKS
Inside your craw to come in TWO

But you should learn that Number TWO
Can have no real meaning, FOR
We all must cross the River STYX
And go where victors never THRIVE,

No winner's rostrum there, so FREE
Your mind from numbers: Death has WON.

The sixth is the last, after that the whole pattern would repeat. All we have to do now is construct the envoi, which contains all the hero words[12] in a strict order: the second and fifth word in the top line, the fourth and third in the middle line, the sixth and first in the bottom line.

Envoi
In order TO improve and THRIVE
Stop yearning FOR success, be FREE
If this rule STICKS then all have WON.

It may have seemed a fiendishly complicated structure and it both is and isn't. The key is to number the lines and follow the 6, 1, 5, 2, 4, 3 formula with (2–5, 4–3, 6–1 for the envoi). If you don't like numbers you might prefer to *letter* the lines alphabetically and make a note of this scheme:

ABCDEF, FAEBDC, CFDABE, ECBFAD, DEACFB, BDFECA
(BE/DC/FA)

If you want to understand the sestina's shape, you might like to think of it as a spiral. Go back and put the tip of your forefinger on STICKS in *Stanza 1*, without taking it off the page move it in an anticlockwise circle passing through 1, 5, 2, 4 and 3. Do it a couple of times so you get the idea. I have made a table which you might find useful. It contains the end-lines of the sestina we built together, as well as ABC equivalents.

12 In its strictest form, the word *Sestina* should also appear in the *envoi*. Crazy, huh?

Sestina Table

ONE	A	STICKS	F	FREE	C	STRIVE	E	FOUR	D	TOO	B
TOO	B	ONE	A	STICKS	F	FREE	C	STRIVE	E	FOUR	D
FREE	C	STRIVE	E	FOR	D	TOO	B	ONE	A	STICKS	F
FOR	D	TOO	B	ONE	A	STICKS	F	FREE	C	STRIVE	E
STRIVE	E	FOR	D	TOO	B	ONE	A	STICKS	F	FREE	C
STICKS	F	FREE	C	STRIVE	E	FOUR	D	TOO	B	ONE	A

Stanza 1   Stanza 2   Stanza 3   Stanza 4   Stanza 5   Stanza 6

I was rather fascinated by why a sestina works the way it does and whether it could be proved mathematically that you only need six stanzas for the pattern to repeat. Being a maths dunce, I approached my genius of a father who can find formulas for anything and he offered an elegant mathematical description of the sestina, showing its spirals and naming his algorithm in honour of Arnaud Daniel, the form's inventor, who was something of a mathematician himself, so legend has it. This mathematical proof can be found in the Appendix. If like me, formulae with big Greek letters in them mean next to nothing, you will be as baffled by it as I am, but you might like, as I do, the idea that even something as ethereal, soulful and personal as a poem can be described by numbers . . .

Sestinas are still being written by contemporary poets. After their invention by the twelfth-century mathematician and troubadour Arnaud Daniel, examples in English have been written by poets as varied in manner as Sir Philip Sidney, Rossetti, Swinburne, Kipling, Pound, W. H. Auden, John Ashbery, Anthony Hecht, Marilyn Hacker, Donald Justice, Howard Nemerov and Kona Macphee (see if you can find her excellent sestina 'IVF'). Swinburne's 'A Complaint to Lisa' is a *double sestina*, twelve stanzas of twelve lines each, a terrifying feat first achieved by Sir Philip Sidney. I mean surely that's just showing off . . . . I shall present two examples to show the possibilities of a form which my sample verse has made appear very false and stagy. The first is by Elizabeth

Bishop, entitled simply 'Sestina', flowing between ten-, nine- and eight-syllable lines, ending with a final line of twelve:

September rain falls on the house.
In the failing light, the old grandmother
sits in the kitchen with the child
beside the Little Marvel Stove,
reading the jokes from the almanac,
laughing and talking to hide her tears.

She thinks that her equinoctial tears
and the rain that beats on the roof of the house
were both foretold by the almanac,
but only known to a grandmother.
The iron kettle sings on the stove.
She cuts some bread and says to the child,

It's time for tea now; but the child
is watching the teakettle's small hard tears
dance like mad on the hot black stove,
the way the rain must dance on the house.
Tidying up, the old grandmother
hangs up the clever almanac

on its string. Birdlike, the almanac
hovers half open above the child,
hovers above the old grandmother
and her teacup full of dark brown tears.
She shivers and says she thinks the house
feels chilly, and puts more wood in the stove.

It was to be, says the Marvel Stove.
I know what I know, says the almanac.
With crayons the child draws a rigid house
and a winding pathway. Then the child
puts in a man with buttons like tears
and shows it proudly to the grandmother.

But secretly, while the grandmother
busies herself about the stove,
the little moons fall down like tears
from between the pages of the almanac
into the flower bed the child
has carefully placed in the front of the house.

Time to plant tears, says the almanac.
The grandmother sings to the marvelous stove
and the child draws another inscrutable house.

It is not considered *de rigueur* these days to enforce the end-word order of the envoi. This next (also called 'Sestina') is by the poet Ian Patterson – wonderful how his end-words slowly cycle their multiple meanings:

Autumn as chill as rising water laps
and files us away under former stuff
thinly disguised and thrown up on a screen;
one turn of the key lifts a brass tumbler –
another disaster probably averted, just,
while the cadence drifts in dark and old.

Voices of authority are burning an old
car on the cobbles, hands on their laps,
as if there was a life where just
men slept and didn't strut their stuff
on stage. I reach out for the tumbler
and pour half a pint behind the screen.

The whole body is in pieces. Screen
memories are not always as sharp as old
noir phenomena. The child is like a tumbler
doing back-flips out of mothers' laps
into all that dark sexual stuff
permanently hurt that nothing is just.

I'm telling you this just
because I dream of watching you behind a screen
taking your clothes off for me: the stuff
of dreams, of course. Tell me the old, old
story, real and forgetful. Time simply laps
us up, like milk from a broken tumbler.

A silent figure on the stage, the tumbler
stands, leaps and twists. He's just
a figure of speech that won't collapse
like the march of time and the silver screen;
like Max Wall finally revealing he was old
and then starting again in that Beckett stuff.

I'd like to take my sense of the real and stuff
it. There's a kind of pigeon called a tumbler
that turns over backwards as it flies, old
and having fun; sometimes I think that's just
what I want to do, but I can't cut or screen
out the lucid drift of memory that laps

my brittle attention just off-screen
away from the comfortable laps and the velvety stuff
I spilled a tumbler of milk over before I was old.

What seems like a silly word game yields poetry of compelling
mystery and rhythmic flow. What appear to be the difficulties of the
form reveal themselves, as of course they should, as its strengths –
the repetition and recycling of elusive patterns that cannot be quite
held in the mind all at once. Much in experience and thought
deserves a poetic form that can bring such elements to life.

Poetry Exercise 15

Well, all you have to do now is write your own. It will take some time: do not expect it to be easy. If you get frustrated, walk away and come back later. Let ideas form in your mind, vanish, reform, change, adapt. The repetition of end-words in the right hands works in favour of the poem: it is a defining feature of the form, not to be disguised but welcomed. You might harness this as a means of repeating patterns of speech, as we all do in life, or in reflecting on the same things from different angles.

You can do it, believe me you can. And you will be so *proud of yourself*!

THE PANTOUM

The slow throb of an old pantoum	1 A
Resounding like a distant gong	2 B
To summon us to certain doom!	3 C
Repeating fragments of its song,	4 D
Resounding like a distant gong,	2 B
The pantoum tolls in solemn weight.	5 E
Repeating fragments of its song,	4 D
It sounds the measures of our fate.	6 F
The pantoum tolls in solemn weight	5 E
Ringing changes and shifting gear.	7 G
It sounds the measures of our fate.	6 F
In chimes of ancient bells we hear,	8 H
Ringing changes and shifting gear	7 G
To summon us to certain doom.	3 C
In chimes of ancient bells, we hear	8 H
The slow throb of an old pantoum.	1 A

How to explain the rules of this strict fifteenth-century form? A PANTOUM (pronounced *pan-tomb*) must be composed in full cross-rhymed quatrains: *abab, cdcd* and so on. It must begin and end with the same line, and this is how the scheme unfolds – *draw breath*. The second and fourth lines of the first stanza become the first and third lines of the second stanza, the second and fourth lines of the second stanza become the first and third of stanza three and so on until you reach the end. *Where* the end comes is up to you: unlike the sestina or the sonnet there is no prescribed length to the form, but when you do end you must use the two lines you will not yet have repeated, the first and third of the opening stanza, they are *reversed in order* and become the second and fourth of the final quatrain. It sounds loopy, but if you look up and see what I have done it really isn't that hard to follow. I have numbered and lettered the lines to make it clearer.

The effect, as my example suggests, can be quite hypnotic or doom-laden. It can seem like wading in treacle if not adroitly handled. Such a form seems to suit dreamy evocations of time past, the echoes of memory and desire, but it need not be limited to such themes.

How the pantoum arrived in France from the Malayan peninsula in about 1830 I am not entirely sure – its importation is attributed to Victor Hugo. I believe the original form, still alive and well in the Far East, uses an *abba* rhyme-scheme and insists upon eight syllables a line and thematic changes in each quatrain. I have managed the syllable count but stuck to the more usual cross-rhymes and consistency of subject matter. Since its first European use by Hugo, Baudelaire and other French practitioners it became moderately well-known and popular in England and especially America, the best-known examples being by Anne Waldman, Carolyn Kizer, John Ashbery, Donald Justice and David Trinidad. The playwright Peter Shaffer, who clearly relishes the challenge of old forms (he has experimented with villanelles, and sestinas too) composed an excellent pantoum entitled 'Juggler, Magician, Fool'.

Here is the opening of Carolyn Kizer's 'Parents' Pantoum'. She eschews rhyme which, given the lexical repetition demanded by the form, seems perfectly permissible. Note that enjambment and some flexibility with the repeated lines is helpful in refreshing the mood of the piece: the line 'How do they appear in their long dresses' re-appears as 'In their fragile heels and long black dresses' for example, and there are additional buts and thoughs that vary the iterations. All this is usual in the modern, Western strain of pantoum.

Where did these enormous children come from,
More ladylike than we have ever been?
Some of ours look older than we feel.
How did they appear in their long dresses

More ladylike than we have ever been?
But they moan about their aging more than we do,
In their fragile heels and long black dresses.
They say they admire our youthful spontaneity.

They moan about their aging more than we do,
A somber group – why don't they brighten up?
Though they say they admire our youthful spontaneity
They beg us to be dignified like them

If you are a nerdy, anagrammy, crossword puzzler sort of a person, as I tragically and irredeemably am, you will be especially drawn to the pantoum. The art, as with other lexically repetitive and patterned schemes, is to choose 'open-ended' repeating lines allowing ambiguity and room for manoeuvre. It is one thing, of course, to write them as a fun exercise, quite another to make a poem of readable qualities for others. Technically the ideal is to push the normative requirements of the mode hard, sometimes to breaking point. Therein lies the knack – stretching the bubble until *just before* it bursts. Without hard pressure on the inner walls of its membrane the pantoum – and this holds true of the other complex forms – can seem a flaccid, futile exercise in wordsmanship.

THE BALLADE

BALLADE is not an easy form to crack
    No other rhymes, but only A or B;
The paeon, dactyl and the amphibrach,
    The antispast, molossus and spondee
    Will not assist us in the least degree
As through the wilderness we grimly hack
    And sow our hopeful seeds of poetry.
It's always one step forward, two steps back.

But let me be Marvell, not Kerouac
    The open road holds no allure for me.
A garden path shall be my desert track,
    The song of birds my jukebox melody,
    The neighbour's cat my Neil Cassidy.
With just a mower for a Cadillac
    I won't get far, but nor will they. You see –
It's always one step forward, two steps back.

A hammock is my beatnik bivouac
    My moonshine bourbon is a cup of tea.
No purple hearts, no acid trips, no smack
    My only buzz the humble honeybee.
    So let them have their free-verse liberty
And I shall have my handsome garden shack
    We'll see which one of us is truly free,
It's always one step forward, two steps back.

Envoi
    Prince and peasant, workers, peers or bourgeoisie
McGonagall, Lord Byron, Pasternak
    Of mongrel stock or high born pedigree —
It's always one step forward, two steps back.

The BALLADE, not to be confused with the ballad (or with the musical *ballade* devised by Chopin), is a venerable French form of some fiendishness for English poets. The difficulty arises, not from any complexity of patterning or repetition such as is to be found in the sestina, but from the number of rhyme sounds needed. It ends with an envoi which, tradition dictates, must be addressed to a *Prince*. Indeed the very word 'Prince' is usually the envoi's first word: this happy convention, maintained even by modern poets like Dorothy Parker, is a nod to the royal patronage enjoyed by early practitioners such as François Villon and Eustache Deschamps. Those who elected to write sacred ballades would begin their envois with the invocations 'Prince Jesus!', or 'Prince and Saviour!'. Each stanza, the envoi included, ends with the same refrain or *rentrement*. Early ballades were often composed in three seven-line stanzas, but these days an eight-line stanza with an envoi of four lines seems to have been settled upon by English-language poets. The usual rhyme scheme is *ababbabA ababbabA ababbabA babA*, in other words ten *a* rhymes (and a refrain, A, to rhyme with them) and *fourteen b* rhymes. This is no doubt a doddle in French but the very bastard son of a mongrel bitch in English. G. K. Chesterton's 'The Ballade of Suicide' is one of the better-known examples:

> The gallows in my garden, people say,
>> Is new and neat and adequately tall;
> I tie the noose on in a knowing way
>> As one that knots his necktie for a ball;
>> But just as all the neighbours – on the wall –
> Are drawing a long breath to shout 'Hurray!'
>> The strangest whim has seized me. . . . After all
> I think I will not hang myself to-day.
>
> To-morrow is the time I get my pay –
>> My uncle's sword is hanging in the hall –
> I see a little cloud all pink and grey –
> Perhaps the rector's mother will not call –
>> I fancy that I heard from Mr Gall
> That mushrooms could be cooked another way –
>> I never read the works of Juvenal –
> I think I will not hang myself to-day.
>
> The world will have another washing-day;
>> The decadents decay; the pedants pall;
> And H. G. Wells has found that children play,
>> And Bernard Shaw discovered that they squall,
>> Rationalists are growing rational –
> And through thick woods one finds a stream astray

So secret that the very sky seems small –
I think I will not hang myself to-day.

Envoi

 Prince, I can hear the trumpet of Germinal,
The tumbrels toiling up the terrible way;
 Even to-day your royal head may fall,
I think I will not hang myself to-day.

It reminds me of Fagin's song 'I'm Reviewing the Situation' from Lionel Bart's musical *Oliver!* the refrain to which, 'I think I'd better think it out again', forms a similarly memorable decasyllabic chorus. Bart's number is not a ballade, of course, but the similarity demonstrates the form's derivations from, and yearnings towards, music. One of the more successful and regular tillers of the ballade's rhyme-rich soil was the Round Table with Dorothy Parker. Here is her 'Ballade of Unfortunate Mammals':

Love is sharper than stones or sticks;
Lone as the sea, and deeper blue;
Loud in the night as a clock that ticks;
Longer-lived than the Wandering Jew.
Show me a love was done and through,
Tell me a kiss escaped its debt!
Son, to your death you'll pay your due –
Women and elephants never forget.

Ever a man, alas, would mix,
Ever a man, heigh-ho, must woo;
So he's left in the world-old fix,
Thus is furthered the sale of rue.
Son, your chances are thin and few –
Won't you ponder, before you're set?
Shoot if you must, but hold in view
Women and elephants never forget.

Down from Caesar past Joynson-Hicks
Echoes the warning, ever new:
Though they're trained to amusing tricks,
Gentler, they, than the pigeon's coo,
Careful, son, of the cursèd two –
Either one is a dangerous pet;
Natural history proves it true –
Women and elephants never forget.

L'Envoi
Prince, a precept I'd leave for you,
Coined in Eden, existing yet:
Skirt the parlor, and shun the zoo –
Women and elephants never forget.

VII

More Closed Forms

The rondeau – rondeau redoublé – the rondel – the roundel –
the rondelet – the roundelay – the triolet and the kyrielle

Yeah, right. You *really* want to know about all these French Rs. Your
life won't be complete without them. Well, don't be too put off by
the confusing nomenclatorial similarities and Frenchy sound they
seem to share. You are probably familiar with the concept of a musically sung ROUND ('Frère Jacques', 'Row, Row, Row Your Boat',
'London Bridge' etc.) All these forms are based on the principle of
a *poetic* round, a (mercifully) short poem as a rule, characterised by
the nature of its refrain (*rentrement*). The avatar of these genres is the
RONDEAU, pronounced like the musical rondo, but with typical
French equal stress.

RONDEAU

OF MY RONDEAU this much is true:
Its virtues lie in open view,
Unravelled is its tangled skein,
Untapped the blood from every vein,
Unthreaded every nut and screw.

I strip it thus to show to you
The way I rhyme it, what I do
To mould its form, yet still retain
The proper shape and inward grain
OF MY RONDEAU.

As rhyming words in lines accrue
A pleasing sense of déjà-vu
Will infiltrate your teeming brain.
Now . . . here it comes the old refrain,
The beating drum and proud tattoo
OF MY RONDEAU.

Most scholars of the genre seem to agree that in its most common
form, as I have tried to demonstrate, the rondeau should be a poem
of between thirteen and fifteen lines, patterned by two rhymes and
a refrain *R*, formed by the first half of the opening line. The scheme
is represented by *R-aabba aabR aabbaR*. A notable example is the
Canadian poet John McCrae's rondeau, 'In Flanders Fields':

IN FLANDERS FIELDS the poppies blow
Between the crosses, row on row,
That mark our place, and in the sky,
The larks, still bravely singing, fly,
Scarce heard amid the guns below.

We are the dead; short days ago
We lived, felt dawn, saw sunset glow,
Loved and were loved, and now we lie
                    In Flanders fields.

Take up our quarrel with the foe!
To you from failing hands we throw
The torch; be yours to hold it high!
If ye break faith with us who die
We shall not sleep, though poppies grow
                    In Flanders fields.

This very earnest poem subverts the usual characteristic of the form
in French verse, where the rondeau is a light, graceful and merry
thing that refuses to take life very seriously. Although the two
examples you have seen are, so far as my very unscholarly researches

can determine, the 'correct' form, the appellation rondeau has been used through the ages by English-language poets from Grimald to the present day to apply to a number of variations. Leigh Hunt's 'Rondeau: Jenny Kissed Me' adheres to the principle of a refrain culled from the first hemistich of the opening line, but adds a rhyme for it in line 6. The Jenny in question, by the way, is said to have been Thomas Carlyle's wife.[13]

JENNY KISSED ME when we met,
 Jumping from the chair she sat in;
Time, you thief, who love to get
 Sweets into your list, put that in:
Say I'm weary, say I'm sad,
 Say that health and wealth have missed me,
Say I'm growing old, but add,
    JENNY KISSED ME.

A variation exists (don't they always) and here it is.

RONDEAU REDOUBLÉ

THE FIRST FOUR LINES OF RONDEAU REDOUBLÉ
Are chosen with especial skill and care
For each one has a vital role to play
In turn they each a heavy burden share.

Disaster comes to those who don't prepare
The opening stanza in an artful way
So do, dear friends, I beg of you, beware
The first four lines of rondeau redoublé.

13 Anthony Holden, in *The Wit in the Dungeon*, his masterly biography of Leigh Hunt, has this to say about the incident: 'Whether or not Carlyle's crusty old wife actually had given Hunt a kiss, let alone leapt from her chair to do so, we will never know; no such unlikely moment is documented in any of the relevant parties' letters or journals.'

That warning made, it's pretty safe to say
This ancient form's a simply wrought affair,
So long as all your rhymes, both B and A
Are chosen with especial skill and care;

For you'll need rhymes and plenty left to spare –
A dozen words, arranged in neat array
That's six, yes six in every rhyming pair,
For each one has a vital role to play.

So long as you these simple rules obey
You'll have no trouble with the form, I swear.
The first four lines your efforts will repay,
In turn they each a heavy burden share,
                  THE FIRST FOUR LINES.

Here, as I hope my abominable but at least accurately self-referential
example makes clear, each line of Stanza 1 forms in turn an end-
refrain to the next four stanzas. As in the standard rondeau, the
opening hemistich is repeated to form a final coda or mini-envoi.
Each stanza alternates in rhyme between *abab* and *baba*.

    Wendy Cope included an excellent example in her collection
Making Cocoa for Kingsley Amis and here is Dorothy Parker's charm-
ing (and charmingly titled) example 'Rondeau Redoublé (and
Scarcely Worth the Trouble at That)' which has an excellent coda:

THE SAME TO ME are somber days and gay.
    Though joyous dawns the rosy morn, and bright,
Because my dearest love is gone away
    Within my heart is melancholy night.

My heart beats low in loneliness, despite
    That riotous Summer holds the earth in sway.
In cerements my spirit is bedight;
    The same to me are somber days and gay.

Though breezes in the rippling grasses play,
    And waves dash high and far in glorious might,
I thrill no longer to the sparkling day,
    Though joyous dawns the rosy morn, and bright.

Ungraceful seems to me the swallow's flight;
    As well might Heaven's blue be sullen gray;
My soul discerns no beauty in their sight
    Because my dearest love is gone away.

Let roses fling afar their crimson spray,
    And virgin daisies splash the fields with white,
Let bloom the poppy hotly as it may,
    Within my heart is melancholy night.

And this, oh love, my pitiable plight
    Whenever from my circling arms you stray;
This little world of mine has lost its light . . .
    I hope to God, my dear, that you can say
            The same to me.

So let us now meet some of the rondeau's hopeful progeny.

RONDEL

*The **RONDEL** sends the senses reeling,*
And who are we to call it dead?
Examples that I've seen and read
Have given me the strongest feeling
That such a form is most appealing
To those whose Heart controls their Head.
The rondel sends the senses reeling
And who are we to call it dead?
Its lines for ever roundly wheeling,
Make manifest what can't be said.

From wall to wall and floor to ceiling
The rondel sends the senses reeling
And who are we to call it dead?

The RONDEL's first couplet, as you can see, is repeated as a final refrain. There appears to be no set length, but in the later thirteen-line or fourteen-line variants such as mine (known as RONDEL PRIME and now seemingly the standard strain in English verse) the rentrements are also repeated in the *middle* of the poem. Chaucer, Longfellow and others wrote poems they called rondels which appear to vary in all points except that crucial matter of the refrain. There again, Nicholas Grimald, the poet and scholar who just avoided burning under Mary Tudor and gave his name to Sirius Black's family home in the Harry Potter books, wrote a 'Rondel of Love' in *sixains* only the first verse of which has a repeated line. Austin Dobson, who enjoyed experimenting with forms of this nature (indeed, he founded a school of poets in 1876 devoted to the rediscovery of the old French *rondeau* family), demonstrates what we might call the rondel's 'correct' form, whose lineaments my effort also shares (the italics are mine to help point up the *rentrements*):

> *Love comes back to his vacant dwelling,*
> *The old, old Love that we knew of yore!*
> We see him stand by the open door,
> With his great eyes sad, and his bosom swelling.
> He makes as though in our arms repelling
> He fain would lie as he lay before
> *Love comes back to his vacant dwelling,*
> *The old, old Love that we knew of yore!*
> Ah! who shall help us from over-spelling
> That sweet, forgotten, forbidden lore ?
> E'en as we doubt, in our hearts once more,
> With a rush of tears to our eyelids welling,
> *Love comes back to his vacant dwelling,*
> *The old, old Love that we knew of yore!*

It is a requirement of this 'correct' form (one that both Dobson and I met) that of the two rhymes, one should be masculine, the other feminine, contributing to the overall call-and-response character of the form.

ROUNDEL

Swinburne developed an English version of his own which he called the ROUNDEL, as you see it is closer to a rondeau than a rondel:

> *A roundel is wrought* as a ring or a starbright sphere,
>   With craft of delight and with cunning of sound
>   unsought,
> That the heart of the hearer may smile if to pleasure his ear
>   *A roundel is wrought.*
>
> Its jewel of music is carven of all or of aught –
>   Love, laughter, or mourning – remembrance of rapture or
>   fear –
> That fancy may fashion to hang in the ear of thought.
>
> As a bird's quick song runs round, and the hearts in us hear
>   Pause answer to pause, and again the same strain caught,
> So moves the device whence, round as a pearl or tear,
>   A roundel is wrought.

RONDELET

> *I cannot sing*
> A **RONDELET** of love to thee
> *I cannot sing*
> I try to let my voice take wing,

It never seems to stay in key
And if you heard me, you'd agree
I cannot sing

Pretty clear, clear and pretty, the RONDELET goes *AbAabbA* as mine demonstrates. I don't know of any spectacular examples (aside from my own) of the rondelet, pronounced as if it were a Welsh valley song (or indeed sexual experience) a *Rhondda Lay*. The good old English version of the word might promise a similar form, you would be entitled to think.

ROUNDELAY

Actually the ROUNDELAY is rather different:

My hee-haw voice is like a bray
Nothing sounds so asinine
Little causes more dismay
Than my dreadful donkey whine.
Hear me sing a ROUNDELAY
There is no fouler voice than mine.

Little causes more dismay
Than my dreadful donkey whine.
People hold their heads and say
Shut your mouth you filthy swine.
Hear me sing a roundelay
There is no fouler voice than mine.

People hold their heads and say
Shut your mouth you filthy swine,
Stop your singing right away,
Else we'll break your fucking spine.
Hear me sing a roundelay
There is no fouler voice than mine.

As you see, pairs of lines repeat in order. Here is 'A Roundelay' by the late seventeenth-century poet Thomas Scott:

> *Man, that is for woman made*
> *And the woman made for man.*
> As the spur is for the jade.
> As the scabbard for the blade
> As for liquor is the can,
> *So man is for the woman made*
> *And the woman made for man.*

And so on for two more stanzas: for Scott and his contemporaries a roundelay seemed to be any poem with the same two-line refrain at the beginning and end of each stanza, but Samuel Beckett did write a poem called 'roundelay' with full and fascinating internal line repetition. Your task is to find a copy of it and discover its beauties and excellence. Award yourself twenty points if you can get your hands on it within a week.

TRIOLET

> This **TRIOLET** of my design
> Is sent with all my heart to you,
> Devotion dwells in every line.
> This triolet of my design
> Is not so swooningly divine
> As you, my darling Valentine.
> This triolet of my design
> I send with all my heart to you.

The TRIOLET is pronounced in one of three ways: to rhyme with 'violet', or the halfway house *tree-o-lett*, or *tree-o-lay* in the full French manner: simply stated it is an eight-line poem whose first (*A*) and second (*B*) lines are repeated at the end: the first line also repeats as the fourth. *ABaAbbAB* in other words. It is, I suppose, the *threefold* repeat of that first line that give it the 'trio' name. Do you remember Frances Cornford's 'To a Fat Lady Seen from a Train' which we looked at when thinking about rhymes for 'love'? If we look at it again, we can see that it is in fact a triolet.

> O why do you walk through the fields in gloves,
>   Missing so much and so much?
> O fat white woman whom nobody loves,
> Why do you walk through the fields in gloves,
> When the grass is soft as the breast of doves
>   And shivering sweet to the touch?
> O why do you walk through the fields in gloves,
>   Missing so much and so much?

Here is another, written by the unfortunately named American poet Adelaide Crapsey:

> I make my shroud but no one knows,
> So shimmering fine it is and fair,
> With stitches set in even rows.
> I make my shroud but no one knows.
> In door-way where the lilac blows,
> Humming a little wandering air,
> I make my shroud and no one knows,
> So shimmering fine it is and fair.

W. E. Henley (on whom Stevenson based the character of Long John Silver) believed triolets were easy and was not afraid to say so. He also clearly thought, if his rhyming is anything to go by, that they were pronounced English-fashion, probably *tree-o-let*:

> EASY is the Triolet,
>   If you really learn to make it!
> Once a neat refrain you get,
> Easy is the Triolet.

As you see! – I pay my debt
  With another rhyme. Deuce take it,
Easy is the Triolet,
  If you really learn to make it!

They are certainly not easy to master but – as my maudlin attempt suggests, and as Wendy Cope's 'Valentine' rather more stylishly proves – they seem absolutely tailor-made for light love poetry:

My heart has made its mind up
And I'm afraid it's you.
Whatever you've got lined up,
My heart has made its mind up
And if you can't be signed up
This year, next year will do.
My heart has made its mind up
And I'm afraid it's you.

One more repeating form to look at before we atrophy.

KYRIELLE

The chanting of a **KYRIELLE**
Tolls like the summons of a bell
To bid us purge our black disgrace.
Lord a-mercy, shut my face.

Upon my knees, I kiss the rod,
Repent and raise this cry to God –
I am a sinner, foul and base
Lord a-mercy, shut my face.

And so I make this plaintive cry:
'From out my soul, the demons chase
Prostrate before thy feet I lie.'
Lord a-mercy, shut my face.

There is no health or good in me,
Nor in the wretched human race.
Therefore my God I cry to thee.
Lord a-mercy, shut my face.

Let sins be gone without a trace
Lord have mercy, shut my face.

You've heard my pleas, I rest my case.
Lord have mercy! Shut my face.

The name and character of the KYRIELLE derive from the Mass, whose wail of *Kyrie eleison!* – 'Lord, have mercy upon us' – is a familiar element. For those of us not brought up in Romish ways it is to be heard in the great requiems and other masses of the classical repertoire.

The final line of every stanza is the same, indeed *rime en kyrielle* is an alternative name for repeated lines in any style of poetry. Most examples of the kyrielle to be found in English are written, as mine is, in iambic tetrameter. As I have tried to demonstrate, quatrains of *aabB* and *abaB* or couplets of *aA*, *aA* are all equally acceptable. There is no set length. The Elizabethan songwriter and poet Thomas ('Cherry Ripe') Campion wrote a 'Lenten Hymn' very much in the spirit, as well as the letter, of the kyrielle:

With broken heart and contrite sigh,
A trembling sinner, Lord, I cry:
Thy pard'ning grace is rich and free:
O God, be merciful to me.

I smite upon my troubled breast,
With deep and conscious guilt opprest,

Christ and His cross my only plea:
O God, be merciful to me.

Incidentally, many kyrielles were written in 1666. Not just to apologise to God for being so sinful and tasteless as to perish in plague and fire, but because numbers were considered important and the Roman numerals in 'LorD haVe MerCIe Vpon Vs' add up to 1666: this is called a CHRONOGRAM.

The kyrielle need not exhibit agonised apology and tortured pleas for mercy, however. The late Victorian John Payne managed to be a little less breast-beating in his 'Kyrielle' as well as demonstrating the scope for *slight* variation in the repeat:

A lark in the mesh of the tangled vine,
A bee that drowns in the flower-cup's wine,
A fly in sunshine, – such is the man.
All things must end, as all began.

A little pain, a little pleasure,
A little heaping up of treasure;
Then no more gazing upon the sun.
All things must end that have begun.

Where is the time for hope or doubt?
A puff of the wind, and life is out;
A turn of the wheel, and rest is won.
All things must end that have begun.

Golden morning and purple night,
Life that fails with the failing light;
Death is the only deathless one.
All things must end that have begun

Well, *haven't* we learned a lot! Bags of French forms beginning with 'r' that repeat their lines *en kyrielle*. To be honest, you could call them all rondeaux and only a pedant would pull you up on it. It is not too complicated a matter to invent your own form, a regular pattern of refrains is all it takes. You could call it a *rondolina* or *rondismo* or a *boundelay* or whatever you fancied. Destiny and a place in poetic history beckon.

Poetry Exercise 16

Your FIRST task is to write a less emetic triolet than mine for your true love, as sweet without being sickly as you can make it, your SECOND to compose a RONDEAU REDOUBLÉ on any subject you please.

VIII

Comic Verse

The cento – the limerick and the clerihew – reflections on comic verse, light verse and parody

CENTO

Wordsworth Comes Out
My heart leaps up when I behold
The pansy at my feet;
Ingenuous, innocent and bold
Beside a mossy seat.

For oft when on my couch I lie
Upon the growing boy,
A little Cyclops with one eye
Will dwell with me – to heighten joy.

CENTOS are cannibalised verse, collage poems whose individual lines are made up of fragments of other poetry. Often each line will be from the same poet. The result is a kind of enforced self-parody. In mine above, all the lines are culled from different poems by Wordsworth. Ian Patterson has produced some corkers. Here are two, one from A. E. Housman, the other a cento stitched from Shakespeare sonnets. Just to emphasise the point: *all* the lines are genuine lines from the poet in question, panels torn from their own work to make a new quilt. First, his Housman Cento:

The happy highways where I went
    Warm with the blood of lads I know
Have willed more mischief than they durst
    A hundred years ago.

Clay lies still, but blood's a rover
    Safe through jostling markets borne;
The nettle nods, the wind blows over,
    With hurts not mine to mourn.

When you and I are spilt on air,
    What's to show for all my pain?
Duty, friendship, bravery o'er,
    And Ludlow fair again.

Extraordinary how much sense it seems to make. This is Patterson's Shakespeare Cento:

When in the chronicles of wasted time
That thy unkindness lays upon my heart,
Bearing the wanton burthen of the prime
To guard the lawful reasons on thy part,
My heart doth plead that thou in him dost lie
The perfect ceremony of love's rite,
And scarcely greet me with that sun thine eye
To change your day of youth to sullen night,
Then in the number let me pass untold
So that myself bring water for my stain,
That poor retention could not so much hold
Knowing thy heart torment me in disdain:
    O cunning love, with tears thou keep'st me blind,
        Since I left you my eye is in my mind.

They are, I suppose, no more than a game, but one which can be surprisingly revealing. If nothing else, they provide a harmlessly productive way of getting to know a particular poet's way with phrase and form. Centos that mix completely dissimilar poets' lines are another harmless kind of comic invention.

The Clerihew

ELIZABETH BARRETT
Was kept in a garret.
Her father resented it bitterly
When Robert Browning took her to Italy.

ALFRED, LORD TENNYSON
Preferred Victoria Sponge to venison.
His motto was 'Regina semper floreat'
And that's how he became Poet Laureate.

OSCAR WILDE
Had his reputation defiled.
When he was led from the dock in tears
He said 'We are all in the gutter, but some of us are looking
    at two years.'

D. H. LAWRENCE
Held flies in abhorrence.
He once wrote a verse graffito
Deploring the humble mosquito.

TED HUGHES
Had a very short fuse.
What prompted his wrath
Was being asked about Sylvia Plath.

The CLERIHEW is named after Edmund Clerihew Bentley, father of Nicolas, that peerless illustrator who always signed his work 'Nicolas Bentley Drew the pictures'. The rules state that clerihews be non-metrically written in two couplets, the first of which is to be a proper name and nothing else. The best-known originals include:

Christopher Wren
Said 'I am going to dine with some men,
'If anyone calls
Say I am designing St Paul's.'

Sir Humphrey Davy
Abominated gravy.
He lived in the odium
Of having discovered sodium.

John Stuart Mill,
By a mighty effort of will,
Overcame his natural bonhomie
And wrote 'Principles of Economy'.

Metrical clumsiness is very much a desideratum; indeed, it is considered extremely bad form for a clerihew to scan. Properly done,
they should tell some biographical truth, obvious or otherwise,
about their subject, rather than be sheer nonsense. Sir Humphrey's
dislike of gravy, for example, may well be whimsical tosh, but he
did discover sodium: I have tried to cleave to this requirement in
my clerihews on the poets. Clerihews have therefore some utility
as biographical mnemonics.

THE LIMERICK

There was a middle-aged writer called Fry
Whose book on verse was a lie.
  For *The Ode Less Travelled*
  Soon unravelled
To reveal some serious errors in its scansion and rhy . . .

Unlike clerihews, LIMERICKS, as we discovered when considering
their true metrical nature (we decided they were anapaestic, if you

recall), do and must scan. I am sure you need to be told little else about them. The name is said to come from a boozy tavern chorus 'Will you come up to Limerick?'. Although they are popularly associated with Edward Lear, anonymous verses in the 'There was an old woman of . . .' formulation pre-dated him by many years:

> A merry old man of Oporto,
> Had long had the gout in his fore-toe;
>   And oft when he spoke
>   To relate a good joke,
> A terrible twinge cut it short-O.

> Said a very proud Farmer at Reigate,
> When the Squire rode up to his high gate
>   'With your horse and your hound,
>   You had better go round,
> For, I say, you shan't jump over my gate.'

That pair was accompanied by Cruikshank illustrations in a children's 'chap-book' of around 1820 when Lear was just eight or nine years old. Oddly, these examples accord more closely to the modern sense of what a limerick should be than Lear's own effusions, in which the last line often lamely repeats the first.

> There was an Old Man of the West,
> Who wore a pale plum-coloured vest;
>   When they said, 'Does it fit?'
>   He replied, 'Not a bit!'
> That uneasy Old Man of the West.

Rather flat to the modern ear, I find. We prefer a punchline:

> Girls who frequent picture palaces
> Set no store by psychoanalysis.
>   And although Sigmund Freud
>   Would be greatly annoyed,
> They cling to their long-standing fallacies.

Or *phalluses*, ho-ho-ho. It was W. S. Baring-Gould's collection *The Lure of the Limerick* that really understood the base (in both senses) nature of the form. I remember owning a Panther Books edition (an imprint known for publishing risqué but classy works, Genet and the like) and finding their scabrous and cloacal nature hilarious, as any unhealthy ten-year-old would. This anonymous (so far as I can tell) limerick puts it well:

> The limerick packs laughs anatomical
> Into space that is quite economical.
>   But the good ones I've seen
>   So seldom are clean
> And the clean ones so seldom are comical.

When I began collecting the works of Norman Douglas I was delighted to find a copy of his 1928 anthology, *Some Limericks*, which remains deeply shocking to this day. Most of them are simply disgusting. Hard to believe that an antiquarian *belle-lettriste* like Douglas (you may remember his 'Wagtail' anacreontics) would dare risk attaching his name to them at a time when *Ulysses* was being impounded by customs officers on both sides of the Atlantic. Please do *not* read these four examples of Douglas's literary excavations. Skip to the next paragraph instead.

> There was an old fellow of Brest,
> Who sucked off his wife with a zest.
>   Despite her great yowls
>   He sucked out her bowels
> And spat them all over her chest.

> There was a young man of Nantucket
> Whose prick was so long he could suck it
>   He said, with a grin
>   As he wiped off his chin:
> 'If my ear were a cunt, I could fuck it.'

There was an old man of Corfu,
Who fed upon cunt-juice and spew.
　　When he couldn't get this,
　　He fed upon piss –
And a bloody good substitute too.

There was an old man of Brienz,
The length of whose cock was immense.
　　With one swerve he could plug
　　A boy's bottom in Zug
And a kitchen-maid's cunt in Koblenz.

Reflections on Comic and Impolite Verse

Comic forms such as the limerick and the clerihew are the pocket
cartoons of poetry. Often they fail dismally to provoke the slightest
smile – although those collected by Norman Douglas can certainly
provoke cries of outrage and s(t)imulated disgust. It seems to me
that the City of Poesy, with its associations of delicacy, refined
emotion and exquisite literacy is all the richer for having these
moral slums within its walls. No metropolis worth visiting is without its red-light district, its cruising areas and a bohemian village
where absinthe flows, reefers glow and love is free. W. H. Auden
wrote obscene comic verse which you will not find anthologised
by Faber and Faber,[14] and even the retiring Robert Frost had the
occasional reluctant (and unconvincing) stab at being saucy.
Obscenity is a fit manner for comic verse; without it the twin
horrors of whimsy and cuteness threaten. There is surely no word
in the language that causes the heart to sink like a stone so much
as 'humorous'. Wit is one thing, bawdy another, but *humorousness*
. . . Humorousness is to wit what a suburban lawn is to either
Sissinghurst *or* a rubbish-heap, what an executive saloon is to an

14 See if you can get hold of 'A Platonic Blow' for example.

Aston Martin *or* a cheerful old banger. Wit is either a steel rapier or a lead cosh, rarely a cutely fashioned paper dart. Wit is not *nice*, wit is not affirmative or consoling. Jonathan Swift describing how 'A Beautiful Young Nymph Goes to Bed' is unafraid of being disgusting in his disgust:

> CORINNA, Pride of Drury-Lane,
> . . .
> Returning at the Midnight Hour;
> Four Stories climbing to her Bow'r;
> Then, seated on a three-legg'd Chair,
> Takes off her artificial Hair:
> Now, picking out a Crystal Eye,
> She wipes it clean, and lays it by.
> Her Eye-Brows from a Mouse's Hide,
> Stuck on with Art on either Side,
> Pulls off with Care, and first displays 'em,
> Then in a Play-Book smoothly lays 'em.
> Now dexterously her Plumpers draws,
> That serve to fill her hollow Jaws.
> Untwists a Wire; and from her Gums
> A Set of Teeth completely comes.
> Pulls out the Rags contriv'd to prop
> Her flabby Dugs and down they drop.
> Proceeding on, the lovely Goddess
> Unlaces next her Steel-Rib'd Bodice;
> Which by the Operator's Skill,
> Press down the Lumps, the Hollows fill,
> Up hoes her Hand, and off she slips
> The Bolsters that supply her Hips.
> With gentlest Touch, she next explores
> Her Shankers, Issues, running Sores,
> Effects of many a sad Disaster;
> And then to each applies a Plaster.

But must, before she goes to Bed,
Rub off the Daubs of White and Red;
And smooth the Furrows in her Front,
With greasy Paper stuck upon't.
She takes a Bolus e'er she sleeps;
And then between two Blankets creeps.

. . .

CORINNA wakes. A dreadful Sight!
Behold the Ruins of the Night!
A wicked Rat her Plaster stole,
Half eat, and dragged it to his Hole.
The Crystal Eye, alas, was miss'd;
And Puss had on her Plumpers piss'd.
A Pigeon pick'd her Issue-Peas;
And Shock her Tresses fill'd with Fleas.
The Nymph, tho' in this mangled Plight,
Must ev'ry Morn her Limbs unite.
But how shall I describe her Arts
To recollect the scatter'd Parts?
Or show the Anguish, Toil, and Pain,
Of gath'ring up herself again?
The bashful Muse will never bear
In such a Scene to interfere.
Corinna in the Morning dizen'd,
Who sees, will spew; who smells, be poison'd.

Heroic verse indeed. Even more scabrous, scatological and down-right disgraceful was the seventeenth-century's one-man Derek & Clive, John Wilmot, Earl of Rochester:

She was so exquisite a whore
That in the belly of her mother
She turned her cunt so right before
Her father fucked them both together.

Mm, nice.

Light Verse

It is revealing that in polls to find the most popular poets, names like Shel Silverstein, Wendy Cope, Spike Milligan, Roald Dahl, Roger McGough, Benjamin Zephaniah, John Betjeman, Glyn Maxwell and Langston Hughes consistently appear high in the charts (not that all their work is comic, of course). Certainly Emily Dickinson, Dylan Thomas, Philip Larkin, Sylvia Plath and Pablo Neruda feature too (not that all their work is serious, of course). There seems to be an inexhaustible appetite for verse whose major rhetorical instrument is wit or lightness of touch. It is notable also that *long* poems seem a great deal less appealing to the public. Perhaps this is something to do with our culture of immediacy: fast food verse for fast food people. Whatever the reason, it seems to me self-evident that if you wish your poetry to make a noise outside the world of academia, poetry magazines and private *Gesellschaften*, your chances are greatly increased by their possession of an element of esprit. Perhaps the description that best fits the work of the more popular poets is not comic, but *light*. 'Angels can fly because they take themselves lightly,' said Chesterton.

Light Verse does not need to be comic in intent or witty in nature: it encourages readers to believe that they and the poet share the same discourse, intelligence and standing, inhabit the same universe of feeling and cultural reference, it does not howl in misunderstood loneliness, wallow in romantic agony or bombard the reader with learning and allusion from a Parnassian or abstrusely academic height. This kind of poetry, Auden argues in his intro-duction to *The Oxford Book of Light Verse*, was mainstream until the arrival of the romantics. With the exception of sacred verse, Miltonic epics, drama and the more complex metaphysical poems of the seventeenth century, almost all poetry was, more or less, light. It was adult, it could be moving, angry, erotic and even religious, but it was digestible, it was not embarrassed by the idea of likeability and accessibility. A poem could be admired because it was prettily made and charming to read, Mozartian qualities if you like. Modernism appeared to drive lightness out of poetry for ever. These popularity polls, irksome as they be, seem to indicate that it is far from dead, however. In the knowledge that Gravity will destroy us in the end, perhaps Levity is not so trivial a response.

Parody

Neither are parody and pastiche an unfit manner for the poet. Chaucer began the trend in English with a scintillating parody of badly versified epical romance called *Sir Thopas*. Shakespeare parodied Marlowe, as did Donne (in praise of angling in the style of 'The Passionate Shepherd'); Byron parodied and was parodied, Dryden, Johnson, and Swift parodied and were parodied and so it went on. Trends in the actual nuts and bolts of versification were ruthlessly guyed by Pope in the *Dunciad*: George Canning and John Hookham Frere (the former of Castlereagh, the latter of *Whistlecraft* fame and the pair of them high Tory 'Anti-Jacobins') made great sport of the democrat Southey's experiments in dactylics:

> Wearisome Sonnetteer, feeble and querulous,
> Painfully dragging out thy democratic lays –
> Moon-stricken sonneteer, 'ah! for thy heavenly chance!'

> Sorely thy Dactylics lag on uneven feet:
> Slow is the syllable which thou would'st urge to speed,
> Lame and o'erburden'd, and 'screaming its wretchedness'.

They had a go at his Sapphic verse too:

> Needy Knife-grinder! whither are you going?
> Rough is the road, your wheel is out of order –
> Bleak blows the blast; your hat has got a hole in 't,
>   So have your breeches.

Byron was always savage at the expense of the 'Lakers'. It is fair to observe that he, silver-spoon nobleman as was, remained a true radical all his life, while both Southey and Wordsworth accepted the King's shilling and butt of malmsey as Poets Laureate, ending their lives as comfortable establishment grandees. Byron seemed to detect an air of fraudulence early on. Here is his parody of Wordsworth's 'Peter Bell'.

> There's something in a stupid ass:
> And something in a heavy dunce;
> But never since I went to school
> I saw or heard so damned a fool
> As William Wordsworth is for once.

They say the modern literary world is full of squabbling hatred and simmering resentments, but it is as nothing to the past.

The individuality and restless stressed energy of Hopkins makes him ripe for pastiche. Anthony Brode was inspired to write a perfect Hopkins parody after reading this on his cereal packet one morning: 'Delicious heart-of-the-corn, fresh-from-the-oven flakes are sparkled and spangled with sugar for a can't-be-resisted-flavour.'

> Parenthesis proud, bracket-bold, happiest with hyphens
>   The writers stagger intoxicated by terms, adjective-unsteadied –
>   Describing in graceless phrases fizzling like soda siphons
>   All things crisp, crunchy, malted, tangy, sugared and shredded.

Parodies are rife in popular culture, a staple of television comedy, but literary and verse parodies seem to have fallen from fashion, Wendy Cope being one of the few practising poets who plays happily and fruitfully with the style of other poets. Now it's your turn.

Poetry Exercise 17

I am sure you have a favourite poet. Write a parody of their style and prosodic manner. Try and make it comically inappropriate: if you like Ted Hughes, try writing a fearsome, physically tough description of a Barbie doll or something else very un-Hughesy. I know this is a bit of a *Spectator* Competition sort of exercise, but it is a good way of noticing all the metrical, rhyming and formal mannerisms of a poet. If you are really feeling bold, try writing a cento. You will need the collected works of the poet you choose, otherwise a cento mixing different verses from an anthology might be worth trying. Surprise yourself.

IX

Exotic Forms[15]

Haiku — senryu – tanka – ghazal – luc bat – tanaga

Haiku

Five seven and five:
Seventeen essential oils
For warm winter nights.

The HAIKU, as you may already know, is a three-line poem of Japanese origin whose lines are composed of five, seven and five syllables. There is much debate as to whether there is any purpose to be served in English-language versions of the form. Those who understand Japanese are strong in their insistence that haikus in our tongue are less than a pale shadow of the home-grown original. English, as a *stress*-timed language, cannot hope to reproduce the effects of *syllable*-timed Japanese. I define these terms (rather vaguely) in the section on Syllabic Verse in Chapter One.

Just so that you are aware, there is a great deal more to the haiku than mere syllable count. For one thing, it is considered *de rigueur* to include the season of the year, if not as crassly as mine does, then at least by some other reference to weather or atmosphere, what is known as a *kigo* word. A reverence for life and the natural world is another apparent sine qua non of the form, the aim being to provide a kind of aural, imagistic snapshot (a *shasei* or 'sketch of nature'). The senses should be engaged and verbs be kept to a minimum, if not expunged entirely. The general tenor and

15 I mean *exotic* in its original sense of 'from far away' not in the travel brochure sense.

thrust of the form (believe me, I am no expert) seems to be for the poet (*haijin*) to await a 'haiku moment', an epiphany or imaginative inspiration of some kind. The haiku is a distillation of such a moment. In their native land haikus are written in one line, which renders the idea of a 5–7–5 syllable count all the more questionable. They also contain many puns (*kakekotoba*), this not being considered a groan-worthy practice in Japanese. A caesura, or *kireji*, should be felt at the end of either the first or second 'line'.

Haiku descends from *haikai no renga*, a (playful) linked verse development of a shorter form called *waka*. The haikai's first stanza was called a *hokku* and when poets like Masaoka Shiki developed their new, stand-alone form in the nineteenth century, they yoked together the words *haikai* and *hokku* to make *haiku*. We now tend to backdate the term and call the short poems of seventeenth-century masters such as Matsuo Basho *haikus*, although they ought really to be called *hokkus*. Clear?

A haiku which does not include a *kigo* word and is more about *human* than *physical* nature is called a SENRYU which, confusingly, means 'river willow'.

Those who have studied the form properly and write them in English are now very unlikely to stick to the 5–7–5 framework. The Japanese *on* (sound unit) is very different from our syllable and most original examples contain far fewer words than their English equivalents. For some the whole enterprise is a doomed and fatuous mismatch, as misguided as eating the Sunday roast with chopsticks and calling it sushi. Nonetheless non-Japanese speakers of some renown have tried them. They seemed to have been especially appealing to the American beat poets, Ginsberg, Ferlinghetti, Corso and Kerouac, as well as to Spanish-language poets like Octavio Paz and Jorge Luis Borges. Here are a couple of Borges examples (it is possible that haikus in Spanish, which like Japanese is syllabically timed, work better than in English) – my literal translations do not obey the syllabic imperatives.

La vasta noche
no es ahora otra cosa
que una fragancia.

(The enormous night
is now nothing more
than a fragrance.)

Callan las cuerdas.
La música sabía
lo que yo siento.

(The strings are silent.
The music knew
What I was feeling.)

Borges also experimented with another *waka*-descended Japanese form, the TANKA (also known as *yamato uta*). I shall refrain from entering into the nuances of the form, which appear to be complex and unsettled – certainly as far as their use in English goes. The general view appears to be that they are five-line poems with a syllable count of 5, 7, 5, 7, 7. In Spanish, in the hands of Borges, they look like this:

La ajena copa,
La espada que fue espada
En otra mano,
La luna de la calle,
Dime, ¿acaso no bastan?

(Another's cup,
The sword which was a sword
In another's hand,
The moon in the street,
Say to me, 'Perhaps they are not enough.')

The form has recently grown in popularity, thanks in large part to the publication *American Tanka* and a proliferation of tanka sites on the Internet.

GHAZAL

The lines in GHAZAL always need to *run, IN PAIRS*.
They come, like mother-daughter, father-*son, IN PAIRS*

I'll change the subject, as this ancient form requires
It offers hours of simple, harmless *fun, IN PAIRS*.

Apparently a Persian form, from far-off days
It needs composing just as I have *done, IN PAIRS*

And when I think the poem's finished and complete
I STEPHEN FRY, pronounce my work is *un-IMPAIRED*.

My version is rather a bastardly abortion I fear, but the key principles are mostly adhered to. The lines of a GHAZAL (pronounced a bit like *guzzle*, but the 'g' should hiccup slightly, Arab-stylie) come in metrical couplets. The rhymes are unusual in that the *last phrase* of the opening two lines (and second lines of each subsequent couplet) is a refrain (*rhadif*), it is the word *before* the refrain that is rhymed, in the manner shown above. I have cheated with the last rhyme-refrain pairing as you can see. Each couplet should be a discrete (but not necessarily discreet) entity unto itself, no enjambment being permitted or overall theme being necessary. It is usual, but not obligatory, for the poet to 'sign his name' in the last line as I have done.

The growth in the form's popularity in English is largely due to its rediscovery by a generation of Pakistani and Indian poets keen to reclaim an ancient form with which they feel a natural kinship. As with the haiku, it may seem to some impertinent and inappropriate to try to wrench the form out of its natural context: like taking a Lancashire hotpot out of a tandoori oven and serving it as Asian food. I see nothing intrinsically wrong with such attempts at cultural cross-breeding, but I am no authority.

LUC BAT

LUC BAT is rather _cute_
It keeps the mind as**tute** and *pert*
It doesn't really *hurt*
To keep the mind al**ert**ly *keen*
You'll know just what I *mean*
When you have gone and **been** and *done*
Your own completed *one*
It's really rather *fun* to *do*
Full of subtlety *too*,
I hope that yours earn *you* re_pute_.

This is a Vietnamese form much easier to do than to describe. LUC BAT is based on a syllable count that alternates 6, 8, 6, 8, 6, 8 and so on until the poet comes to his final pair of 6, 8 lines (the overall length is not fixed). The sixth syllables rhyme in couplets like my *cute/astute* but the eight-syllable lines have a second rhyme (*pert* in my example), which rhymes with the sixth syllable of the next line, *hurt*. When you come to the final eight-syllable line, its eighth syllable rhymes with the first line of the poem (re*pute* back to *cute*). I don't expect you to understand it from that garbled explanation. Here is a scheme: maybe that will be easier to follow.

●●●●*a*   *cute*
●●●●*a*●*b*   *astute* and *pert*
●●●●*b*   *hurt*
●●●●*b*●*c*   *alert*ly *keen*

●●●●*c*	*mean*
●●●●*c*●*d*	*been* and *done*
●●●●*d*	*one*
●●●●*d*●*e*	*fun* to *do*
●●●●*e*	*too*
●●●●*e*●*a*	*you* re*pute*

Luc bat is the Vietnamese for 'six eight'. The form is commonly found as a medium for two-line riddles, rhyming as above.

Completely round and *white*
After baths they're *tight* together.

Milk inside, not a *yak*
Hairy too, this *snack* is fleshy

Plates and coconuts, in case you hadn't cracked them.[16] Proper poems in Vietnamese use a stress system divided into the two pleasingly named elements *bang* and *trac*, which I cannot begin to explain, since I cannot begin to understand them. Once more the Internet seems to have been responsible for raising this form, obscure outside its country of origin, to something like cult status. It has variations. SONG THAT LUC BAT (which literally means *two sevens*, *six-eight*, although it begs in English to have the word 'sang' after it, as in 'The Song That Luc Bat Sang') consists of a seven-syllable rhyming couplet, followed by sixes and eights that rhyme according to another scheme that I won't bother you with. I am sure you can search Vietnamese literature (or *van chuong bac hoc*) resources if you wish to know more.

---

16 *Cracked* them! Coconuts, you see. And china plates. Cracked them! Ho, ho. No but really, ho *ho*.

TANAGA

The TANAGA owes its genes
To forms from the Philippines.
To count all your words like beans
You may need adding machines.

The TANAGA is a short non-metric Filipino form, consisting of four seven-syllable lines rhyming *aaaa*, although modern English language tanagas allow *abab*, *aabb* and *abba*.[17] I am not aware of any masterpieces having yet been composed in our language. But there it is for your pleasure.

Poetry Exercise 18

Four haikus in the usual mongrel English form: one for each season, so do not forget your *kigo* word.

---

17 A manila envelope rhyme?

X

The Sonnet

PETRARCHAN AND SHAKESPEAREAN

I wrote a bad **PETRARCHAN SONNET** once,
   In two laborious weeks. A throttled stream
   Of words – sure following the proper scheme
Of Abba Abba – oh, but what a dunce
I was to think those yells and tortured grunts
    Could help me find an apt poetic theme.
  The more we try to think, the more we dream,
The more we whet our wit, the more it blunts.
But give that dreaming part of you release,
   Allow your thrashing conscious brain a break,
Let howling tom become a purring kitten
   And civil war dissolves to inward peace;
A thousand possibilities awake,
    And suddenly your precious sonnet's written.

The sonnet's fourteen lines have called to poets for almost a thousand years. It is the Goldilocks form: when others seem too long, too short, too intricate, too shapeless, too heavy, too light, too simple or too demanding the sonnet is always just right. It has the compactness to contain a single thought and feeling, but space enough for narrative, development and change.

The sonnet was, they say, invented in the thirteenth century by Giacomo da Lentini in the Sicilian court of the Holy Roman Emperor Frederick II. Dante and d'Arezzo and others experimented with it, but it was Francesco Petrarca, *Petrarch*, who shaped it into the form which was to have so tremendous an impact on European and English poetry. In the papal court of Avignon he composed his cycle of sonnets to Laura, a girl he always claimed was flesh and blood, but whom many believed to be a conjured ideal. His sonnets made their way over to god-fearing medieval England and lay there like gleaming alien technology: dazzling in their sophistication, knowledge, mastery and promise, frightening in their freedom, daring and originality.

Chaucer knew of them and admired them but their humanism, their promotion of personal feeling and open enquiry, the vigour and self-assertion of their individual voice would have made any attempt on his part to write such works, if indeed he had that desire, a kind of heresy or treason. We had to wait two hundred years for the warm winds of the Renaissance truly to cross the channel and thaw us out of our monkish and feudal inertia. In the hundred and twenty or so years between the Reformation and the Restoration the sonnet had, like some exotic plant, been grafted, grown, hothoused and hybridised into a flourishing new native stock, crossbred to suit the particular winds and weather of our emotional and intellectual climate. This breeding began under Wyatt and Surrey, great pioneers in many areas of English verse, and was carried on by Sidney, Shakespeare, Drummond, Drayton, Donne, Herbert and Milton. The next century saw an equally rapid decline: it is hard to think of a single sonnet being written between the death of Milton in the 1670s and the publication of Wordsworth's first sonnets a hundred and thirty years later. Just as Wren and the Great Fire between them redesigned half-timbered, higgledy-piggledy Tudor London into a metropolis of elegant neoclassical squares and streets, so Dryden, Johnson and Pope preferred to address the world from a Palladian balcony, the dignified, harmonious grandeur of the heroic couplet replacing what they saw as the vulgar egoism of the lowly sonnet and its unedifying emotional wrestling matches. Those very personal qualities of the sonnet were precisely what attracted Wordsworth and the romantic poets of course, and from their day to ours it has remained a popular verse forum for a poet's debate with himself.

The structure of the PETRARCHAN SONNET, preferred and

adapted by Donne, Milton and many others, is easily expressed. The first eight lines *abba-abba* are called the OCTAVE, the following six lines *cdecde* (or *cddccd* or *cdccdc*) the SESTET.

The ninth line, the beginning of the sestet, marks what is called the VOLTA, the turn. This is the moment when a contrary point of view, a doubt or a denial, is often expressed. It is the sonnet's pivot or fulcrum. In mine at the top of this section the ninth line begins with 'But', a rather obvious way of marking that moment (although you may recall Donne uses the same word in his 'At the round earth's imagined corners' cited in Chapter Two). In Wordsworth's 'The world is too much with us' below, the volta comes in the middle of the ninth line, at the 'en dash': it is precisely here, after 'It moves us not' that, overlooking the sea, having pondered the rush of the modern Christian world in its commerce and crassness and its blindness to nature, Wordsworth as it were draws breath and makes his point: he would rather be a pagan for whom at least nature had life and energy and meaning. A volta can be called a *crisis*, in its literal Greek sense of 'turning point' as well as sometimes bearing all the connotations we now place upon the word.

The world is too much with us; late and soon,
    Getting and spending, we lay waste our powers:
    Little we see in Nature that is ours;
We have given our hearts away, a sordid boon!
The Sea that bares her bosom to the moon;
    The winds that will be howling at all hours,
    And are up-gathered now like sleeping flowers;
For this, for everything, we are out of tune;
It moves us not. – Great God! I'd rather be
    A Pagan suckled in a creed outworn;
So might I, standing on this pleasant lea,
    Have glimpses that would make me less forlorn;
Have sight of Proteus rising from the sea;
    Or hear old Triton blow his wreathèd horn.

Within the Petrarchan form's basic octave–sestet structure there are other sub-divisions possible. Two groups of four and two of three are natural, two quatrains and two tercets if you prefer.

Here now is Shakespeare's twenty-ninth Sonnet.

When, in disgrace with Fortune and men's eyes,
I all alone beweep my outcast state,
And trouble deaf heaven with my bootless cries,
And look upon myself and curse my fate,
Wishing me like to one more rich in hope,
Featured like him, like him with friends possessed,
Desiring this man's art, and that man's scope,
With what I most enjoy contented least;
Yet in these thoughts myself almost despising,
Haply I think on thee, and then my state,
Like to the lark at break of day arising
From sullen earth, sings hymns at heaven's gate;
For thy sweet love remembered such wealth brings,
That then I scorn to change my state with kings.

This contains one of the strongest voltas imaginable: it arrives in the breath between *Haply* and *I think of thee* in line 10, pivoting from the very first word of the sonnet, *When*. The whole first part of the poem is a vast conditional clause awaiting the *critical* turn. But the difference in rhyme-scheme and lack of octave and sestet structure will already have shown you that, volta or no volta, this is far from a Petrarchan sonnet.

For the Tudor poets one of the disadvantages of the Petrarchan form was that *abba abba* requires two sets of four rhyming words. While this is a breeze in Italian where every other word seems to end *-ino* or *-ella*, it can be the very deuce in English. Drayton, Daniel and Sidney radically reshaped the rhyme-scheme, using a new structure of *abab cdcd efef gg*. This arrangement reached unimaginable heights in the hands of Shakespeare, after whom it is named. His great sonnets stand with Beethoven's piano sonatas as supreme expressions of the individual human voice using and fighting the benign tyranny of form, employing form itself as a metaphor for fate and the external world. Sonata and sonnet share the same etymology, as it happens – 'little sound'. Little sounds that make a great noise.

The SHAKESPEAREAN SONNET offers, aside from less troublesome rhyming searches, twelve lines in its main body, three quatrains or two sestets and a couplet and other permutations thereof – twelve is a very factorable number. The cross-rhyming removes the characteristic nested sequence of envelope rhyming found in the Petrarchan form (*bb* inside *aa* and the following *aa* inside *bb*) but the reward is a new freedom and the creation of a more natural debating chamber.

For this is primarily what the Shakespearean sonnet suits so well, interior debate. I have mentioned before the three-part structure that seems so primal a part of human thinking. From the thesis, antithesis, synthesis of the earliest logicians, the propositions, suppositions and proofs of Euclid and the strophe, antistrophe and epode of Greek performance and poetic ode to our own parliaments and senate chambers, boardrooms, courtrooms and committee rooms, this structure of proposal, counterproposal and vote, prosecution, defence and verdict is deep within us. It is how we seem best to frame the contrary flows of thought and feeling that would otherwise freeze us into inaction or propel us into civil war or schizophrenic uncertainty. The sonnet shares with the musical sonata a rhetorical fitness for presentation, exploration and return. While the Petrarchan sonnet's two divisions separated by a strong volta suit a proposition and a conclusion, the nature of the Shakespearean form allows of three quatrains with a final judgemental summing up in the trademark final couplet. Do bear in mind when I talk of a 'dialectical structure' that the sonnet is, of course, a poetic form, not a philosophical – I oversimplify to draw attention to the internal movement it offers. Clearly a closing couplet can often seem glib and trite. The romantics preferred the

Petrarchan sonnet's more unified scheme, finding the Shakespearean structure of seven rhyme pairs harsh and infelicitously fractured compared to the Petrarchan's three.

In modern times the sonnet has undergone a remarkable second English-language renaissance. After its notable health under Elizabeth Barrett Browning (*Sonnets from the Portuguese*) and Hopkins ('The Windhover', 'All Nature is a Heraclitean Fire'), Daryush wrote some syllabic sonnets ('I saw the daughter of the sun' is very fine) and the form was 'rediscovered' by Auden, Berryman, Cummings, Edna St Vincent Millais, Elizabeth Bishop, Carol Ann Duffy and many others, including Seamus Heaney whose superb sonnets in *The Haw Lantern* are well worth exploring. In this century it is more popular than ever: you will find one written every minute on the profusion of websites devoted to it.

SONNET VARIATIONS AND ROMANTIC DUELS

There are as many arguments about what constitutes a sonnet as there are arguments about any field of human activity. There are those who will claim that well-known examples like Shelley's 'Ozymandias' are anamorphic, not true sonnets but types of *quatorzain*, which is just another way of saying 'fourteen-line poem'. This is an argument we need not enter. There are those who recognise poems of less than fourteen lines as being CURTAL SONNETS (Hopkins's 'Pied Beauty' reproduced in full in Chapter One being an example and perhaps Yeats's 'The Fascination of What's Difficult' is another).

There is also a seventeen-line variant. These are called CAUDATE SONNETS (from the Latin for 'tail', same root as 'coda') which feature a three-line envoi or *cauda*. The convention here is for the first line of the cauda to be trimetric and to rhyme with the last line of the main body of the sonnet, and for the next two lines to be in the form of a rhyming couplet in iambic pentameter. Milton's sonnet 'On the New Forcers of Conscience Under the Long Parliament' is an example: here are its final couplet and cauda, with line numbers, just so that you are clear:

> May with their wholesome and preventative shears   13
> Clip your phylacteries,[18] though baulk your ears,   14
>   And succor our just fears,   15
> When they shall read this clearly in your charge: 16
> New *Presbyter* is but old *Priest* writ large.   17

Those last two words, of course, *writ large*, have entered the language.

In the nineteenth century the poet and novelist George Meredith developed a form of sixteen line sonnet with four sets of envelope rhymes *abba cddc effe ghhg*.

There are traditions in the writing of SONNET SEQUENCES, such as Elizabeth Barrett Browning's forty-four *Sonnets from the Portuguese* and Meredith's sequence 'Modern Love' (in his own Meredithian sixteen-line form). Christina Rossetti's *Monna Innominata*, being a sequence of fourteen sonnets, is known as a SONNET OF SONNETS. More complex sequences exist, such as one of indeterminate length in which each new sonnet opens with the last line of the previous until you reach the final sonnet which terminates with the opening line of the first. This is called a CORONA SEQUENCE. John Donne wrote such a sequence in seven sonnets, called 'La Corona'. More complex variations on that include the SONNET REDOUBLÉ, a corona sequence of fourteen sonnets terminating with a fifteenth which is wholly composed of each linking line of the corona in sequence. If there is no good reason for such complexity it will look like showing off, I feel.

---

18 Jewish readers may wonder why Milton is writing about the *tefillin*: 'phylacteries' here actually refer to religious trinkets used by Presbyterians, whose intolerance the sonnet attacks. *Presbyterians*, as you may know although Milton probably did not, is an anagram of *Britney Spears*.

Donne's corona had a purposeful religious structure, to make a crown of poetry to match Christ's crown of thorns.

There are two very well-known examples of SONNET COMPETITIONS which reveal, among other things, the form's special place in poetry. The ability to write them fluently was, and to some extent still is, considered the true mark of the poet.

On the evening of 30 December 1816, John Keats and his friend Leigh Hunt challenged each other to write a sonnet on the subject of 'The Grasshopper and the Cricket'. Legend has it that they each took just fifteen minutes to write the following. I shall not tell you straight away who wrote which. All I ask is that you decide which you prefer:

1

Green little vaulter in the sunny grass,
Catching your heart up at the feel of June,
Sole voice that's heard amidst the lazy noon,
When even the bees lag at the summoning brass;
And you, warm little housekeeper, who class
With those who think the candles come too soon,
Loving the fire, and with your tricksome tune
Nick the glad silent moments as they pass;
Oh sweet and tiny cousins, that belong
One to the fields, the other to the hearth,
Both have your sunshine; both, though small, are strong
At your clear hearts; and both were sent on earth
To sing in thoughtful ears this natural song:
Indoors and out, summer and winter, – Mirth.

2

The poetry of earth is never dead:
When all the birds are faint with the hot sun,
And hide in cooling trees, a voice will run
From hedge to hedge about the new-mown mead;

That is the Grasshopper's – he takes the lead
In summer luxury, – he has never done
With his delights; for when tired out with fun
He rests at ease beneath some pleasant weed.
The poetry of earth is ceasing never:
On a lone winter evening, when the frost
Has wrought a silence, from the stove there shrills
The Cricket's song, in warmth increasing ever,
And seems to one in drowsiness half lost,
The Grasshopper's among some grassy hills.

Our second two sonnets share the subject of an inscription on the
great statue of Rameses II (Greek name Ozymandias): one is by
Percy Byssche Shelley and the other by his friend Horace Smith.
Shelley's is more than a little well known, but which 'Ozymandias'
do you like best?

1

I met a traveller from an antique land,
Who said – 'two vast and trunkless legs of stone
Stand in the desert . . . near them, on the sand,
Half sunk a shattered visage lies, whose frown,
And wrinkled lips, and sneer of cold command,
Tell that its sculptor well those passions read
Which yet survive, stamped on these lifeless things,
The hand that mocked them, and the heart that fed;
And on the pedestal these words appear:
"My name is Ozymandias, King of Kings,
Look on my works ye Mighty, and despair!"
Nothing beside remains. Round the decay
Of that colossal Wreck, boundless and bare
The lone and level sands stretch far away.'

2

In Egypt's sandy silence, all alone,
Stands a gigantic Leg, which far off throws
The only shadow that the Desert knows: –
'I am great OZYMANDIAS,' saith the stone,
'The King of Kings; this mighty City shows
The wonders of my hand.' – The City's gone, –
Naught but the Leg remaining to disclose
The site of this forgotten Babylon.
We wonder, – and some Hunter may express
Wonder like ours, when thro' the wilderness
Where London stood, holding the Wolf in chase,
He meets some fragments huge, and stops to guess
What powerful but unrecorded race
Once dwelt in that annihilated place.

Of 'The Grasshopper and the Cricket' pair, the first is by Leigh Hunt and the second by Keats. In a recent Internet poll (for what it is worth) seventy-five per cent preferred the Leigh Hunt and only a quarter went for the Keats. As a matter of fact Keats would have agreed with them; he thought Leigh Hunt's clearly the superior poem. One the other hand, 'The poetry of earth is never dead' is one of the finest opening lines imaginable. If you have read Keats before, 'one in drowsiness half lost' would be a dead giveaway as to authorship. Leigh Hunt's sonnet scores, we feel, as a whole poem; even if it doesn't contain such moments of perfect music, the progression of ideas (which is so much of what a sonnet is there to exhibit) seems clearer and more satisfactory. They are both Petrarchan, and both have clear voltas at the beginning of their ninth lines. The Leigh Hunt sestet rhymes *cdcdcd*, while Keats sticks to the more traditional *cdecde*.

Of the next pair, Shelley's is the first, Smith's second, as I'm sure you guessed even if you didn't already know. They were both published in *The Examiner* in 1818 and are both entitled

'Ozymandias'. They each, as you can see, tell the same story – the opening descriptions being, in their basic outlines, identical. There all similarity ends. There is something dreadfully comic about 'In Egypt's sandy silence, all alone,/Stands a gigantic Leg . . .'. If Shelley's sonnet outlasts even the ancient monument it commemorates, Smith's will be fortunate to endure as a curiosity. His is not a *terrible* poem, but immensely ordinary by comparison. Perhaps you disagree? Shelley and Smith, as you may have noticed if you have been a good and attentive girl or a boy, have both dreamt up their own rhyme schemes.

Whether you choose to write Petrarchan or Shakespearean sonnets in blank, full or slant-rhyme, or adapt or reinvent as many poets have, the form is there for you to explore. I find it hard to imagine anyone calling themselves a poet who has not at least experimented with the sonnet and, like Wordsworth, found –

> In sundry moods, 'twas pastime to be bound
> Within the Sonnet's scanty plot of ground;
> Pleased if some Souls (for such there needs must be)
> Who have felt the weight of too much liberty,
> Should find brief solace there, as I have found.

So now it is your turn.

Poetry Exercise 19

♦ Write a Petrarchan Sonnet on *Electoral Apathy*. Use the octave to complain about how lazy and uninterested voters are and then, at the volta, decide that apathy is probably the best response.

♦ Now write a Shakespearean Sonnet on exactly the same subject. Use the first four lines for a description of apathy, the second four for a complaint against it, the third for an admission of your own apathy and then, in the final couplet express the concluding thought that, what the hell, it makes no difference anyway.

If you don't like this subject, do write your own sonnet anyway. I think it would be a big mistake to leave this chapter without having tried to write at least one of each major form.

XI

Shaped Verse

Pattern poems — concrete poetry: a few words concerning Imagism — gamesome forms — rictameter, rhopalics, lipograms — silly syllabic forms — tetractys and nonet — acrostics and more

PATTERN POEMS

the
QUEEN
can do
almost
what
ever
she
wishes
up down
side to side
the world is hers

but

a
small
PAWN
gets
the
chance
to be a king

The idea of shaping your poem on the page to make a picture, symbol or pattern is a very old one. The best-known example in English verse is George Herbert's 'Easter Wings' which, rotated ninety degrees, takes on the shape of two angels' wings:

Lord, who createdst man in wealth and store
Though foolishly he lost the same,
Decaying more and more
Till he became
Most poore:

With Thee
O let me rise
As larks, harmoniously,
And sing this day thy victories:
Then shall the fall further the flight in me.

My tender age in sorrow did beginne;
And still with wickedness and shame
Thou didst so punish sinne,
That I became
Most thin.

With Thee
Let me combine
And feel this day thy victorie;
For, if I imp my wing on thine,
Affliction shall advance the flight in me.

Another of Herbert's pattern poems, 'The Altar', reveals the shape of its title, an altar table.

When I was small I remember endlessly looking through my parents' copy of the collected poems of e e cummings and being fascinated and appalled by the things he did with punctuation, his blithe disregard for majuscules and spaces and the general appearance of childish illiteracy his work presented. My teachers, I felt, would never allow me to get away with such liberties and yet there he was, sharing shelf-space with Robert Browning and John Keats. The collection included this poem; I found the slippage of the 'l' from 'loneliness' unbearably sad.

```
                    1(a

                    le
                    af
                    fa
                    ll

                    s)
                    one
                    l

                  iness
```

It is, incidentally, the only poem I know of whose title contains all
the words of the poem: *1(a . . . (a leaf falls on loneliness),* yet of course
the poem is not the words, it is the sum of the words *and* their layout, a truth in all poetry but one most obviously declared in this
kind of patterned or shaped verse. cummings was a Cubist painter
as well as a poet: 'The symbol of all art is the Prism,' he wrote. 'The
goal is unrealism. The method is destructive. To break up the white
light of objective realism into the secret glories which it contains.'
I am not sure how one would categorise such a work as the famous
'r-p-o-p-h-e-s-s-a-g-r':

```
r-p-o-p-h-e-s-s-a-g-r
who
a)s w(e loo)k
upnowgath
PPEGORHRASS
eringint(o-
aThe):l
eA
!p:
S            a
(r
rIvInG .gRrEaPsPhOs)
to
rea(be)rran(com)gi(e)ngly
,grasshopper;
```

Unscrambled, the words reveal 'the grasshopper, who, as we look now upgathering into [himself], leaps, arriving to become, rear-rangingly, a grasshopper'. Those may be the words, but the poem attempts to embody the movement, complexity, camouflage, wind-up and release, the whole *whatness* of a grasshopper's leap. It is not meant visually to imitate the appearance of a grasshopper on the page, rather to force the reader to slow down and look and feel and think and unpick all the dynamics of a grasshopper's launch and spring. A conventional poem can use words and all their qualities descriptively and sonorously, a painting can freeze a moment in time, a sculpture can imitate texture, density and mass, music can reproduce sound and shape, but what cummings has done is to cre-ate a mechanism whose moving parts are operated by the reader in the act of reading. A verbal sculpture, if you like, containing a potential energy which releases its kinetic force only at the moment of the reader's engagement. Some of you may find this either a pre-tentious game or a stultifying dead end. I am sorry if this is so. I would agree, however, that as with much modern conceptual art the very specificity of the work's originality allows little opportu-nity for development by others. cummings has had that idea, it is now ticked off in the box of high concepts and anything else in that line would look like cheap imitation. This is what separates such works from *forms*. The sonnet and the villanelle are certainly not played out, such poetic self-release mechanisms probably are.

I suppose 'r-p-o-p-h-e-s-s-a-g-r' qualifies as CONCRETE POETRY, a term that came out of a movement in São Paolo in the 1950s. Its manifesto states that

> the old formal syllogistic-discursive foundation, strongly
> shaken at the beginning of the century, has served again as a
> prop for the ruins of a compromised poetic, an anachronistic
> hybrid with an atomic heart and a medieval cuirass.[19]

19 The full manifesto can be read at:
   http://www2.uol.com.br/augustodecampos/concretepoet.htm

So there. Ezra Pound and the Imagists were concrete poets *avant la lettre*: Pound was influenced by the writings of T. E. Hulme and by Ernest Fenollosa's pioneering work, *The Chinese Written Character as a Medium for Poetry*. Pound (Fenollosa's literary executor) found himself inspired by the idea that the Chinese ideogram, rather than displaying its meaning *syntagmatically* (rolling it out phonetically and phonemically in sequence as this sentence does) actually *contained* meaning, held it in one visual unit. This tallied with Hulme's idea of reality being *process*. 'There are no nouns in the universe,' he had declared, 'only verbs.' The upshot of this – and academics will forgive my blithe generalities – was to attempt poems that were kinds of ideogram. The best-known example is 'In a Station of the Metro' written in 1911:

> The apparition   of these faces   in the crowd   :
> Petals   on a wet, black   bough   .

Pound went into some detail concerning the composition of this poem in an influential article called 'Vorticism'. He had been overwhelmingly moved by the sight of a succession of beautiful women and children on the Paris Metro, 'and I could not find any words that seemed to me worthy, or as lovely as that sudden emotion,' he wrote, until

> ... that evening, as I went home along the Rue Raynouard,
> I was still trying, and I found, suddenly, the expression. I do
> not mean that I found words, but there came an equation ...
> not in speech, but in little spotches of colour. It was just that
> – a 'pattern', or hardly a pattern, if by 'pattern' you mean
> something with a 'repeat' in it. But it was a word, the
> beginning, for me, of a language in colour. ... I dare say it is
> meaningless unless one has drifted into a certain vein of
> thought. In a poem of this sort one is trying to record the
> precise instant when a thing outward and objective
> transforms itself, or darts into a thing inward and subjective.

The new poetics suggested by Pound's thoughts on colour, image, quiddity and ideogram engendered a new kind of 'iconographic' poetry which culminated in his cantos, most especially *The Pisan Cantos*, notable for their use of hieroglyphs and ideograms and, so far as most of us are concerned, their almost total unreadability. There is huge gusto and bravado in their best moments, but much to make the reader feel foolish and unlettered.

I am not here to attempt a history lesson, nor am I qualified to do so, but I mention all of this as a background to the concepts that have propelled much modern poetry, most of these ideas being osmotically absorbed by succeeding generations of course, not acquired intellectually: but that holds true of our grasp of, for example, gravity, evolution, the subconscious mind and genetics. Our understanding of much in the world is more poetic than noetic. We let others do the work and take their half-understood ideas for a ride, all unaware of the cognitive principles that gave birth to them. That those principles and their corollaries would have shocked and perplexed us had we lived in other times is interesting but irrelevant for our purposes. You do not have to understand Faraday's and Maxwell's electromagnetic theories of light to operate a light switch, or even to become a professional lighting designer.

The upshot of Imagism, Vorticism, Cubism, Neo-Plasticism, Constructivism, Acmeism, Futurism, Dadaism and all the other -isms that flooded art in the twentieth century was to allow a new kind of poetry, of which concrete poetry is one, the work of cummings another. Such practices now inform the works of thousands of poets around the globe. Since, unlike traditional metrical poetry, they descend from conscious ideas rather than techniques evolved (by way of music and dance) out of the collective unconscious of three millennia, their genesis did seem worth a small excursion.

The point that seems to me most relevant is the notion of *quiddity* or whatness. I mentioned this when we were looking at Gerard Manley Hopkins, who had been deeply influenced by the medieval theologian Duns Scotus and his concept of *haecceity*, or *thisness*. Novels can develop stories and character and much else besides, but poetry uniquely gives itself the opportunity to enter the absolute truth of a phenomenon (whether it be a feeling, an object, a person, a process, an idea or a moment) through language itself. How many times will you, as poet, look at a fly, watch a tap dripping, examine an inner feeling, listen to the wind and grow immensely frustrated at the inability of language exactly to capture it, to *become* it? All the stock phrases and clichés enter your frantic mind, all the footling onomatopoeia, rhymes and rhythmic patterns that we have heard before and none of them will do. Painters, too, look from their subject to the tip of their paintbrush and their palette of paints and despair.

That's not it at all, that's not what I meant at all.

So poor J. Alfred Prufrock whines, and so do we.

Aside from Pound, the works of H. D. (Hilda) Doolittle are perhaps the purest conscious attempt to adhere to the imagist project: here is her 'Sea Poppies':

> your stalk has caught root
> among wet pebbles
> and drift flung by the sea
> and grated shells
> and split conch-shells.

> Beautiful, wide-spread,
> fire upon leaf,
> what meadow yields
> so fragrant a leaf

It fascinates me that a medievalist like Hopkins and a modernist like Doolittle could both arrive at so similar a poetic destination from such utterly opposing points of origin. Doolittle's technique and effect are wildly different from those of Hopkins, of course, but I am sure you can feel the same striving to enter the identity of experience.

SILLY, SILLY FORMS

Enough, already. There are ludic and ludicrous forms, a world away from ideology and ideogram, which play on syllable length, shape and pattern, some of them bafflingly specific. What is the point of RICTAMETERS, one is forced to wonder? They are poems in the shape of a diamond.

```
                              im
            it              sweet
  ice      forms         enough to
they call  slowly in     give you ice never
them – rocks  all the rubbish  drop it on the floor
million-year-old  of the forest  of the forest for
crystals made  floor and     time to re-
of carbon     thus          claim
   but         if            it
```

In stricter versions (as if there is any reason to be strict about so childish a form. I mean *ferrankly* . . .) the diamond is structured by a syllable count of 2, 4, 6, 8, 10, 8, 6, 4, 2. A variation is the DIAMANTE where the purpose, as in some absurd weekend puzzle magazine, is to go from one object or phenomenon to an opposite or complementary one, by way of a succession of related words.

wolf

grey shaggy

slavering howling ripping

violent hunter innocent quarry

frisking grazing bleating

white woolly

lamb

The 'rule' is that the second line is composed of related adjectives and the third of related *participles*; the first two words of the middle line are nouns or nominal phrases connected to the top of the diamond, the next pair connect to the bottom. You then repeat the process symmetrically down to your end-word. The whole thing is daffy and hardly qualifies as a form for poetry, but I include it anyway. Something to do on long train journeys.

Another bizarre form, bizarrely popular if the Internet is anything to go by, is to be found in RHOPALICS. A rhopalic line is one in which each successive word has one more syllable than its predecessor. *This sentence cleverly exemplifies rhopalicism.* There are variations, like increasing each word in a line letter by letter (*I am not sure about trying variant rhopalics*) and decreasing rather than increasing the count (*stultifying staggering tediously complete bloody waste, fuck off* . . .). Or there is this kind of thing:

My feelings and emotions
In their restless motions
Seethe and swell like oceans
Of the kind a Stoic shuns,
Better find some calmer 'uns

The dwindling but aurally congruent rhyme-returns yielded from *emotions, motions, oceans, shuns* and *'uns* constitute DIMINISHING RHYME, which may seem arid and futile, but George Herbert, the deeply religious and verbally playful poet whose 'Easter Wings' we have seen, used them with great seriousness in his poem 'Paradise':

I bless Thee, Lord, because I grow
Among the trees, which in a row
To Thee both fruit and order ow.

Certain other pointless forms demand a prescribed diminishing or ascending syllable count. The TETRACTYS asks the poet to produce five lines of 1, 2, 3, 4 and 10 syllables. Where's the *tetra* in that, for heaven's sake, you may be wondering. I believe it may be to do with a 'mystic tetrad' in Pythagoreanism and kabbalism and some arse-dribble or other connected to Tarot card layout and the four elements. 1+2+3+4=10 is the sum on which Ray Stebbing, the form's inventor, based the poetic tetractys. No doubt he meant well by it. Tetractys, appropriately enough, is pronounced to rhyme with *wet practice*.

Those

who choose

to compose

tetractyses

are welcome to them, far as I'm concerned

and I really cannot see the virtue

in flipping them:

too heavy

on top

no?

Mr Stebbing is a serious and accomplished poet, and if he believes his form to be the new native haiku then I wish him well. An even arsier form is the NONET:

death
to those
who compose
such wastes of breath
they have no graces
at least in my poor eyes
they suggest useless traces
of ancient forms more pure and wise
when people start to count, true verse dies.

The syllabic count starts at one and increases until it reaches nine. Mine, in desperation, rhymes. Syllabics? Silly bollocks, more like.

ACROSTICS

ACROSTICS have been popular for years; nineteenth-century
children produced them instead of watching television – those who
were lucky enough not to be sent down chimneys or kidnapped by
gangs of pickpockets did, anyway.

> So you want a dedication then?
> For you I'll do my very best
> Read the letters downwards, darling, then
> You'll see I've passed your little test.

What is going on below, you might wonder?

> age is a
> real bugger
> so few years
> ending up white
> wrinkled weak as straw
> incontinence comes and i
> piss myself in every way – stop
> eternity's too short too short a time

That is a DOUBLE ACROSTIC, both the *first* and *last* letters of each
line spell out the same defiance and physical disgust. I haven't
highlighted the letters; you can trace them down yourself. In case
you are wondering, I have not reached that stage yet – it is an
imaginative leap, we are allowed those from time to time: all
functions working smoothly last time I checked. You could in
theory spell words down from the middle of a line – this is called
a *mesostich* and is just plain silly.

The French seem to be the people most interested in acrostics
and other poetic wordplay. Salomon Certon wrote a whole sonnet
omitting the letter 'e': this is known as a LIPOGRAM. *Not* the same
root as liposuction, as it happens, despite the apparent similarity of

meaning. These days, you might feel, a poem that never uses an 'I' would be a real achievement . . .

PARONOMASIA is a grand word for 'pun': Thomas Hood, whose rich rhyme effusion you have read, was famous for these: 'He went and told the sexton and the sexton tolled the bell,' that kind of thing.

Keats slips most of the name of his hero into a line in the poem Endymion: this is known as a PARAGRAM:

> . . . I
>
> Will trace the story of Endymion.
> The very music of the name has gone

There are those who loathe puns, anagrams and wordplay of any description. They regard practitioners as trivial, posey, feeble, nerdy and facetious. As one such practitioner, I do understand the objections. Archness, cuteness, pedantry and showoffiness do constitute dangers. However, as a non-singing, non-games-playing, -dancing, -painting, -diving, -running, -catching, -kicking, -riding, -skating, -skiing, -sailing, -climbing, -caving, -swimming, -free-falling, -cycling, -canoeing, -jumping, -bouncing, -boxing sort of person, words are all I have. As the old cliché has it, they are my *friends*. I like to say them, weigh them, poke them, tease them, chant their sound, gaze at their shape and savour their juiciness, and, yes, play with them. Some words are made up of the same letters as others, some can fit inside others, some can be said the same backwards as frontwards, some rhyme outrageously, some seem unique and peculiar like *yacht* and *quirk* and *frump* and *canoodle*. I take pleasure in their oddities and pleasures and contradictions. It amuses me that a *cowboy* is a boy who rounds up cows, but a *carboy* is a flagon of acid, that *conifer* is an anagram of *fir cone* and *esoteric* of *coteries*, that *gold* has a hundred rhymes but *silver* has none.[20] It saddens me that the French talk of the *jouissance* of language, its joyousness, juiciness, ecstasy and bliss, but that we of all peoples, with English as our mother tongue, do not. Such frolicsome larkiness may put you off, but if you wish to make poems it seems to me necessary that some part of your verse, however small, will register the sensuousness, oddity and pleasure of words themselves, as words, regardless of their semantic and communicatory duties. Not all paintings draw attention to their brushwork – art can, of course, as validly make transparent its process as exhibit its presence – but each tradition has value and none represents the only true aesthetic.

In fact, I shall start the final chapter with an exploration of the idea that there are no limits to the depth of commitment to language that a poet can have. Not before you have completed . . .

Poetry Exercise 20

Write *one* PATTERN POEM in the shape of a cross, and *another* in the shape of a big capital 'I' (for ego) (obviously it should be a Roman I with serifs, otherwise it would just be a block of verse). Make the words relevant to their shape. When you have finished that, write a rhyming ACROSTIC VERSE spelling either your surname or forename.

---

20 Save the rich-rhyme *sylva* of course . . .

CHAPTER FOUR

Diction and Poetics Today

I

How I learned to love poetry – two stories – diction

The Whale, the Cat and Madeline

I was fortunate in my own introduction to poetry. My mother had, and still has, a mind packed with lines of verse. She could recite, like many of her generation but with more perfect recall than most, all the usual nursery rhymes along with most of A. A. Milne, Beatrix Potter, Lewis Carroll, *Struwwelpeter*, Eleanor Farjeon and other hardy annuals from the garden of English verse. This standard childhood repertoire somehow slid, without me noticing and without any didactic literary purpose, into bedtime recitations, readings or merry snatches of Belloc, Chesterton, Wordsworth, Tennyson and Browning. Then one birthday a godfather gave me *Palgrave's Golden Treasury*. This solid, Empire-made anthology (published in 1861, the same year as *Mrs Beeton's Household Management* and regarded by some as its verse equivalent) had been updated by the then Poet Laureate, Cecil Day Lewis, and included works by Betjeman, Auden and Laurie Lee, but its greatest emphasis was still on the lyrical and the romantic. That year I won the first and only school prize of my life, an edition of the *Collected Poems* of John Keats. In this I found a line, just one line, that finished the job my mother started and made me for ever a true slave to poetry. I will come to it in a minute, but first, a story about Keats himself and then an instance of poetry in motion.

THE WHALE

When Keats was a teenager (so the story goes), he came across a line from Spenser's *Faerie Queen*. Not even a line, actually: a phrase:

> . . . the sea-shouldering whale.

Some versions of the story maintain that Keats burst into tears when he read this. He had never known before what poetic language could *do*. He had no idea it was capable of making images spring so completely to life. In an instant he was able to see, hear and feel the roar, the plunging, the spray, the great mass and slow colossal upheaving energy of a whale, all from two words yoked together: 'sea' and 'shouldering'. From that moment on Keats *got* poetry. He began to understand the power that words could convey and the metaphorical daring with which a poet could treat them. We might say now that it was as if he had grasped their atomic nature, how with the right manipulation, and in the right combinations, words can release unimaginable energy. If not nuclear physics, then perhaps a living *magick*, whose verbal incantations conjure and summon a live thing out of thin air. Duke Theseus in *A Midsummer Night's Dream* put it this way:

> And, as imagination bodies forth
> The forms of things unknown, the poet's pen
> Turns them to shapes, and gives to airy nothing
> A local habitation and a name.

For Keats the grand plan of *The Faerie Queen*, its narrative, its religious, metaphysical, political and philosophical allegory and high epic seriousness dwindled to nothing in comparison with the poetic act as realised in two words. He 'would dwell in ecstasy' on the phrase, his friend Charles Cowden Clarke wrote later. This may sound rather extreme – there goes another typically high-strung nancy-boy poet in a loose neckcloth, swooning at a phrase – but I think the story goes to the heart of poetry's fundamental nature. I am sure there must have been moments like this for painters struck, not by the composition and grand themes of a masterpiece, but by one brush stroke, one extraordinary solution to the problem of transmitting truth by applying pigment to canvas. Poetry is constructed by the conjoining of words, one next to the other. Not every instance of poetic language will yield so rich an epiphany as Spenser's did for Keats – there are muddy backgrounds in poems as in paintings – and poetry can never hope to rival the essay, the novel or a philosophical treatise when it comes to imparting thought, story and abstract truths, but it can make words live in a most particular way, it can achieve things like 'the sea-shouldering whale'. You may not think it the finest poetic phrase ever wrought, but it unlocked poetry for the young Keats. Most of us have an inexplicably best-loved film or book that opened our eyes to the power of cinema and literature, and these favourites may not necessarily be part of the canon of Great Cinema or Great Literature, they just happened to be the ones that were there when we were ready for them. First Love comes when it comes and often we are hard put to explain later just why such and such a person was the object of our ardent youthful adoration when photographs now reveal just how plain they really were.

The Cat and the Act

Let me give you another example, this time it is from a poem by Ted Hughes called 'Wilfred Owen's Photographs'. Hughes tells the story, simply and directly, of how Parnell's Irish Members of

Parliament in the late nineteenth century called for a motion to abolish the cat-o'-nine-tails as a punishment in the Royal Navy:

> Predictably, Parliament
> Squared against the motion. As soon
>
> Let the old school tie be rent
> Off their necks . . .

Absolutely. 'Noble tradition! Trafalgar, what?' The cat-o'-nine-tails was, the old guard in Parliament cried, 'No shame, but a monument . . .'

> 'To discontinue it were as much
> As ship not powder and cannonballs
> But brandy and women' (Laughter). Hearing which
> A witty profound Irishman calls
> For a 'cat' into the House, and sits to watch
> The gentry fingering its stained tails.
> Whereupon . . .
>   quietly, unopposed,
> The motion was passed.

There, to some extent, you have it all. Poetry (literally) in Motion. Poetry (literally again) *enacted*, passed into Act. Hughes calls the unnamed Irishman who cried for the cat to be brought in 'witty and profound' for good reason. That Irishman did in life what poems try to do in words: to make the idea fact, the abstract concrete and the general particular.

The politicians run their fingers over the stained leather, real human blood flakes off and the Idea of the cat is no longer an idea, it is now a real whip which has scourged very flesh and drawn very blood. That obscene carrier of flesh and blood passes along the benches and the motion is, of course, passed unopposed and in silence. Essays, journalism and novels can parade political, philosophical and social ideas and arguments about corporal punishment or any other damned thing, but such talk has none of the power of the real. We use prose words to describe, but poetic language attempts, like the magician or the profound Irishman, to body forth those notions into their very *act*, to reify them. Poetry, the art of making, pushes the Idea into becoming the Thing Itself. Witty and profound. This wit and profundity might be harnessed to release a real whale to appear before us, or to compel us to handle the stained tails of a barbaric whip. Hughes made a poem that celebrated an act that tells us what poetry does, which is why he entitled his poem not 'Death of the Cat' or something similar, but 'Wilfred Owen's Photographs', for Owen gave us not the *idea* of war but the torn flesh and smashed bone of 'limbs so dear achieved', he gave us the *fact* of war. He called for photographs of the ruined minds and bodies of soldiers to be brought into *our* houses and passed along for inspection. The patriotic cheers stuck in our throats.

MADELINE

Madeline, ah, Madeline. I wish I could tell you that the line of verse that awoke me to the power of poetry was as perfectly contained and simple in its force as Spenser's, or that it had all the cold rage and perfection of the Hughes description of the Irish member's act of wit. It was a line of Keats's, an alexandrine as it happens, not that I knew that then, of a sensuousness and melodic perfection that hit me like a first lungful of cannabis, but without the great arcs of vomit, inane giggling and clammy paranoia attendant upon ingestion of that futile and overrated narcotic. The line is from 'The Eve of Saint Agnes':

And Madeline asleep in lap of legends old.

It is very possible that you will see nothing remarkable in this line at all. I had been dizzily in love with it for months before I became consciously aware of its extraordinary consonantal symmetry. Moving inwards from each extremity, we see the letter D at either end, moving through a succession of Ls, Ss, Ps and Ns. D-L-N-S-L-P-N-L-P-L-N-D-S-L-D. This may be bollocks to you, but I thought it a miracle. I *still* think it remarkable. It has none of the embarrassing obviousness of over-alliterated lines, but its music is as perfectly achieved as any line of verse I know. It was not, however, the sonorous splendours of the words that had first captivated me, but the image evoked by them. I found the line as completely visual as anything I had ever read. I suppose that subconsciously *diction* had been as responsible as *description*, which is to say the nature and physical attributions of the words chosen had made the image vivid in my mind quite as much as their literal meanings. 'It ain't what you say, it's the way that you say it,' the song goes. It is *both* of course. And what *had* Keats said? That a girl was asleep in the lap of . . . not a person, but some old legends. It had never occurred to me before that you were allowed to do this. It was like a nonsense joke or a category mistake. You can sleep in a *person's* lap, but not a *legend's*. Legends don't have laps any more than whales have shoulders. Yet straight into my head came a suffused and dreamy picture of a long-haired maiden, eyes closed, with armoured knights and dragons rising up from her sleeping head. An image, I was later to discover, that greatly influenced the works of Rossetti and the Pre-Raphaelite Brotherhood of painters. Music and paint-ing in one twelve-syllable line, but something more than either and this 'something more than either' is what we mean, I suppose, by poetry.

I know this is all very fey and mockable. Very sensitive cardigan-wearing reading-glasses on a thin gold chain old poof who runs an antique business and yearns for beauty. Ah, my beloved Keats, such a solace to me in this world of reality television and chicken nuggets. They don't understand, you know. Well, perhaps. I am not sure that it is in truth any more mockable than bloodless mirror-shaded cool in black jackets or disengaged postmodern quotation marks or sneery journalism or any style of cheap social grading one wishes to indulge in. I am not going to waste time trying to claim that a line of sensuous romantic poetry is cool and hard and powerful and relevant and intellectually muscled: it is quite enough for me that it astonishes with its beauty. Christopher Ricks wrote a book called *Keats and Embarrassment* and while his thesis went far beyond the usual implications of the word, a sense of embarrassment will always cling to poetry that isn't hip like Bukowski.

'Oh, play that thing!' says Larkin in his poem to the jazz saxophonist and clarinettist, Sidney Bechet:

On me your voice falls as they say love should,
Like an enormous yes.

I reckon an enormous yes beats seven kinds of crap out of an enormous no.

DICTION

How does the foregoing, illuminating as it may or may not have been, help with the writing of our poetry? I suppose I was trying with those examples to promote a high doctrine of poetic diction. I am not for a minute suggesting that some high poeti*cal* language be reserved for poetry. The language of the everyday, the vulgar, the demotic and the technical have as much place in poetry as any other diction or discourse. I am suggesting that language be worked, as a painter works paint, as a sculptor works marble. If what you are writing has no quality that prose cannot transmit, then why should you call it a poem? We cannot all play the game of 'it is art because I say it is, it is art because it hangs in a gallery, so there'. David Hockney once said that his working definition of a piece of art was a made object that if left in the street, leaning against a bus shelter, would cause passers-by to stop and stare. Like all brave stabs at defining the indefinable it has its limitations, I suppose – it is not, as Aristotle would say, necessary and sufficient[1] – but we might agree that it is not so bad. Perhaps poetry is the same: insert some poetry inside a body of prose and surely people should notice?

The poet Robert Graves offered the Game of Telegrams as a way of defining poetry. I suppose we would make that the Game of Texting now. A telegram, sometimes called a telegraph, wire or cable, for those of you too young to remember, was a message sent via the post office (or Western Union in the States). You would pay by the word, so they tended to be shorn of ornament, detail and connective words, asyndetic if you prefer: 'Arriving Wed pm stop leg broken stop' that sort of thing. Much as 'r u gng out 2nite?' might now be sent by SMS. Graves's theory was that poetry should be similar. If you could take a word out without losing any sense, then the poet was indulging himself unacceptably. He made great sport of Wordsworth's 'The Reaper':

> Behold her, single in the field,
> Yon solitary Highland Lass!
> Reaping and singing by herself
> Stop here, or gently pass!
> Alone she cuts and binds the grain . . .

Graves pointed out (with some glee as I remember, I am afraid I don't have a copy of his essay to hand and haven't been able to locate it in the library) that Wordsworth tells us the same thing four times in five lines – that the girl is not sharing her society with anyone else. She is *single*, *solitary*, *by herself* and *alone*. A needlessly extravagant telegram, then. Therefore bad poetry. Well, yes. In his callous way Graves is right, of course, but only right according to the terms of his own definition. I could erect a theory that all poets whose surnames rhyme with Waves are dunderheads. Ha! Robert Graves, you are a dunderhead, I have proved it. The fact is, the

1 After all, a large bowl of strawberry trifle or a buzzing electric dildo would make most people look twice . . .

Telegram Theory is nothing like good enough. We all know that repetition is a valuable and powerful rhetorical and poetical tool. What happens to 'The woods decay, the woods decay and fall' and 'Break, break, break'? Sometimes profusion and repetition are the very point. That is why we have words like anaphora, antimetabole, epanalepsis, epanodos, epistrophe, palilogy, polyptoton, repetend and rentrement among many other technical rhetorical words for kinds of repetition. Certainly I would agree that in most good lines of poetry the thing said could not be said *any other way*, but that does not necessarily mean that each word or phrase must be semantically different. One man's pleonasm is another man's plenty.

Commandments that categorically insist upon contemporary language and syntax are just as open to doubt as Graves's telegram rule. Keats himself, as I have mentioned, abandoned *Hyperion* because he hated all the old-fashioned *inversions* 'his features stern' for 'his stern features', for example, or 'For as among us mortals omens drear/Fright and perplex, so also shuddered he –' instead of 'For as drear omens fright and perplex us mortals, so he shuddered' and so on. Wrenched syntax, he felt, is no better than wrenched metre, or wrenched rhyme. Of course, he is generally speaking right, as we saw all too clearly with McGonagall. But here is a line from that definitively modern poem *The Waste Land*:

He, the young man carbuncular, arrives

Why not 'He, the carbuncular young man, arrives'? It would actually scan better, perfect iambic pentameter with a trochaic first foot, in fact. So if Eliot has not wrenched the syntax to fit the metre, why did he write it the way he did? T. S. Eliot of all people, so old-fashioned? I could not possibly explain why the line is so musical and funny and perfect and memorable when inverted and so feeble and uninteresting when not. It just is. I feel the same about Frost's unusual syntax in 'Mending Wall':

Something there is that doesn't love a wall

These are the kinds of lines non-singers like me chant to ourselves in the shower instead of belting out 'Fly Me to the Moon'. Here is Wallace Stevens in 'Le Monocle de Mon Oncle' with a wondrous pair of double negatives:

> There is not nothing, no, no, never nothing,
> Like the clashed edges of two words that kill,
>
>   . . . and then
> A deep up-pouring from some saltier well
> Within me, bursts its watery syllable.

Poetic Diction is about two things, it seems to me: taste and concentration. The concentration of language Graves talks about in his telegram game, yes, but also the concentration of mind that never gives up on arranging and rearranging words and phrases until taste tells you that they are right. Sometimes, of course, they will come right first go but often they take work. Much as you might walk briskly to work every day to get fit instead of using a treadmill and getting nowhere, so poets can work on their poetic diction every day, not just when they are sitting down with pen in hand practising sonnets.

BEING ALERT TO LANGUAGE

Be always alert to language: it is yours as a poet in a special way. Other may let words go without plucking them out of the air for consideration and play, we do not. Every word has its own properties. There is the obvious distinction in meaning between a word's denotation and its connotation. For example, odour, fragrance, aroma, scent, perfume, pong, reek, stink, stench, whiff, nose and bouquet all denote smell, but they by no means connote that meaning in the same way. The more aware you are of the origins, derivations, history, evolution, social usage, nuances and character of words the better. Their *physical* qualities are as important to a poet as their meaning – their weight, density, euphony, quantity, texture and appearance on the page. Their *odour*, in fact. And as with odours, notice what physically occurs when words are combined. Not just the obvious effects of alliteration, consonance and assonance (my 'occurs' being close to 'words' just now is a rather infelicitous assonance, for example. Perhaps I should have used 'happens' instead) but be alive to more subtle collisions too: 'west' and 'side' are easy words to say, but who doesn't say 'Wesside Story' dropping the 't'? 'Black glass' takes extra time to say because of the contiguity of the hard 'c' and 'g' – this kind of effect, whether euphonious or cacophonous, is something you should always be aware of. You cannot pay too much attention to every property of every word in your poems.

Imagine the intensity of painters' understanding and knowledge of all the colours in their paintbox. There is no end to the love affair they have with their paints, no limit to the subtleties and alterations achieved by mixing and combining. Just because we use them every day, it is no reason to suppose that we do not need to pay words precisely the same kind of attention. I believe we have to be *more* alert. Colours have a pure and absolute state: cerulean is cerulean, umber is umber, you can even measure their frequency as wavelengths of light. Words have no such purity or fixity. So be alert to poetic diction past and present, but be no less alive to the language of magazines, newspapers, radio, television and the street.

I do not mean that in your engagement with language you should become the kind of ghastly pedant who writes in to complain about confusions between 'fewer' and 'less', 'uninterested' and 'disinterested' and so on. Irritating as such imprecision can be, we all know perfectly well that when we see or hear letters damning them they only make us think how sad the writers of them are, how desperate to be thought of as knowledgeable and of account. No, I certainly do not mean to suggest that you need to become a grammarian or adopt an academic approach to language. Keats and Shakespeare were far from academic, after all. Keats left formal studies at fourteen and trained for a career in medicine. Wordsworth did go to university, where he studied not classical verse and rhetoric, but mathematics. Yeats went to art school. Wilfred Owen as a boy worked as a lay assistant in a church and had no further education at all. Tennyson was educated till the age of eighteen by his absent-minded clergyman father. Browning, too, was educated by his father and left university after one term. Edgar Allan Poe managed a year at his university before running off to join the army. Shelley was expelled from Oxford (for atheism, rather splendidly) and Byron was more interested in his pet bear and his decadent social life at Cambridge than in his studies. But they were all passionately interested in the life of the mind and above all in every detail and quality of language that could be learned and understood.

English is a language suited to poetry like no other. The crunch and snap of Anglo-Saxon, the lyric romanticism of Latin and Greek, the comic, ironic fusion yielded when both are yoked together, the swing and jazz of slang . . . the choice of words and verbal styles available to the English poet is dazzling.

Think of cityscapes. In London, thanks to a mixture of fires, blitzes, ludicrous mismanagement and muddled planning, the medieval, Tudor, Georgian, Victorian and modern jostle together in higgledy-piggledy confusion. The corporate, the ecclesiastical, the imperial and the domestic coexist in blissful chaos. Paris, to take the nearest capital to London, was planned. For reasons we won't go into, it managed to escape the attentions of the *Luftwaffe*. It remains a city of grand, tasteful boulevards laid out in a consistent style where, with the exception of a few self-consciously designed contemporary projects, the modern, commercial, vulgar and vernacular are held at bay beyond the outer ring of the city, like barbarians at its gates.

The English language is like London: proudly barbaric yet deeply civilised too, common yet royal, vulgar yet processional, sacred yet profane: each sentence we produce, whether we know it or not, is a mongrel mouthful of Chaucerian, Shakespearean, Miltonic, Johnsonian, Dickensian and American. Military, naval, legal, corporate, criminal, jazz, rap and ghetto discourses are mingled at every turn. The French language, like Paris, has attempted, through its Academy, to retain its purity, to fight the advancing tides of *franglais* and international prefabrication. English, by comparison, is a shameless whore.

This is partly what is meant by the *flexibility* of English: it is more than a question of the thousands more words available to us, it is also a question of the numberless styles, modes, jargons and slangs we have recourse to. If by poetry we mean something more than the decorative, noble and refined, then English is a perfect language for poetry. So be alert to it at all times.

II

Poetic vices – ten habits to acquire – getting noticed –
Poetry Today, a final rant – goodbye

Poetic Vices

LAZINESS is the worst vice a poet can have. Sentimentality, cliché, pretension, falsity of emotion, vanity, dullness, over-ambition, self-indulgence, word-deafness, word-blindness, clumsiness, technical ineptitude, unoriginality – all of these are bad but they are usually subsets and products of laziness. Laziness in prose you can get away with. There are, it is true, Flaubert-style novelists who search for ever for *le mot juste*, but they take their inspiration from poets and try to claim for novels precisely the same linguistic diligence and perfectionism that is an absolute essential in poetry. The real reason why McGonagall's 'Tay Bridge' is such a disaster is that he did not have the first idea how much *labour* goes into the making of a poem. I do not believe that he was even dimly aware of the extremes of effort and concentration that poets a hundred thousand times more talented poured into their work. Much easier to indulge in the belief that the world is against you, that everyone else is a member of some club whose doors are closed to you because you didn't go to the right school or have the right parents, than to realise that you *simply do not work hard enough*.

The first Golden Rule you signed up to when you started to read this book emphasised the necessity of taking time with poetry, as a reader and a maker of it. I emphasise that rule again with redoubled force.

I have shown you some techniques and forms of poetry, and discoursed a little on diction, but I am in no position to tell you how to write poetry that will provide you with an audience for your work. Beyond technique, the call to concentration, linguistic awareness, hard toil and the taking of time, with all the benefits of developed taste and judgement that these will bring, there is, of course, such a thing as talent. I cannot give you that and only you can judge whether you possess enough of it to make poems that others will want to read. For me, the pleasure of the thing is enough. Here, though, for what little they are worth, are a few more things to consider before we say goodbye.

TEN HABITS OF SUCCESSFUL POETS THAT THEY DON'T TEACH YOU AT HARVARD POETRY SCHOOL, OR CHICKEN VERSE FOR THE SOUL IS FROM MARS BUT YOU ARE WHAT YOU READ IN JUST SEVEN DAYS OR YOUR MONEY BACK

Concentration and total commitment to language are far and away the most important qualities needed for poetry writing. These other pieces of advice I have for you, hedged about with ifs and buts as they are, offer little more than obvious common-sense observations. They may seem too simple to be attractive. A complicated regimen is easy and (for a while) fun to follow, but the plain dictum *don't eat so much*, while an infinitely better way of losing weight than any diet ever devised, is much harder and usually less fun.

1 CONSIDER YOUR READERS: it is only good manners to do so. Are you giving them a good time? Are you confusing them, upsetting them, boring them? Maybe you are and this is part of a deliberate poetic strategy. Just be sure you know what you are doing. This leads to my next suggestion . . .

2 KEEP A JOURNAL: sometimes only by talking to ourselves do we discover what we are up to. 'Today I wrote a poem that was confusing and incoherent. But it was what I meant. Or was it? Hm. I must go back to it.'

3   CONSIDER THE VOICE OF YOUR POEM: who is speaking? You or a pretend authorial version of you?

4   READ POETRY: I did warn you that I was going to be obvious. Most popular musicians I know are fans first and foremost, owners of enormous record collections. I do not know of any poets who are not readers of poetry. You are allowed to *hate* some poets and be indifferent to others. But get to know as many as you can. Variety is important or you end up as an imitative shadow of your favourites.

5   TRUTHFULNESS: are the emotions (disgust, joy, anger, terror and so on) in your poem *really felt*, or are you feigning them for effect? Readers can tell bullshit and pretence as easily as we can detect it in someone we meet at a party. Of course, artifice is a part of poetry but again, be sure you know what you are doing.

6   CONTROL: 'All bad poetry springs from genuine feeling,' Oscar Wilde wrote. Which is *absolutely not* the same as saying that *all* genuine feeling produces bad poetry, or that all *good* poetry springs from *false* feeling. But genuine feeling is not *enough* in poetry any more than it is in painting or music. Genuine feeling which isn't pressed into some sort of shape is a tantrum or a sentimental mess. *Negative capability* and the *objective correlative* are (rather hackneyed) phrases you may want to check out, via the glossary and your own researches.

7   ENJOY YOURSELF: poetry might be a need in you, but it should not be a penance. Unless you believe yourself to be cursed by an unwanted vocation, the labour involved should be one of love.

8   FORGIVE YOURSELF: everyone writes shit from time to time. Don't get all hysterical about it. Keep your poetic toys in the pram and start again when you feel better. Write some light and stupid verse to take the taste away.

9   THE MUSE IS CAPRICIOUS: the Greek idea of a real, living Muse whispering in your ear is a good one and it works quite

well. Sometimes it truly is as if we are inspired. The work flows, we concentrate yet we are supremely relaxed, beta and theta waves are active in the brain. We are in a true creative state – the Muse is at our shoulder. BUT: next morning we may well discover that she has poured not wine but ullage into our ears. You never know with her. Our own judgement cannot go to sleep. It is the same with writing when under the influence of drugs or alcohol: we may think they are giving us poetic nectar but it can turn out next morning to be prosaic arse-gravy.

10 SAY IT OUT LOUD: however much your poetry is meant for the page, most readers will *say* it, out loud or in their heads. Read your work to yourself all the time, even as you are composing it.

Well, I did warn you that the points would be obvious. Suppose you have learned all you have learned from my book, read all you have read, followed all the precepts and avoided all the vices? Suppose you now have a body of work, however small, that languishes unread and suppose you wish to do something about this. What to do?

GETTING NOTICED

Most people who paint and play musical instruments do so at home, not for profit or attention but for their own pleasure. This is how I write my poetry, entirely for myself. I am therefore not qualified to enlarge upon ways to get yours noticed, published and talked about. There are many competitions, poetry clubs and societies, not to mention thousands of websites, chat-rooms and online bulletin boards which offer net-based or face-to-face advice, workshops and courses. Poetry Slams and public reading events of a similar nature have migrated from the United States and appear to be growing in popularity here. There are outlets and venues for performance poetry not unlike, and often connected to, the stand-up comedy circuit. New poets can be heard, applauded or gonged off like comics if they have the courage. I must add the obvious caveat that such outlets tend to promote a rather crowd-pleasing line in off-the-peg wit and ready-made satire, but this may suit your ambitions.

The first opinion you should trust, I believe, is your own, so long as it is pitilessly honest. Ask yourself, through your journal or face to face with yourself in a mirror, whether you think what you have written truly deserves a readership or audience. If the answer is an absolutely honest yes – then you will already have the confidence to proceed. If you are sincerely unsure, find someone you trust and who is patient enough and kind enough to look at your poetry or have it read to them and offer a serious and uncon-ditionally candid response. Choose such a person well.

POETRY TODAY

Sounds like the title for a quarterly magazine, doesn't it? *Poetry Today*. Well, in what kind of condition *is* poetry today? How is its circulation? Aside from the big guns – Seamus Heaney, Andrew Motion, Craig Raine, Alan Brownjohn, Simon Armitage, Wendy Cope, Peter Porter, Carol Ann Duffy, Tony Harrison, Les Murray and others, there are hundreds and hundreds more published poets who continue to furrow their brows and plough their furrows in the service of the art. Are there 'schools' of verse; is there a distinctive voice that in fifty years' time we will know speaks in unmistakable early twenty-first century tones? If there is, I have yet to hear it. I am not sure that any poem written now, social refer-ences and changes in language aside, could not have been written fifty years ago. Perhaps this is just my own deafness or ignorance.

I am aware that much in this book will enrage or stupefy some.

The very idea of clinging to ancient Greek metrical words for the description of rhythm, the use of such phrases as 'poetic taste' and 'diction', the marshalling of so many lines from dead poets – all these will cause expostulations of contempt or slow shakings of the head from those with very certain ideas about where poetry should be going and how it should be written about. If we lived in a rich time of bountiful verse and a live contemporary poetics then I would agree with them. Allow me to become a little heated and unreasonable for a moment and see if you agree with anything I am saying.

I think that much poetry written today suffers from anaemia. There is no iron in its blood, no energy, no drive. It flows gently, sometimes persuasively, but often in a lifeless trickle of the inwardly personal and the rhetorically listless. This lack of anima does not strike me as anything like the achieved and fruitful lassitude of true decadence; it is much more as if the volume has been turned down, as if poets are frightened of boldness. Lots of delicate miniatures, but few gutsy explosions of life and colour. That, perhaps, is why the colour and life in the work of poets like Armitage stand out so brightly in a dull world. The poet and critic Ian Patterson, who was kind enough to correct some of the more egregious errors in the first draft of this book, points out that there are of course many contemporary poets writing 'terrific poetry with amazingly live (and literary) engagement with contemporary language in the UK.' He cites John James, Tom Raworth, Denise Riley, Jeremy Prynne, John Wilkinson and the tragically short-lived Veronica Forrest-Thomson, but is (wrongly) too modest to include himself. I concede that I may have exaggerated this epidemic of pernicious anaemia, but cling to my view that far too many practising poets default to a rather inward, placid and bloodless response to the world.

The Victorians, for all their faults, had energy to spare. We see it clearly in the novel with Thackeray and Dickens and in the verse of Browning, Tennyson and Whitman. The Augustans, too, for all their grandeur, had a real charge running through their couplets. Virtuosity, strength and assurance seem not to be qualities of our age. There are obvious reasons for this, doubt, relativism, social sensitivity, blah, blah, blah. The short bursts of twentieth-century experimentalism (Dadaist aleatory verse, Ginsberg and chums up at Big Sur with their acid-induced Automatic Writing and cut-up poetry) are now all older than the hat Tristan Tzara drew his random words from. There is some electricity in the verse that takes its language and attitude from the streets,[2] certainly, but is literary poetry, ghastly as the phrase may be, all played out? Is it a kind of jingoistic fascism to bemoan the failure of nerve of our distinctive cultural voice? Fuck me, I do hope not.

For my own taste, I would rather read the kinds of often extreme and technically flawed but always dynamic verse of a Blake, a Whitman or a Browning than the tastefully reined in works that seem to be emerging today. It may appear contradictory of me to write a book that concentrates on metrics and form in some detail, and then argue the case for wildness. Perhaps this is the most valuable and poetically fruitful paradox of formal writing – technical perfection may be the aim, but it is out of the living and noisy struggle to escape the manacles of form that the true human voice in all its tones of love, sorrow, joy and fury most clearly emerges. 'So free we seem, so fettered fast we are,' says Browning's Andrea del Sarto, before adding the now well-worn *cri de coeur* I have already quoted.

> Ah, but a man's reach should exceed his grasp,
> Or what's a heaven for?

Or what's a *poem* for?

---

2 Though also a great danger that such demotic diction dates even more rapidly than old-fashioned 'poetical' language.

GOODBYE

We have come to the end of *The Ode Less Travelled*. I hope you have enjoyed the journey and that you will write and read poetry with a new energy and commitment, and with deep, deep pleasure. Please do not send me your poems. I am horribly poverty-stricken when it comes to time. Before it was ever announced in any public arena that I was writing this book, word somehow got out and I have already been flooded with more unsolicited verses than I can cope with. If you were to send samples of your work to me it is possible that I might skim through one or two lines, but it is desperately unlikely that I could ever give them the concentration they deserve or be able to write back to you. It is all I can do to find time to go to the lavatory these days.

As for my poetry. I have already said often enough that I do not write for publication or recital. This is partly cowardice and embarrassment, partly a problem connected to the fact that I am well-known enough to feel that my poems will be given more attention than they deserve, whether negative or positive makes no difference, they cannot be read without the reader being likely to hear my voice not as an individual poetic voice, but as the voice of that man who publicly disports himself in assorted noisome ways. My poems come from another me, a me who went down a road I did not take. He never entered the loud public world but became, I suspect, a teacher and eventually, in his own small way, a poet.

Incomplete
Glossary of Poetic Terms

I hope I haven't left out anything vital: not all terms for metric feet are here, since they are gathered in the table of metric feet at the end of Chapter One.

abecedarian Pointless style of *acrostic* q.v. in ABC order.

acatalectic Metrically complete: without *clipping* or *catalexis*, *acephalic* or *hypermetric* alteration q.q.v.

accent The word used for the natural push given to words within a sentence. In poetry, accent is called *stress*. q.v.

accentual Of verse, metre that is defined by stress count only, irrespective of the number of weak syllables. Comic and non-literary ballads and rhymes etc.

accentual-alliterative Poetry derived from the Anglo-Saxon and Middle English traditions of four-stress alliterated lines divided into two, where the first three stressed syllables alliterate according to the *bang, bang, bang – crash* rule, q.v.

accentual-syllabic Poetry ordered by metre *and* syllabic count. Iambic pentameter, trochaic tetrameter etc.

acephalous Lit. 'headless'. A line of poetry lacking its initial metrical unit. Same as *clipped*, q.v.

acrostics Kind of verse whose first letters, when read downwards, spell out a name, word or phrase: What A Nonsensical Kind, you might think.

Adonic line The final short line of a *Sapphic (Ode)*. Classically, the dactyl-trochee (named after Sappho's line 'O for Adonis').

alba Alt. name for an *aubade* q.v.

alcaics Named after Alcaeus, another poet from Lesbos, greatly admired by Horace. Some English versions of his rather complex metre have been attempted, Tennyson's 'Milton' being a well-known example. *Alcaics* now seem to be settled as a quatrain form. I will leave you to discover more.

aleatory Lit. 'of dice' – *a. verse* uses chance (drawing of words from a hat, sticking a pin in a random word from a dictionary etc.) to determine word choices.

alexandrine A line of iambic hexameter, typically found in English as the last line of a *Spenserian Stanza* or similar pentametric verse arrangement.

allegory, allegorical The device of using a character or narrative element symbolically to refer to something else, either abstract (the quest for the Holy Grail is an allegory of Man's search for spiritual grace), or specific (Gloriana in the *Faerie Queen* is an allegory of Elizabeth I).

alliteration, alliterative The repetition of the sound of an initial consonant or consonant cluster in stressed syllables close enough to each other for the ear to be affected.

amphibrach, -ic A *ternary* metrical unit expressed as ○●○, ro**man**tic de**lud**ed etc.

amphimacer A *ternary* metrical unit expressed as ●○●, **hand** to **mouth**, **pack**ing **case** etc.

anacoluthon Change of syntax within a sentence.

anacreontics Short-lined (often seven-syllable trochaics), celebrating erotic love, wine and pleasure.

anacrusis Extra weak syllable(s) at the start of a line.

anadiplosis Repetition of the last word of one clause or line as the first of the next, e.g. Keats's use of 'forlorn' in 'Ode to a Nightingale'.

anapaest, -ic A *ternary* metrical unit expressed as ○○●, uncon**vinced**, in a *spin*.

anaphora Rhetorical or poetic repetition of the first word or phrase at the beginning of successive clauses or stanzas.

anceps A metrical unit that can be either short or long, stressed or unstressed according to the poet's whim. Only really found in classical verse, such as *quantitative* imitations of Sappho etc.

anthology Collection of poems, literally of flowers – a posy of poesy, in fact.

antimetabole Rhetorical repetition by inversion and *chiasmus* q.v. – e.g. 'I pretty and my saying apt? or 'I apt and my saying pretty?' from *Love's Labour's Lost*.

antiphon Sung verse.

antistrophe The 'counter-turn', used as the second part of a triad in *Pindaric Odes*.

aphaeresis, aphaeretic The omission of a syllable at the beginning of a word: 'gainst, 'neath etc.

aphorism Wise saying, often witty. Like an *epigram* but with a more universal truth. An epigram could be made about the appearance of a particular bride at a wedding, say, but this would not be an aphorism unless its wit and truth held for any occasion.

apocope, apocopation An elision or omission of the final letter or syllable of a word, 'i'the' for 'in the', 'seld' for 'seldom' and the Chaucerian 'bet' for 'better' etc.

apostrophe Aside from the obvious reference to a punctuation mark, a moment when a poet turns to address some person, object or principle, often preceded by a (pro)vocative 'O', as in 'O attic shape!' as Keats liked to say to his favourite Grecian urns.

apothegm A short aphorism, q.v.

assonance, assonantal A repetition of vowel sounds either used internally, or as a *partial rhyme* q.v. 'Most holy Pope', 'slurred first words', etc.

asyndeton, asyndetic The omission of conjunctions, personal pronouns and other particles: 'hoping see you tomorrow', 'not fond turkey, prefer goose,' etc.

aubade A poetic celebration of dawn or a lament at daybreak's interference with lovers and their private bliss e.g. *Romeo and Juliet*: 'But soft what light at yonder window breaks?', Donne's 'The Sun Rising' etc. Also called an *alba*.

ballad Traditional verse form, often sung, usually in four-stress cross-rhyming quatrains, often alternating with three-stress lines. Not to be confused with *ballade* or *salad* q.v.

ballade Verse form of three stanzas, three rhymes and envoi: *ababbabA ababbabA ababbabA babA*.

bang, bang, bang – crash! Michael Alexander's phrase describing the alliterative principle behind Anglo-Saxon verse. Three alliterated stresses followed by a non-alliterated one.

bathos, bathetic A (comic or pathetic) failure to achieve dignity, a banal anticlimax.

binary A metrical foot of two units: *iambic, trochaic, spondaic* or *pyrrhic*.

blank verse Non-rhyming verse: most often applied to iambic pentameter, such as that found in Shakespeare's plays, Milton's *Paradise Lost* and Wordsworth's *The Prelude*.

burden A *refrain*, q.v.

cadence Lit. 'falling', the natural rhythm derived from accentuation, i.e. the rise and fall of stress. The sound that precedes a pause.

caesura Of metrical verse: a pause or breath in mid line.

canto A series of long poems.

canzone A lyric poem, usually with envoi.

catalexis, catalectic Truncation: the docking of a final metrical unit, such as the last *feminine* syllable of a trochaic line.

cataplexis, cataplectic Hardly relevant, but a fun word. It means a poetical or rhetorical threatening of punishment, horror or disaster. Like King Lear's 'I will do such things, What they are, yet I know not; but they shall be The terrors of the earth'.

cauda, caudate sonnet Lit. *tail*. A three-line coda to a *sonnet*, consisting of a *trimeter* and two *pentameters*.

cento A collage poem made up of lines of real verse from different poems.

chant royal A sixty-line poem with envoi. I spared you it in
    Chapter Three out of care for your sanity.

chiasmus From the Gr. letter *chi*, meaning a 'crossing' of sense.
    A common rhetorical figure, 'It's not the men in my life,
    it's the life in my men', 'one should eat to live, not live to
    eat', 'Real pain for sham friends, Champagne for real friends'
    etc.

choliamb A *scazon* q.v. – kind of metrical substitution, usually with
    ternary feet replacing binary. Forget about it.

chronogram A *gematric* q.v. poem or motto whose letters when
    added as Roman numerals make up a significant number,
    such as a date: e.g. *Lord have mercie vpon vs* = 1666 (or 1464
    or permutations thereof).

cinquain A stanza of five lines. Esp. in reference to the verse of
    Adelaide Crapsey.

clerihew From Edmund Clerihew Bentley. A non-metrical comical
    and biographical quatrain whose first line is the name of its
    subject.

clipped As *acephalous* q.v., omission of the first metrical unit in a
    line of verse.

closed form Any form of verse whose stanza length, rhyme scheme
    and other features are fixed.

closet drama Not, as you might think, the hysterics attendant upon
    coming out, but a play written to be read, not performed. A
    genre invented by the Roman playwright Seneca.

Cockney School Blackwood (of Magazine fame) and the *Quarterly
    Review* q.v. used this snobbish and wholly inappropriate
    appellation to describe the 'bad' poetic diction of Keats and
    Leigh Hunt and their circle. Byron, too, 'disapproved of that
    School of Scribbling' and believed Keats guilty of wasting his
    talents in 'Cockneyfying and Suburbing' (letter to John
    Murray, 1821).

common metre ballad metre, i.e. 4-3-4-3, rhyming *abab* or *abcb*
conceit An extended metaphor or fanciful image.

connotation The associative, implied meaning of a word, as opposed to its *denotation* q.v.

consonance A loose or exact repetition of consonant sounds either used internally, or as partial rhyme. 'And Madeline asleep in lap of legends old', *fuck/fork*, *pushing/passion*, *past the post* etc.

corona sequence A sonnet sequence where the last line of a sonnet is used as the first line of the next. The final sonnet will end with the opening line of the first in the sequence.

coronach A *threnody* or funeral dirge.

counter-turn Ben Jonson's word for *antistrophe* q.v.

couplet A pair of rhyming lines.

cretic Alternative name for the *amphimacer* q.v., after the Cretan poet Thaletas.

cross-rhyme End-rhyming of alternate lines: *abab cdcd* etc.

curtal Name for a *sonnet* that falls short of the usual fourteen lines, if such a thing can be said to exist. Properly speaking, the Hopkins stanza with an octave reduced to a sestet.

cynghanedd From Welsh poetry, a style of interlaced *alliteration*: as employed by Hopkins.

dactyl Ternary foot. ●○○, or long-short-short in classical prosody.

denotation The strict, literal meaning of a word, stripped of its *connotation* q.v., colour, suggestion, implications etc.

diacritic -al A sign, such as an accent or cedilla, that goes above or below a letter to indicate a change in pronunciation.

diamante Wretchedly silly diamond-shaped verse form in which one word becomes its opposite or antithesis according to pointless rules that I can't be bothered to go into again.

diction In poetry, the choice of words. The discourse, frame of reference, atmosphere, coloration and other aspects of word choice are all elements of poetic *d*.

didactic Lit. 'teaching' – writing that intends (usu. moral) instruction.

dieresis Diacritical mark – the two dots used to show that a *diphthong*'s vowel sounds should be pronounced separately,

'Noël', 'naïve'; etc. In metre, a word meaning a natural *caesura* (i.e. one that does not break a word or clause).

dimeter A verse line of two metric feet.

diminishing rhyme A rhyme scheme where each new rhyme takes a syllable or letter less than its predecessor: *promotion, emotion, motion, ocean* and *passing, arsing, sing* etc.

diphthong Two vowels together.

dipodic Composed of two feet (as most humans are).

dirge A mourning, wailing lament.

dithyramb, dithyrambic Wild choral Dionysiac celebratory verse. Often used to describe overblown poetic *diction* q.v.

divine afflatus (Now mock comic) phrase used to describe poetic inspiration.

dramatic monologue (Non theatrical) verse in the voice of a character, often addressing another imaginary character or the reader him/herself. 'My Last Duchess', 'Andrea del Sarto', sections of *The Waste Land* etc.

eclogue From Virgil, pastoral poem.

elegiac Of mourning. The elegiac quatrain *abab* in iambic pentameter was developed by Thomas Gray for his country churchyard.

elision The omission of words or parts of words.

encomium Praise song or ode for a (usu. living) person.

endecasíllabo Italian name for a *hendecasyllabic* line of iambic pentameter.

end-rhyming The rhyming of final words, or final stressed syllables in lines of verse. Usual rhyming, in fact.

end-stopped Lines of verse which do not run on in sense, but whose thought ends with the line. Lines without *enjambment* q.v.

enjambment The running-on of sense over the end of a line of verse. Verse that is not *end-stopped* q.v.

entry Just testing to see whether you had got to *q.v.* q.v. yet.

envelope rhyme A couplet nested in two outer rhymes, as in *abba*.

envoi A short stanza of summation or conclusion at the end of a poem. Found in certain closed forms, such as the *sestina* and *ballade* q.q.v.

epanalepsis General word for repetition or resumption of a theme.

epanaphora Extreme *anaphora* q.v. As in Wendy Cope's 'My Lover' in which every line begins with the word 'For'.

epanodos Recapitulation and expansion of an image or idea.

epigram Memorably witty remark, saying or observation.

epistrophe Repetition at the end of clauses or sentences: 'When I was a child, I spake as I child, I understood as a child, I thought as a child' etc.

epithalamium A poem celebrating a wedding: nuptial or hymeneal verse. No specific formal requirements. Much the same as *prothalamium* to be honest.

epode The third part of the *Pindaric Ode*'s triad. Called by Jonson the *stand*.

esemplastic Rather fine word coined by Coleridge to describe an unlike imaginative union of two qualities or things.

expletive A word or words used to fill the metrical requirements of a line. The iambic pentameter 'He thus did sit him down upon the rock', is saying no more than 'he sat on the rock', the other five words are expletives.

fabliau A (sometimes comic) tale, originally medieval French, now applied to any short moral fable in verse or prose.

falling rhythm Metre whose primary movement is from stressed to unstressed, dactylic and trochaic verse, for example.

false friend Word or phrase whose meaning is confused with other words or phrases (often from another language) which sound similar. 'To meld' is used often to mean to 'fuse' or 'unite' through false friendship with 'melt' and 'weld' – it actually means 'to announce'. Similarly 'willy-nilly' is used to mean 'all over the place' where in reality it means 'whether you like it or not', i.e. 'willing or unwilling'. Only sad pedants like me care about these misuses which are now common enough to be almost correct.

feedback See *loop*.

feminine ending An unstressed ending added to an iamb, anapaest or other usually rising foot. *Hanging, waiter, television* etc.

feminine rhyme The rhyming of feminine-ended words. The rhyme is always on the last stressed syllable. Rhymes for the above could be *banging, later, derision*.

fescennine Indecent or scurrilous verse.

filidh An Irish bard.

foot A metrical division: five feet to a *pentameter*, four to a *tetrameter* etc.

fourteeners Iambic heptameter. Seven iambs make fourteen syllables.

free verse Verse that follows no conventional form, rhyming scheme or metrical pattern.

ghazal Middle Eastern couplet form following special rules as described in Chapter Three.

gematri-a, -ic (Originally Kabbalistic) assignation of numerical value to letters – as in *chronogram* q.v.

glyconic Latin style of verse usu. with three trochees and a dactyl.

haijin A *haiku* practitioner.

haikai (no renga) The ancestor of *haiku*. Playful linked Japanese verse developed from the *waka* in the sixteenth century.

haiku Three-line verses (in English at least) with a syllable count of 5-7-5 and adhering to certain thematic principles.

hemistich A half-line of verse: the term is most often found in reference to Anglo-Saxon and Middle English poetry.

hendecasyllabic Composed of eleven syllables.

hendiadys Lit. 'one through two': a trope where a single idea is expressed by two nouns where usually it would be a qualified or modified noun: 'nice and warm' for 'nicely warm', 'sound and fury' for 'furious sound'. Also phrase where 'and' replaces infinitive 'to' as in 'try and behave' for 'try to behave'.

heptameter A line of verse in seven metrical feet. *Fourteeners*, for example.

heroic couplets Rhyming couplets in iambic pentameter.

heroic line Iambic pentameter.

heroic verse Poetry cast in heroic couplets.

hexameter A line of verse in six metrical feet.

hokku The opening verse of *haikai*, from which the *haiku* is descended.

homeoteleuton Repetition of words ending in like syllables: e.g. 'readable intelligible syllables are horrible', 'a little fiddle in a pickle' etc.

homostrophic Arrangement of identically structured stanzas, esp. as in *Horatian* and other ode forms.

Horatian Ode Ode in the manner of the Roman poet Horace, adopted, adapted, translated and imitated in English verse esp. in the seventeenth and eighteenth centuries.

Hudibrastic Used to describe the kind of tortured polysyllabic rhyming found in Samuel Butler's mock-epic *Hudibras*.

hypermetric A line with an extra syllable. Technically, a hendeca-syllabic line of pentameter is hypermetric.

hypermonosyllabic Optional *synaeresis* q.v. A word that can be sounded with either one or two syllables, i.e. 're´al', 'flo´wer' and 'li´ar' (can be said as 'reel', 'flour' and 'lyre').

ictus The unit of stress within a foot. The second element in an *iamb*, the first in a *trochee*, the third in an *anapaest* etc.

idyll A short pictorial poem, chiefly lyrical or pastoral: 'idyllic' is often now used to mean 'ideal' and 'perfect'.

internal rhyme Oh for heaven's sake it's obvious, isn't it?

inversion Reversal of usual sentence structure. 'Happy am I', etc.

jeu d'esprit Merry word play or similar gamesome larkiness.

kenning A Norse and Anglo-Saxon metaphorical or metonymic yoking of words, such as 'whale road' for sea.

kigo The 'season word' placed in a *haiku* to tell the reader in which time of year the verse is set.

tomato A red savoury fruit sometimes known as a love-apple
    which has a place in many sauces and salads but none
    whatever in a glossary of poetical terms. Especially when it
    has not been inserted in the correct alphabetical order.

kireji The caesura that should occur in the first or second line of a
    haiku.

kyrielle A *refrain* verse form descended from an element of
    Catholic mass.

lay Narrative poem or short song.

leonine rhyme Internal rhyming in verse of long measure where
    the word preceding the caesura rhymes with the end-word.

limerick You know perfectly well.

lineation The arrangement of lines in a poem, how they break and
    how their length is ordered. Prescribed in metrical verse but
    at the poet's discretion in free verse. See *stichic*.

lipograms Verse or writing where for some reason best known
    to himself the poet has decided to omit one letter through-
    out. As I have unquestionably done with the letter q here.
    Damn.

litotes Understatement for comic effect, often cast in negatives to
    indicate a positive: 'a not unsatisfactory state of affairs' for 'a
    splendid outcome' etc. Same as *meiosis* q.v.

loop See *feedback*.

luc bat A Vietnamese form described in Chapter Three.

lyric ode An open form of rhymed, stanzaic verse, usually in
    iambic pentameter, descended as much from the *sonnet* as
    from the *Horatian Ode*. Used to describe the odes of Keats
    and other romantic poets.

majuscule Capital letters. Upper Case.

masculine ending A stressed word end.

masculine rhyme The rhyming of same.

meiosis Cell division to a biologist, understatement to a grammarian.
    Often comical. See *litotes*.

melon Sweet pleasant fruit. What possible reason can it have for being in this glossary? Andrew Marvell stumbled on them as he passed, but otherwise they have no business being here. Please ignore this entry.

melopoeia Word coined by Ezra Pound to describe the overall soundscape of a poem.

mesostich Halfway point of a line – used to apply to acrostics that descend therefrom.

metaphor Figurative use of a word or phrase to describe something to which it is not literally applicable. 'The ship ploughed through the waves', 'Juliet is the sun', 'there's April in her eyes' etc.

metonym A metaphoric trope in which a word or phrase is used to stand in for what it represents: 'the bottle' is a metonym for 'drinking', 'the stage' for 'theatrical life', 'Whitehall' for the civil service etc. *Kennings* q.v. and *synecdoche* are often metonymic.

minuscule non capital letters. lower case.

molossus A ternary foot of three long, or stressed, units. 'Short sharp shock', etc.

monody Ode or dirge sung or declaimed by a single individual.

monometer A metric line of one foot.

monosyllable Let me say this in words of one sill ab uhl.

mora From Lat. for 'delay'. In syllable-timed languages the duration of one short syllable. Two *morae* make a long syllable. Equivalent of crotchet and minim in music.

Muses Nine multi-domiciled girls (the daughters of *Mnemosyne* or Memory) who shuttle between Pieria, Parnassus and Mount Helicon and give poets and others inspiration. *Erato* helps us with our Love Poetry, *Calliope* with our epics, *Melpomene* with our tragedies, *Polyhymnia* is good for sacred verse and *Thalia* for comedy. For non-poets *Clio* looks after History and *Renault* motor cars, *Euterpe* is in charge of music, *Terpsichore* is the dance mistress and *Urania* teaches astronomy.

near rhyme Echoic devices such as *assonance, consonance* and *homeoteleuton* q.q.v

negative capability Keats's phrase (used in a letter of 1818 and referring to Shakespeare after being inspired by Kean's performance as Richard III) 'when a man is capable of being in uncertainties, mysteries, doubts, without any irritable reaching after fact and reason'. A phrase now used to describe the poetic ability to efface self and take on the qualities being described.

nonce word A word coined for use on one occasion: *not* a nonsense word – that would be a false friend q.v.

nonet No, no. Silly verse form of ascending or diminishing syllabic count.

numbers A now archaic word for lines of verse.

objective correlative Phrase coined by T. S. Eliot in a 1919 essay on *Hamlet* to refer to the context of an emotion, the pattern of events, diction etc. leading to an emotional response. Now often used to mean the poet's intended emotional effect. Eliot felt that *Hamlet* lacked an o. c.

octameter A metric line of eight feet.

octave The first eight lines of a (usually Petrarchan or Petrarchan variant) sonnet.

ode Verse form on one theme, now usually applied to lyric poems.

Old English Anglo-Saxon (approx. fifth–twelfth century). Applies to four-stress hemistichal alliterative accentual verse, e.g. *Beowulf.*

onomatopoei-a, -ic Of words whose sounds imitate their meaning: e.g. 'click', 'hiss', 'susurration' etc.

open form Metrical rhymed verse where issues like the number of stanzas are not fixed, but up to the poet.

ottava rima An open form of eight-line verse rhyming *abababcc*. Byron's *Don Juan*, late Yeats etc.

oxymoron Lit. 'sharp blunt' a contradictory phrase: as in *Romeo and Juliet*'s 'O loving hate! O heavy lightness!', or a paradoxical phrase such as 'eloquent silence', 'living death' or 'military intelligence' (ho-ho).

paean A song of praise, encomium.

palilogy Repetition – what a lot of words for it there are.

panegyric Writing in praise of a character's specific qualities or achievements.

pantoum Malayan closed form with refrained lines. See Chapter Three.

paragram To hide a name or word inside text. 'A cut and paSTE PHENomenon', or' SuiTablE Poetic HiddEN word'.

paralepsis To say something while pretending not to: 'I shall not mention his appalling table manners' etc.

para-rhyme Partial rhyme, assonance or consonance rhyming, for example, *head/bet, foul/stout, feel/full*. Also called *slant-rhyme* or *off-rhyme*.

parody Imitation of the style of another.

paronomasia Wordplay, punning.

particle Small word like a conjunction (and, or, but), preposition (for, of, with, by), pronoun (they, his, me, who, that) and so on.

pathetic fallacy John Ruskin's term for the romantic attribution of life and a soul to inanimate objects or principles, Nature esp.

pattern poem A poem whose physical shape on the page represents an object of some kind. Same as shaped poetry.

pentameter A metrical line of five feet.

periphrasis A roundabout way of speaking, circumlocution.

Petrarchan sonnet A sonnet form adapted from Petrarch's original cycle of poems to his Laura: the octave rhymes *abba abba* and the sestet in English can be anything from the original *cdecde* to *cdcdcd, cdcdee* and other variations.

phaleucian A Greek metre consisting of a spondee, dactyl and three trochees.

phanopoeia Name Pound gave to Imagism in action – a revelatory or reified image.

phoneme Base unit of sound.

Pindaric Ode From the Greek poet Pindar; celebratory or praise songs that developed into formal *triadic* odes in English.

pleonasm Tautology, use of redundant words, unnecessary repetition – as in this entry. Not to be confused with 'neoplasm' which means a morbid new growth or tissue.

poesie, poesy Now poncey word for poetry.

polyptoton Repetition of the same word, but using different endings and inflexions e.g. 'It's socially unacceptable in society to socialise with an unsociable socialist' etc.

prosody The art of versification: the very subject of this magnificent little book.

prothalamium An *epithalamium*, specifically one to be recited before entry into the bridal chamber (Spenser).

pyrrhic A binary foot of two unstressed units.

quantitative Of quantity. A word's quantity is the sum of its vowel lengths. In quantitative verse, feet are not elements of stress but of sound duration (*morae* q.v.). 'Smooth' is long, 'moth' is short and so on. The stuff of classical verse, quantitative poetry was never much more than an experiment in the stress-timed English language. Longfellow's *Evangeline* and Southey's dactylic hexameters remain possibly the best-known examples.

Quarterly Review Tory magazine begun in 1809. Shelley held a 'homicidal article' in it responsible for Keats's early demise: 'Who killed John Keats? I, said the Quarterly, So savage and Tartarly, 'Twas one of my feats.' Byron adapted S's squib in *Don Juan* (but see under *Cockney School*).

quaternary Divided into four: in prosody this refers to metrical feet that have four units, such as the choriamb and the antispast.

quatorzain Name given to a fourteen-line poem that is not considered by the prosodist or critic using the term to be a 'true' sonnet. A subjective matter, to be honest.

quatrain A four-line stanza.

quintain A five-line stanza, or *cinquain*.

q.v. From Latin *quod vide* meaning 'which see' or 'take a look at that one', used in fancy glossaries like this to follow a word in the body of a definition which has its own *entry* q.v.

rann A quatrain in Irish verse.

redondilla Spanish verse cast in octosyllables.

refrain Line repeated at set intervals within a song or poem.

reify, reification To concretise the abstract, to embody an idea.

rentrement Refrain, burden or single-lined chorus.

repetend Any word or phrase that is (to be) repeated.

rhadif The *refrain* line of a *ghazal*.

rhapsody The sung part of an epic or saga. Applied to moments of lyricism in otherwise non-lyric verse, i.e. the 'Isles of Greece' section in Byron's *Don Juan*.

rhopalic Progression of words whereby each word is longer by one syllable than its predecessor.

rhopalics Too silly to bother with.

rhyme royal, rime royal An open stanza form following the scheme *ababbcc*. Chaucer's *Troilus and Criseyde* and Auden's 'Letter to Lord Byron' are written in this form.

rhyme-scheme The pattern of rhyming in a stanza or passage of verse, *abba abab*, *aa* etc represent various examples of r. s.

rich rhyme The rhyming of words that either look and sound the same but have a different meaning (*homonyms*), 'the *sound* is very *sound*', *or* words that sound the same but look different, (*homophones*) like *blue/blew* or *praise/preys*, *or* words that look the same but sound different, 'he wore a *bow* and made a *bow* to the audience' etc.

rictameter See *rhopalics*.

rime en kyrielle Used to describe any *rentrement* q.v. or poetic refrain.

rime retournée Backwards rhyme, but of *sound* not spelling: i.e. not *emit* and *time*, *Eros* and *sore* but *mite* or *might* and *time*, *Eros* and *sorry* etc.

rising rhythm Metre whose primary movement is from unstressed to stressed, iambs and anapaests for example.

rondeau Closed French form with various English guises. *R-aabba aabR aabbaR* seems to be the most common form, where *R* is the first half of the opening line. 'In Flanders Fields' by John McCrea is a well-known example of this kind of *r*.

rondeau redoublé Variation of *rondeau* q.v. where the last lines of each stanza become refrain lines for the following stanzas. See the 'More Closed French Forms' section of Chapter Three.

rondel Another French *rentrement* form. Check it out in Chapter Three, as above.

rondel prime Ditto basically.

rondelet And again.

rondine The name of Shiraz's sister in *Footballer's Wives*. No, but shush at once.

roundel Swinburne's name for his adaptation of one or other of the French letter-R forms.

roundelay Refrained verse of some bloody kind.

Rubai, ruba'iat, ruba'iyat At last, sense. *Quatrain* verse of Persian origin, rhyming *aaba, ccdc* etc.

salad Summery vegetable assemblage not to be confused with *ballad* or *ballade* q.v. Often contains *tomatoes* q.v.

Sapphic metre In classical verse, a hendecasyllabic line composed of a *trochee*, an *anceps*, a *dactyl*, a *trochee* and a *spondee*.

Sapphic Ode A stanza of three lines in Sapphic metre as above, followed by an Adonic line. The English stress-based adaptation as seen in Pope and others is usually in iambic pentameter or tetrameter with an iambic dimeter instead of a true Adonic.

Satanic School Southey's petulant name for poets like Byron, Shelley and Leigh Hunt who were better than he was and had more integrity.

scazon Substitution of a ternary foot for a binary. See *choliamb*.

schwa The phonetic character ɘ that stands for a scudded *uh* sound, as in the weak vowel sounds in words like actɘ and commɘn and grammɘ.

scop Old English or Nordic storyteller, bard or poet.

Scriblerus, Martin Group pseudonym under which satirical verses were published in the eighteenth century. Prominent members included Swift and Pope. Also known as the Scriblerus Club.

scud To skip lightly over a syllable imparting no stress.

sdrucciolo Cool word for *triple-rhyme*.

semantics The study of linguistic meaning.

semeion A basic metrical unit, either stressed or unstressed.

semiotics, semiology The study of linguistic (and by extension social, cultural etc.) signs. The base study in structuralism, formalism, Saussurian linguistics, Lévi-Strauss-style social anthropology etc.

senryu, senriu A *haiku* that is more about people than nature.

septain A stanza of seven lines.

sestet A stanza of six lines; also the final six lines of a (usually) Petrarchan sonnet.

sestina A closed verse form in six stanzas and an envoi determined by rules of some complexity. See the section devoted to it in Chapter Three.

Shakespearean sonnet The native English sonnet form adapted by Drayton, Sidney and others which found its apotheosis at the hands of Will. It rhymes *abab cdcd efef gg*.

shaped poem See *pattern* poems.

shasei The 'sketch of nature' that a *haiku* is supposed to render.

Skeltonics Merry, rather clumsy subversive and scurrilous irregular verses, named after John S. (fifteenth–sixteenth-century English poet). Sometimes called *tumbling* verse.

slam Originally Chicagoan poetry contests or public recitals of verse held as entertainment events.

slant-rhyme See *partial* rhyme.

song that luc bat A version of *luc bat*.

sonnet A poem of fourteen lines, usually following a particular

scheme, e.g. Petrarchan, Shakespearean, Spenserian or
variations thereof.

sonnet of sonnets A sequence of fourteen sonnets.

sonnet redoublé A fifteen-poem *corona* sequence in which the
fifteenth is made of the last lines of the previous fourteen.
Something to do between lunch and tea.

Spenserian sonnet Close to Shakespearean s., but with vestigial
Petrarchan internal couplets: *abab bcbc cdcd ee.*

Spenserian stanza An open stanzaic form in iambic pentameter
developed by Spenser for *The Faerie Queen* and later used by
Keats and Tennyson. It rhymes *ababbcbcc* and features a final
line in iambic hexameter, an *alexandrine.*

spondee A metrical unit of two stressed feet. Or long feet if you're
an ancient Greek.

sprung rhythm A phrase coined by Gerard Manley Hopkins to
describe verse in which only the stresses are counted. See the
section on it towards the end of Chapter One.

stand A place to put a cake. *Or,* Ben Jonson's word for *epode.*

stanza, stanzaic What a verse is to a hymn or song, so a *stanza* is
to a poem.

stave Sometimes used to refer to a *stanza.*

stichic Of or in *lines*: how a poem is presented as distinct to prose.
Christopher Ricks once said the real defining difference
between prose and poetry was that whereas prose *has* to go
to the end of a line, with poetry it's an option. Reductive
logic at its best.

stichomythia Verse presented as dialogue, often rapidly alternating
between speakers. In verse drama refers to dialogue of single
lines rather than speeches.

stress The feeling that comes upon an author when he knows
he must deliver a book to his publisher when it isn't quite
finished yet and there's a glossary to be completed.

strophe The first part of a Pindaric Ode's *triad.* What Jonson called
the *turn.*

substitutions The use of an alien metric foot in a line of otherwise regular metrical pattern. *Pyrrhic* and *trochaic* substitutions are common in iambic verse, for example.

suspension of disbelief Term coined by Coleridge to describe a reader's willingness to accept as true what clearly is not.

syllable, syllabic The basic sound unit of a word. Come on, you know perfectly well. Of poetry it refers to forms that are predicated on their syllabic count rather than any metric considerations. The *haiku* and the *tanaga*, for example.

syllepsis Kind of *zeugma* q.v. where a verb governs two unlikely nouns or phrases: as in 'he left in a cab and a temper', and Pope's 'Or stain her Honour, or her new Brocade'.

synaeresis A gliding of two syllables into one: in the opening line of *Paradise Lost* 'Of man's first *disobedience* and the fruit' *d* becomes the four-syllable 'disobedyence'. Also called *synaloepha*.

synaloepha Look up at the preceding entry.

syncope The *elision* of a syllable from a word: 'prob'ly' for 'probably' etc.

synecdoche A figure of speech in which the part stands in for the whole or vice versa: e.g. 'England won the Ashes' where 'England' means the English Cricket XI, 'twenty hands', where 'hand' stands for a crewman etc.

syzygy High score at Scrabble that means a pair of connected or corresponding things. Two hemistichs make a syzygy, you might say, or a plug and a socket together. In poetics also refers to multiple alliteration and consonance, as in the Ms in Tennyson's 'The moan of doves in immemorial elms/And murmuring of innumerable bees' (from 'The Princess').

tanaga A syllabic Filipino verse form.

tanka A syllabic Japanese cinquain form of verse. The count is 5-7-5-7-7.

telestich An *acrostic* where it is the last letters that do the spelling out.

teleuton The terminating element of a line.

tercet A three-line stanza.

ternary A foot composed of three metrical elements. *Anapaest, dactyl, amphimacer* etc.

terza rima An open stanzaic form with interlocking cross-rhyming. Used by Dante for his *Inferno*.

tetractys Bizarre form of syllabic verse developed by Mr Stebbing.

tetrameter A four-stress line.

transferred epithet Illogical (often comic) use of image, transferring meaning from mood of person to object: 'I lit a moody cigarette', 'sad elms' etc.

triad, triadic The three-part structure of Pindaric Odes. Each triad consists of *strophe, antistrophe* and *epode* or *turn, counter-turn* and *stand* as Ben Jonson dubbed them. Originated as actual physical movements in Greek choric dances.

tribrach Ternary unit of three unstressed syllables. Forget it.

trimeter A three-stress line.

triolet A closed French form of some sweetness. Or perhaps it's just the name. It rhymes *ABaAbbAB* where *A* and *B* are *rentrements*.

triple rhyme Tri-syllabic (usually dactylic) rhyme, *merited/inherited, eternal/infernal, merrier/terrier* etc.

triplet Three-line couplet, *aaa, bbb* etc. Augustan poets braced them in a curly bracket.

trochee A binary metrical unit of stressed and unstressed syllables: ●○.

trope Any rhetorical or poetic trick, device or figure of speech that changes the literal meaning of words. *Metaphor* and other common figures are tropes.

tumbling verse See *Skeltonics*.

turn Ben Jonson's word for a *strophe*.

twiner Term used by Walter de la Mare to describe a kind of double limerick form.

ubi sunt Lit. 'where are they?' Poetic formula addressing something vanished: 'Where are the songs of Spring?' (Keats, 'Ode to Autumn'), '*Où sont les neiges d'antan*? Where are the snows of yesteryear?' (Ballade by François Villon).

vatic A poetic prophecy.

Venus and Adonis Stanza A six-line stanzaic form of iambic pentameter that takes its name from Shakespeare's *Venus and Adonis*. It rhymes *ababcc*. Wordsworth's 'Daffodils' etc.

vers libre French for free verse.

vignette In poetry, a delicate but precise scene or description.

villanelle See section devoted to it in Chapter Three.

virgule In metrics, the mark used for foot division.

volta The 'turn' marking the change of mood or thought between the (Petrarchan) sonnet's *octave* and *sestet* q.q.v.

Vorticism Word coined by Pound for British phalanx of the modernist movement. Most often used to refer to work (in paint and verse) of Wyndham Lewis. They had their own fanzine – *Blast!*. Rejection of sentimentality and verbal profusion.

waka Original Japanese verse from which *haikai* and *haiku* descended.

weak ending See *feminine ending*, but take no offence therefrom.

wrenched accent Sound and sense of words vitiated by the need for them to fit the metre.

wrenched rhyme A word forced out of its natural pronunciation by its need to rhyme.

wretched rhyme Bad rhyme.

wretched sinner Me.

zeugma Lit. 'yoking': 'she wore a Chanel dress and an expression of disappointment'. Essentially the same as *syllepsis* q.v. The differences between them are trivial and undecided.

zymurgy Word that always tries to get into glossaries and dictionaries last but is often beaten by *zythum*, which, ironically perhaps, it helps create. Something to do with fermentation. More connected to Yeast than Yeats.

zythum Ancient Egyptian beer.

Arnaut's Algorithm

The line-ends of the first stanza (A, B, C, D, E and F) are chosen for the second and subsequent stanzas according to a 'spiral' algorithm illustrated in Figure 1. It can be seen that the position and relative order of the line ending alters in a complex manner from stanza to stanza.

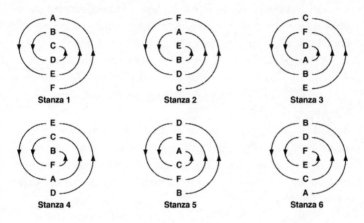

Figure 1: The 'spiral' algorithm

Consider line-end A: it moves down one line for the second stanza and then down two lines for the third stanza, down one line again for the fourth stanza and so on. The algorithm can therefore be considered as the sequence of displacements from the starting position, namely, +1; +2; +1, −2; +3; −5. The last displacement returns the first line-end (A) from the last line of the last stanza to the starting position.

Defining the sequence of translations as a we see that:

$$\sum_{i=1}^{i=6} a_i = 0 \tag{1}$$

How do the other line-ends behave after six iterations? Well, consider the situation after the first iteration; line-end A now occupies the position previously occupied by line-end B. Now carry out six iterations, namely $+2; +1; -2; +3; -5$ and finally the first of the next cycle: $+1$. This sequence also sums to zero, meaning that the line-end returns to where it was. In general therefore we can say for all line ends in the first stanza corresponding to the position of line-end A after interation m;

$$\sum_{i=m+1}^{i=6} a_i + \sum_{i=1}^{i=m} a_i = \sum_{i=1}^{i=6} a_i = 0 \tag{2}$$

which proves that the entire set of line-ends returns to the original position and order after a full cycle of six iterations, or in other words a seventh stanza would be identical (in respect of line-ends) to the first.

Acknowledgements

My thanks, as always, go to JO CROCKER for running my life with such efficiency, understanding and good humour while I have been engaged upon this book. My publisher SUE FREESTONE has shown her usual blend of patience, kindness, enthusiasm and accommodation, as have ANTHONY GOFF and LORRAINE HAMILTON, my literary and dramatic agents. Thanks to JO LAURIE for her game guinea-piggery in reading early sections on metre and trying out some of the exercises, and to my father for his baffling but beautiful sestina algorithm. Especial gratitude must go to IAN PATTERSON, poet, Fellow and Director of Studies in English at Queens' College, Cambridge, for casting his learned and benevolent eye over the manuscript – all errors are mine, not his. I thank him also for allowing me to include his excellent centos and sestina. My thanks to his predecessors at Queens', Professors A. C. SPEARING and IAN WRIGHT, and to PETER HOLLAND of Trinity Hall, who between them did their doomed best to make a scholar of me during my time there. Aside from my mother, the person who most awoke me to poetry was RORY STUART, a remarkable teacher who has now retired to Italy. I send him my eternal thanks. If every schoolchild had been lucky enough to have a teacher like him, the world would be a better and happier place.

The author and publisher acknowledge use of lines from the following works:

Simon Armitage, 'Poem', *Kid*, Faber, 1999
W. H. Auden, 'Letter to Lord Byron, II', 'The Age of Anxiety', 'Meiosis', 'Precious Five', 'In Memory of W. B. Yeats', 'Letter to Lord Byron', 'Miss Gee', 'Lullaby', *Collected Poems*, ed. Edward Mendelson, Faber 1976, rev. 1991

Carolyn Beard Whitlow, 'Rockin' a Man Stone Blind', *Wild Meat*, Lost Roads Publishers, USA, 1986

John Betjeman, 'Death in Leamington', *Collected Poems*, John Murray, 2003

Elizabeth Bishop, 'Sestina', *Complete Poems*, ed. Tom Paulin, Chatto & Windus, 2004

Jorge Luis Borges, Haikus and Tanaka from *Obras Completas* (4 vols), Emecé Editores, Buenos Aires, 2005

Anthony Brode, 'Breakfast with Gerard Manley Hopkins', *The New Oxford Book of Light Verse*, ed. Kingsley Amis, OUP, 1978

Anne Carson, 'Eros The Bittersweet', Dalkey Archive Press, 1998

G. K. Chesterton, 'The Ballade of Suicide', *The Collected Poems of G. K. Chesterton*, Dodd Mead, 1980

Wendy Cope, 'Valentine', *Serious Concerns*, Faber, 1992

—— 'Engineer's Corner', *Making Cocoa For Kingsley Amis*, Faber, 1986

Frances Cornford, 'Fat Lady Seen From A Train', *Collected Poems*, Enitharmon Press, 1996

Cummings, E. E., '1 (a', 'r-p-o-p-h-e-s-s-a-g-r', *Selected Poems*, Liveright Books, 1994

Elizabeth Daryush, 'Still Life', *Collected Poems*, Carcanet, 1972

Hilda Doolittle, 'Sea Poppies', *Selected Poems*, Carcanet, 1997

Norman Douglas, 'Wagtail' and Anacreontics from *Norman Douglas: A Portrait*, Edizioni La Conchiglia, Capri, Italy, 2004

Marriott Edgar, *The Lion and Albert*, Methuen, 1978

T. S. Eliot, 'The Love Song of J. Alfred Prufrock', 'The Waste Land', *Complete Poems and Plays of T. S. Eliot*, Faber, 1969

Robert Frost, 'Spring Pools', 'The Death of the Hired Man', 'Stopping by Woods on a Snowy Evening', 'Mending Wall', *The Poetry of Robert Frost*, Vintage, 2001

Thomas Hardy, 'The Convergence of the Twain (Lines on the Loss of the Titanic)', 'The Lacking Sense', *Collected Poems*, Wordsworth Editions, 1994

Seamus Heaney, 'Blackberry Picking', 'From the Frontier of Writing', *Opened Ground: Poems 1966–96*, Faber, 1998

Michael Heller, 'She', *Exigent Futures: New and Selected Poems*, Salt Publishing, 2003

A. E. Housman, 'The Colour of his Hair', *Collected Poems*, ed. J. Sparrow, Penguin, 1995 (By permission of The Society of Authors as the Literary Representative of the Estate of A. E. Housman)

Ted Hughes, 'Wilfred Owen's Photographs', 'Thistle', 'The Sluttiest Sheep in England', 'Eagle', *Collected Poems*, ed. Paul Keegan, Faber, 2003

Donald Justice, 'The Tourist from Syracuse', *Collected Poems*, Knopf, USA, 2004

Rudyard Kipling, 'Tommy', 'If', *The Collected Poems of Rudyard Kipling*, Wordsworth Editions, 1994

Carolyn Kizer, 'Parents' Pantoum', Copper Canyon Press, USA, 1996

Philip Larkin, 'An Arundel Tomb', 'Toads', 'For Sidney Bechet', 'The Trees', *Collected Poems*, ed. Anthony Thwaite, Faber, 2003

Derek Mahon, 'Antarctica', *Collected Poems*, Gallery Press, 1999

Marianne Moore, 'The Fish', *The Poems of Marianne Moore*, ed. Grace Schulman, Penguin, 2005

Ogden Nash, 'The Sniffle', *Best of Ogden Nash*, ed. Smith and Eberstadt, Methuen, 1985

Dorothy Parker, 'Rondeau Redoublé (and Scarcely Worth the Trouble at That)', 'Ballade of Unfortunate Mammals', *The Collected Dorothy Parker*, Penguin, 2001 (By permission of Gerald Duckworth & Co. Ltd)

Ian Patterson, 'Sestina', *Time to Get Here: Selected Poems 1969–2002*, Salt Publishing, 2003

—— 'Shakespeare Cento' and 'A. E. Housman Cento' are previously unpublished and are reproduced with the author's permission

Ezra Pound, 'In A Station of the Metro', 'The Sea Farer: from the Anglo Saxon', *ABC of Reading*, Norton, 1960

—— 'Apparuit', *Personae: The Shorter Poems of Ezra Pound*, Faber, 2001

Robert Service, 'Dangerous Dan McGrew', *The Best of Robert Service*, A. & C. Black, 1995 (first English edition edited by Ernest Benn, 1978) ©1960 Germaine Service

Wallace Stevens, 'Le Monocle de Mon Oncle', *The Complete Poems*, Vintage, 1990

Dylan Thomas, 'Do Not Go Gentle Into That Good Night', 'In My Craft and Sullen Art', *Collected Poems*, Everyman Edition, Phoenix, 2000

R. S. Thomas, 'The Welsh Hill Country', *Everyman Selected Poems of R. S. Thomas*, ed. Anthony Thwaite, J. M. Dent, 1996

W. B. Yeats, 'Among School Children', 'The Choice', 'Easter 1916', 'Sailing to Byzantium', 'When You Are Old', *The Poems*, ed. Richard Finneran, Macmillan, 1983

Benjamin Zephaniah, 'Talking Turkey', *Talking Turkeys*, Puffin Books, 1995

Further Reading

The Princeton Encyclopedia of Poetry and Poetics, 1993 edition, Preminger and Brogan, is, in my view, the standard work and final authority on all matters prosodic and poetical. Timothy Steel, Professor of English at Cal State, Los Angeles is one of the best living writers on metrics and I would recommend his two sprightly but deeply scholarly books *Missing Measures* and *All the Fun's in How You Say a Thing*. Vladimir Nabokov's *Notes on Prosody* bears all the hallmarks of astuteness, clarity and cogent idiosyncrasy you would expect of the great man – it is essentially an examination of tetrameter (iambic octosyllabics properly), with especial reference to Pushkin's *Eugene Onegin* and you may find one gin is not enough . . .

The Making of a Poem: A Norton Anthology of Poetic Forms by Mark Strand and Eavan Boland contains excellent examples of many of the forms I have examined. I would also recommend John Lennard's student-orientated *The Poetry Handbook, a Guide to Reading Poetry for Pleasure and Practical Criticism*.

W. H. Auden, T. S. Eliot and Ezra Pound wrote on poetry and poetics with great brilliance and knowledge: as illustrious practising poets, their (sometimes polemical) insights naturally have great authority. The most rewarding academics on the subject in my view are Christopher Ricks, Frank Kermode and Anne Barton. I also fall terribly eagerly on Terry Eagleton and with affectionate scepticism on old Harold Bloom whenever they publish.

Poets whose work showed and has shown particular interest in formal writing include Tennyson, Swinburne, Auden, Elizabeth Bishop, Donald Justice, Richard Wilbur, Wendy Cope, J. V. Cunningham and Seamus Heaney. Between them they have written in many of the forms I concentrate on in Chapter Three.

The good old Internet naturally contains all kinds of information: I would be hesitant to recommend any single site as authoritative on matters prosodic, but poemhunter.com has 'Top 500' lists, which indicate fluctuations in popularity as well as offering online poetry for inspection and links to nearly a thousand other poetry-based sites.